BRITISH EMIGRATION POLICY
1815-1830

BRITISH EMIGRATION POLICY
1815–1830
'Shovelling out Paupers'

BY

H. J. M. JOHNSTON

CLARENDON PRESS · OXFORD

1972

Oxford University Press, Ely House, London W. 1

GLASGOW NEW YORK TORONTO MELBOURNE WELLINGTON
CAPE TOWN IBADAN NAIROBI DAR ES SALAAM LUSAKA ADDIS ABABA
DELHI BOMBAY CALCUTTA MADRAS KARACHI LAHORE DACCA
KUALA LUMPUR SINGAPORE HONG KONG TOKYO

PRINTED IN GREAT BRITAIN
BY W & J MACKAY LTD, CHATHAM

PREFACE

THE emigration experiments of Lord Liverpool's government and Wilmot Horton's vision of an extensive system of assisted emigration have been described in the works of R. C. Mills, Helen I. Cowan, W. F. Adams, R. B. Madgwick, Donald Winch, and others. From a number of angles the question of assisted emigration which was raised in the years after Waterloo has been shown to be pertinent. The subject has received sufficient attention to warrant a special study which would go beyond earlier accounts in explaining the process by which the government decided to sponsor emigrants on a few but notable occasions, the manner in which the several experiments were related, the success of those experiments, the views Cabinet ministers and political economists held of Horton's plan of emigration, the support Horton received from his colleagues, and the complete system that Horton advocated. I have been encouraged to attempt such a study by the existence of fresh material in the Wilmot Horton papers which have become available only during the past decade.

This project has been carried out with the assistance of a Fellowship and a further Research Grant from the Canada Council. A number of people have given helpful advice and I would particularly like to mention E. Bletcher and J. S. Sutton, who put their knowledge of the Wilmot Horton Papers at my disposal, and W. E. Williams, B. M. Gough, and Edward Ingram, who read and criticized my manuscript. Through successive stages of research and writing I have had the advantage of Professor G. S. Graham's guidance and encouragement. Finally, I must thank my wife, Patricia, for the many ways in which she has contributed to this work.

Simon Fraser University   H J.M.J.

CONTENTS

LIST OF MAPS

ABBREVIATIONS USED IN FOOTNOTES

Add. MSS.	Additional Manuscripts, British Museum
A.O.	Audit Office Series
B.M.	British Museum
C.O.	Colonial Office Series
F.O.	Foreign Office Series
H.O.	Home Office Series
H.R.A.	*Historical Records of Australia*
O.H.S.P.R.	*Ontario Historical Society Papers and Records*
Parl. Pap.	*Parliamentary Papers*
R.C.C.	*Records of Cape Colony*
W.H.P.	Wilmot Horton Papers

I

INTRODUCTION

BETWEEN 1815 and 1826 the government of Lord Liverpool conducted six separate experiments in state-aided emigration. There was little precedent for these experiments nor was there any exact repetition of them in later decades. They were unique to the period in which they took place. At an earlier time they would have been considered harmful; subsequently they were believed to have been ineffective. In the decade after Waterloo they represented a hesitant response to newly discovered problems. In size the experiments were extremely modest, involving only 10,500 or 11,000 persons or less than one state-aided emigrant for every nineteen who travelled independently or with assistance from private sources during the same period. As outlets for the population of the British Isles, the experiments were of no significance at all. From a colonial viewpoint they were more important. In the eleven years concerned they accounted for one-sixth or one-fifth of the growth by immigration of Upper Canada and brought the first large body of British settlers to the Cape.[1] The experiments were exceptions to a general pattern which

---

[1] There are no firm statistics on immigration to Upper Canada, but it is possible to make a reasonable estimate based on two separate calculations. Between 1815 and 1826 the population increase of the colony was about 65,000. Of this about 33,000 could be explained by a natural increase of 30 per cent per decade which was the rate of increase in the United States. The total number of arrivals at Quebec from 1819 to 1825 was 68,534 according to the Port of Quebec exchange books. With this figure and figures for the annual number of departures for British North America one can place the arrivals at Quebec between 1815 and 1825 at 88,000. Of these a large percentage went to the western states or to New York. Between 1824 and 1826 11,000 British subjects arrived at New York by way of Quebec (*Parl. Pap.* 1826–7, v (550), 574). The *Quebec Official Gazette* reported that one-half of the emigrants who arrived at Quebec in 1828 proceeded to the United States and that one-twelfth stayed in Lower Canada; five-twelfths went to Upper Canada (H. A. Innis and A. R. M. Lower, *Select Documents in Canadian Economic History, 1783–1885* (Toronto, 1933), pp. 104–5). If these proportions apply for the period from 1815 to 1825 then approximately 37,000 British immigrants reached Upper Canada during those years. Some of these people did not stay; their departures were partially counterbalanced by a small immigration to Upper Canada from the United States and by the arrival of some British immigrants who came through the United States. Nevertheless, the 6,700 or more state-aided immigrants to the province were a significant part of the total.

sent most emigrants either directly or indirectly to the United States. But they possessed a wider interest for contemporaries than these statements would indicate. In post-Waterloo Britain there had developed a sudden awareness of the national advantages of emigration. This awareness arose from an appreciation of serious social and economic issues and was not entirely separable from the growth of the movement for parliamentary reform or the rise of the demand for repeal of the Corn Laws. Emigration like parliamentary reform and repeal of the Corn Laws was a question which found roots in the distress of the lower classes. The idea of state-aided emigration had a vigorous champion in R. J. Wilmot Horton, Under-Secretary of State for the Colonies, 1822-8; it reached a pinnacle of public attention with the publication of the reports of Horton's select committees on emigration in 1826 and 1827.

Attitudes towards emigration had undergone a rapid change. In 1815 the belief that emigration could weaken or depopulate Britain was not yet dead. Men still equated population with power and wealth and saw each industrious emigrant as a further loss of national strength. For much of the eighteenth century the expansion of the population had escaped public notice. The belief that numbers had declined since ancient times had a long life. It was understandable that Parliament should have been hostile to emigration and that it should have intervened only to restrict or prohibit. This hostility had been most recently expressed in the Passenger Act of 1803 which was inspired by a fear that emigration from the Highlands was on the increase.[2] At the dawn of an era of mass emigration strong objections were still heard to the departure of even a small number.

The weapons of rebuttal lay in the works of Malthus and of Adam Smith. The first edition of the *Essay on the Principle of Population* had been in print since 1798. Redundant population was a new term in British vocabulary. But events seemed to confirm Malthus's frightening projections: rising unemployment, high prices, grain shortages, and working-class unrest were all to be observed in the opening years of the nineteenth century. In 1801 the first census of England was taken and ten years later the second. Only a perverse mind could deny the increase which was so evident. Malthus looked at the birth-rate rather than the death-rate to explain fluctuations in population

---

[2] Oliver MacDonagh, *A Pattern of Government Growth, 1800–60, the Passenger Acts and their Enforcement* (London, 1961), pp. 54–5.

growth.[3] A high birth-rate, he claimed, was responsible for the present gain of almost 15 per cent in a decade. Unless pestilence or war intervened, population would continue to expand until checked by famine. In the long run famine was inevitable. The supply of food increased in arithmetical proportions, Malthus wrote, while population increased in geometrical proportions. The human race could avoid disaster only if men curbed their sexual appetites or else resorted to prostitutes.

To Malthus the existing system of parish support for the able-bodied poor was reprehensible; it cushioned the pauper against the full consequences of his sexual irresponsibility. Relief should be denied to the children of paupers. Malthus suggested that clergymen should warn brides and grooms of the 'impropriety, and even immorality of marrying' without a prospect of being able to maintain children.[4] This was the only remedy to over-population that he was prepared to offer. Many of those who accepted Malthus's fatalistic diagnosis found his answer too limited. They could not submerge an optimistic faith in remedial measures. Emigration appeared to be a possible solution. Malthus himself conceded that after the passage of a few centuries Britain would be able to feed with ease two or three times its present population.[5] A system of emigration to the colonies would help the nation to adjust its rate of population growth to its increase in agricultural production.

Such a system would meet the problem of over-population in a positive instead of a negative way. It would turn a liability into an asset. There was more to be gained from emigration than simply the expulsion of excess mouths and stomachs. If the colonies acquired a greater population, they would become immensely more valuable to the parent state. At the root of this belief was an understanding of the ideal relationship of colony and mother country acquired from Adam Smith's *Wealth of Nations*. It is customary to attribute anti-colonial thinking after 1776 to two contemporaneous events, the American Revolution and the publication of the *Wealth of Nations*.

[3] *An Essay on the Principle of Population*, ii (London, 1817), 304–5. Since Talbot Griffith published his *Population Problems in the Age of Malthus* in 1926 the question has remained unresolved whether it was a change in the birth-rate or in the death-rate that stimulated population growth. See P. E. Razzell, 'Population Growth and Economic Change in Eighteenth- and Early Nineteenth-Century England and Ireland', E. L. Jones and G. E. Mingay, eds., *Land Labour and Population in the Industrial Revolution* (London, 1967).

[4] *Essay*, iii. 179.

[5] Ibid. 339.

Yet Smith's great work was also an inspiration to designers of a new imperial structure and to advocates of emigration to the colonies. His views provided a rationale for emigration and settlement which was absent in the mercantilist system.

Mercantilist policy had encouraged colonial development only to the extent necessary to ensure Britain with a supply of required materials or food. It had not supported settlement overseas that did not contribute to this limited purpose. Newfoundland, whose settlers waited until 1811 before they were conceded a right to permanent residence, provided an extreme example of this line of reasoning. Smith did not believe that British prosperity depended upon restriction or that the mother country profited by exploiting the colony. In rejecting mercantilist theory he opened up new prospects. Now colonies could be envisaged as purchasers of British goods meeting the mother country in an equal and mutually beneficial trade. As their populations grew, this trade would grow. Moreover, if colonies were settled by British citizens, they would be more likely to want British goods. By emigration a suppliant for public handouts in Britain could become a customer for British manufacturers in the colonies. In this light the process was doubly desirable.

It is a matter of debate whether or not Adam Smith believed that Britain should maintain colonies.[6] His free-trade ideas led disciples like J. R. McCulloch to a rigid opposition to all colonial ties. Yet it was quite possible to argue the advantages of colonies even in a free-trade system. Colonial markets were safer and more predictable than those of foreign states: they were less likely to be closed as a consequence of a sudden change of policy or a new alignment and they were friendly markets which could be depended upon in time of war. It followed that Britain would profit more from emigration to her colonies than to the United States. For most advocates of state-aided emigration this assumption was unquestionable.

However, it was the idea that population problems could be solved by sending away excess numbers rather than the vision of expanding colonial trade which gave impetus to discussion of emigration. No one with eyes to see could overlook the desperate condition of the labouring classes who paid the price of rising population and

---

[6] See Donald O. Wagner, 'British Economists and the Empire', *Political Science Quarterly*, June 1931, pp. 252–74; S. M. Hardy, 'William Huskisson, 1770–1830; Imperial Statesman and Economist' (Ph.D. Thesis, London, 1943), pp. 7–8; Donald Winch, *Classical Political Economy and Colonies* (London, 1965), pp. 14–24.

industrialization. An improved system of farming meant the impoverishment of agricultural labourers in the south and east of England and smallholders and crofters in the Highlands and Western Islands of Scotland; a modernized textile industry meant the degradation of hand-loom weavers in northern England, Scotland, and Ulster. Pauperism was perhaps worst in rural areas but most conspicuous in the cities.[7] Incredible poverty existed in Ireland where a vast and growing rural population was trapped in a subsistence economy in which any capital accumulation fell into the hands of absentee proprietors while the peasantry were forced by higher rents and increased numbers to submit to minute subdivisions of the land and to push the potato culture to its limits.

For Britain the conclusion of the Napoleonic Wars brought an intensification of difficulties. Several hundred thousand men discharged from the army, navy, and transport services sought employment in a country in which unemployment was already a large and permanent feature. Industries that had flourished in wartime now shrank and left thousands more out of work. In rural England peace meant a decline in the price of wheat, a tightening of the screw made all the more effective by a small harvest in 1816. Labourers in city and country alike were caught in the grip of falling wages while the price of bread and fuel remained high. It was estimated that almost 15 per cent of the population of England was indigent.[8] Over 120,000 pauper children ran the streets of London; of these between three and four thousand had been let out by their parents to beggars or systematically employed in pilfering. The problem was present in all large cities and worst in the manufacturing districts.[9]

Compassion for a class considered to be habitually lazy and improvident did not come easily to the gentry. As long as the landlord was unaffected, he could see in pauperism a degree of social justice. When faced with the prospect of chronic lawlessness and rising poor rates, his detachment dissolved. In 1817–18 parish expenditure on poor relief reached nearly £8,000,000 or 84 per cent of the total sum spent by local authorities.[10] The burden was not equal for all parishes. Where it fell most heavily, it was indeed crushing. One of the more unfortunate parishes, Halstead in Essex, perennially exacted a rate

[7] E. J. Hobsbawm, *The Age of Revolution, 1789–1848* (New York, 1962), p. 244.
[8] 'On Improving the Condition of the Poor', *Quarterly Review*, Oct. 1814, p. 152.
[9] Robert Southey, 'The Poor', *Quarterly Review*, Apr. 1816, p. 226.
[10] David D. Douglas, ed., *English Historical Documents, 1783–1832* (London, 1959), p. 413.

of close to 50 per cent of the rents.[11] The example of Halstead and other stricken parishes, coupled with a Malthus-inspired fear of population growth, made pauperism a matter of major public concern.

In Northern Ireland and in the Highlands of Scotland emigration had long been known as an answer to the economic hardships and political repression which bore peculiarly on those areas. Highland emigration was given its original momentum when veterans of the Seven Years War brought accounts of America to friends and relatives who had seen the disintegration of the clan system following the Jacobite rebellion of 1745 and had experienced a sharp rise in rents and an increase in the frequency of evictions as landlords consolidated estates to create sheep-runs.[12] Between 1763 and 1775 about 25,000 Scots sailed for America. More than one in five settled in North Carolina; others went to Georgia and upper New York. This pattern was disrupted only by the Revolution which caused loyal Scots to migrate from the rebel colonies to Canada and to Nova Scotia. Subsequently the main flow of Highland emigration was directed towards Nova Scotia, Cape Breton, and Prince Edward Island.

The total number of Scottish emigrants was never very great: only once between 1783 and 1815 did it exceed 3,000 in a single year and in most years it was less than 1,000.[13] Because Highland emigration was characteristically a communal rather than an individual venture, with parties organized by tacksmen, priests, or clan chieftains, its effect on particular parishes was dramatic. In size, however, it was dwarfed by the older movement out of Ulster.

Until the Union of 1800 Ireland had been allowed only limited access to the markets of England and her colonies; her trade with foreign countries had been restricted when it threatened to compete with the sale of English woollens. Ulster, the principal manufacturing region of Ireland, felt these restraints far more than Leinster, Munster, or Connaught and Ulstermen lived in a state of perpetual depression. The discouragements of an unfavourable economic setting

---

[11] *Parl. Pap.* 1817, vi (462), 125–7.

[12] Gordon Donaldson, *The Scots Overseas* (London, 1966), pp. 46–70; M. A. Jones, 'The Role of the United Kingdom in the Transatlantic Emigrant Trade' (D. Phil. Thesis, Oxford, 1956), pp. 2, 32; I. C. C. Graham, *Colonists from Scotland: Emigration to North America, 1704–1783* (Ithaca, New York, 1956), pp. 188–9; Henry Hamilton, *An Economic History of Scotland in the Eighteenth Century* (Oxford, 1963), pp. 13, 17; W. S. MacNutt, *The Atlantic Provinces: The Emergence of Colonial Societies, 1712–1857* (Toronto, 1965), p. 117.

[13] Jones, 'Transatlantic Emigrant Trade', p. 3.

were reinforced by religious disabilities which affected Presbyterians as well as Roman Catholics. Emigration became a frequent escape.[14] About 225,000 Ulstermen arrived in North America between 1717 and 1775. Most went to America as indentured servants. Their usual destination was Pennsylvania, the flax-growing colony with which Belfast and Newry carried on their greatest trade. Although the American Revolution interrupted this movement, the Irish of Pennsylvania, unlike the Scots of North Carolina, supported the rebel cause and, when the flow of indentured servants from Northern Ireland revived in 1783 it followed the old channel.

While Northern Ireland knew the meaning of emigration in 1815, most of the British Isles did not. The exodus from Southern Ireland did not begin until the 1820s. It was not until late in the same decade that enthusiasm for emigration began to develop in England. Even in Scotland there were few departures from Greenock, the principal emigrant port for the Lowlands, before 1815.[15] The economic pressures of post-Waterloo Britain and Ireland did not produce an immediate flood of emigrants except in regions in which this had been a traditional response. Ten years passed before there was a noticeable change. In that time public concern about pauperism was translated into increased interest in the emigration remedy. Consequently, the national advantages of pauper emigration were widely discussed by members of the privileged classes before members of the lower classes manifested much desire to leave. The possibilities of government action were debated in advance of a spontaneous surge in the transatlantic movement. Wilmot Horton's experiments in Irish emigration in 1823 and 1825 were a step ahead of events.

The idea that emigrants could be directed to the colonies also owed little to the example of the past. Very few British or Irish emigrants had even gone to the overseas possessions that Britain now held. Emigration from Ulster had run almost entirely to the United States. Of all the colonies under the British flag in 1815, only Nova Scotia, Cape Breton, and Prince Edward Island had drawn a regular influx of British immigrants during the late eighteenth and early nineteenth centuries. Lower Canada remained predominantly French, a situation which had been accepted as irremediable by

[14] M. A. Jones, *American Immigration* (Chicago, 1960), pp. 65–6; W. F. Dunaway, *The Scotch-Irish of Colonial Pennsylvania* (London, 1962), pp. 29–46; H. J. Ford, *The Scotch-Irish in America* (Princeton, 1915), pp. 181–203.

[15] Jones, 'Transatlantic Emigrant Trade', pp. 31, 69–74, 99.

British administrators since 1774. Upper Canada, born as an immediate consequence of the American Revolution, had been first settled by American Loyalists from Pennsylvania and New York. Efforts to introduce British settlers during the period of the French Revolutionary and Napoleonic Wars had been largely unsuccessful. Most of the people who came to Upper Canada before 1812 were Americans moving out of New England, New York State, and Pennsylvania in search of land and unconcerned about political boundaries. At the onset of the War of 1812 one Canadian province was French and the other American; the loyalty of neither one could be taken for granted. Even Nova Scotia was essentially American in origin: no group contributed more to its early growth than the New Englanders who began to arrive in 1759; these people were submerged only by the immigration of large numbers of American Loyalists in 1783.[16] New Brunswick, which was separated from Nova Scotia in 1784, was populated almost entirely by American Loyalists and their descendants.

Outside North America the colonies with the greatest settlement potential were Cape Colony and New South Wales. Great Britain had seized the Cape in 1795, returned it to the Dutch in 1803, reoccupied it in 1806, and valuing it as a half-way station to India had kept it when the Treaty of Paris was negotiated in 1814. Except for officials and a few merchants there had been no British immigration and in 1815 the colony's white population of 35,000 was almost entirely of Dutch and French Huguenot descent. New South Wales, which had been founded as a penal settlement in 1788, was equally unknown to free British emigrants. While thousands of convicts had been sent there, voluntary immigration had not developed or been encouraged on any appreciable scale; in 1810 in the whole of eastern Australia there were scarcely more than 400 settlers who had come as free men.[17]

It was not the example of past emigration to the colonies but simply the existence of vast tracts of undeveloped land that prompted discussion of pauper settlement overseas. Plans and projects were inspired by the basic observation that Britain was over-populated while her colonies were under-populated. Of course, those who admitted that the effects of emigration would be positive and bene-

---

[16] MacNutt, pp. 53–62, 89–95.
[17] R. B. Madgwick, *Immigration into Eastern Australia 1788–1851* (London, 1937), p. 30.

ficial did not all think that emigrants should be sent to Canada, Cape Colony, or New South Wales. It was easier to persuade Parliament to remove obstacles to a free and unrestricted movement to the United States, South America, and other areas than to secure its approval for heavy expenditure to assist and direct emigrants to the colonies. For this reason Wilmot Horton, the chief advocate of state-aided emigration, accomplished little. His scheme was too imaginative and outran by too much the prevailing concept of the functions of government.

Yet the Cabinet did sanction experiments in state-aided emigration and encouraged Horton to bring the whole issue before the House of Commons. The attitude of the ministers concerned was ambiguous. They told Horton that his grand ideas were unrealistic but described his efforts as necessary and worth while. They saw emigration as a weapon against the poverty that bred radicalism and revolt, but were unwilling to attempt anything but token measures. They used the term *experiment* without any intention of taking bolder action if the experiments were successful. Ultimately, the reserved support they gave to Horton was a measure of their ability to comprehend social problems without being able to respond effectively to them.

II

THE RIDEAU SETTLEMENT

IN 1814 the Colonial Office was not infected by the idea that pauper emigration could relieve domestic distress. But the Colonial Secretary did see value in a policy of assisted emigration if it turned people away from the United States. The old Thirteen Colonies were no longer just a foreign state: they were an enemy state. The present war might well not be the last one; it ill suited Britain to contribute to the power of an adversary by exporting population to her. If emigration was an evil, it was a lesser evil when it ran in the direction of the colonies. There was no divergence from the traditional, conservative view of population and emigration. Between 1815 and 1819 the Colonial Office offered assistance to emigrants for reasons related to the colonies but without any consideration of the possible benefits at home. Yet, even though the objectives were limited, a great gap existed between what the Colonial Office intended to accomplish and what it was prepared to do. Scarcely more than one thousand emigrants received help from the government while tens of thousands left on their own. The Colonial Secretary and his Under-Secretary did not anticipate the size of the post-war spontaneous and unassisted emigration from Northern Ireland. Moreover, they headed an administrative rather than a spending department and they possessed little capacity for bold action. Their emigration measures were not so much mistaken as inadequate.

It would have been difficult for the Colonial Office in 1814 to have justified a scheme of assisted emigration except in strict reference to colonial requirements. The public had not yet been educated to view emigration as a desirable outlet for redundant population. Indeed, the problems of pauperism and over-population had not previously attracted much attention. For over a generation the war in Europe had been the great focus of national concern while internal crises aroused little excitement. In the late stages of the war a market collapse, the disruption of trade with America, interference with Continental trade, bad harvests, and wartime taxes had brought despair to the poor. The Luddite outbreaks of 1811, 1812, and 1814 were far more serious than the disturbances of the years after the war, but they were not the cause of the same general alarm.[1] Apprehensions about the condition and attitude of the lower classes did not surface until after Napoleon's final surrender.

Even when the existence of widespread unemployment was recognized and pamphleteers began to write volumes of literature on the Poor Laws and over-population, interest in the emigration remedy did not develop immediately. In 1814 Patrick Colquhoun, social philosopher and philanthropist, pointed to the expanse of uncultivated lands in the colonies and observed: 'No nation ever possessed such resources for the beneficial employment of a redundant population as Great Britain at the present moment.'[2] But there was not much discussion of this idea before 1817. The most important remedy in the opinions of many pamphleteers was the one that Malthus had advocated: withholding relief from the able-bodied poor. The author of one representative essay recommended that the provisions of the law for disabled paupers in old age or inflicted with an incurable infirmity should be continued and improved, but that after the passage of ten years no relief should be granted to the healthy except by voluntary subscriptions.[3] The practice which had arisen in the late eighteenth century of giving relief to the underpaid as well as the unemployed was blamed for the depression of wages and the demoralization of the labouring class. It was argued that if relief were abolished wages would rise, the poor would become self-reliant, and young couples would not be tempted to have families in the expectation of parish help. The gentry were encouraged to believe that a reduction of the poor rates could be achieved to the advantage of all members of the community.

Sympathy for the poor was not a strong sentiment. Those who wrote about pauperism tended to measure it by the cost to the taxpayer of providing relief rather than by the numbers out of work or without profitable employment or by the numbers homeless or underfed. They saw the problem first and foremost as one of rising poor rates. Many believed that able-bodied persons could be compelled to contribute to the community. If any relief were found necessary, it should be confined to workhouses; the impoverished should never

---

[1] F. O. Darvall, *Popular Disturbances in Regency England* (London, 1934), p. 319.

[2] *A Treatise on the Wealth, Power, and Resources of the British Empire* (London, 1814), p. 16.

[3] John Davidson, *Considerations on the Poor Laws* (Oxford, 1817), p. 117.

be given anything more than the minimum needed to keep them healthy. In a few instances pamphleteers advocated physical compulsion. Indignation towards 'boys of sixteen and seventeen who marry one week, and demand relief the next' led to a call for the restoration of the practice of branding hands: 'Three or four instances of the use of this emblem would bring a whole parish to its senses.'[4]

Most pamphleteers advanced remedies of a more positive nature: the employment of the jobless in 'real and useful public works'; the establishment of a national bank to which all classes should subscribe and from which depositors should receive help when they were ill and on other occasions; the colonization of waste lands within the British Isles; and the creation in each parish of areas of garden allotments.[5] Robert Owen's plan for co-operative villages was but one of a variety of proposals to give land to the unemployed. Advocates of these reforms stressed the value of permitting paupers to earn self-respect by providing for themselves. But they did not answer the apprehensions of their contemporaries about the consequences of further population growth. Few people were convinced of the practicality of Malthus's solution: moral restraint. 'What!' wrote Robert Gourlay, 'lecture a young couple on that day against intemperance during the honeymoon!! Really, Mr. Malthus, there is no wonder you have stirred up indignation.'[6]

In the early editions of his *Essay* Malthus had contended that emigration would not solve the problem of over-population in the long run. In the fifth edition published in 1817 his position was considerably modified:

If . . . a very great stimulus should be given to a country for ten or twelve years together [a reference to the War] and . . . then comparatively cease . . . labour will continue flowing into the market with almost undiminished rapidity, while the means of employing . . . it have . . . been contracted. It is precisely under these circumstances that emigration is

[4] S. W. Nichol, *A Summary View of the Report and Evidence Relative to the Poor Laws* (York, 1818), p. 98.

[5] For examples see: T. P. Courtenay, *A Treatise upon the Poor Laws* (London, 1818); [Sidney Walker or Robert Lundie], 'Tracts on Saving Banks', *Quarterly Review*, Oct. 1816; Egerton Brydges, *Arguments in favour of the Practicability of Relieving the Able-Bodied Poor, By Finding Employment for Them* (London, 1817); Charles Jerram, *Considerations on the Impolicy and Pernicious Tendency of the Poor Laws* (London, 1818); H. B. Gascoigne, *Suggestions for the Employment of the Poor of the Metropolis* (London, 1817).

[6] *General Introduction to Statistical Accounts of Upper Canada* (London, 1822), p. clxxxii.

most useful as a temporary relief; and it is under these circumstances that Great Britain finds herself at present placed. The only real relief in such a case is emigration; and the subject is well worth the attention of the government, both as a matter of humanity and policy.[7]

In the same year the first papers on government-assisted emigration were placed before the Select Committee of the Commons on the Poor Laws.[8] The authors were Robert Torrens, an economist who was later to become one of Gibbon Wakefield's earliest converts and to play an important role in the colonization history of Australia, and W. G. Hayter, a law student who subsequently followed a political career of minor significance. Both Torrens and Hayter reasoned that, because subsistence could not keep pace with population, the growth of population would need to be retarded. This could be accomplished by moral restraint, Torrens admitted, but time would be needed to educate the labouring classes. To meet the immediate problem government should adopt an extended system of colonization in Canada, the Cape of Good Hope, and New Holland. Torrens did not consider in any detail the means by which such a programme could be carried out. He merely proposed that able-bodied persons who were accepting relief should be offered grants of land in the colonies on condition that they repay the expense of their passage after their arrival. Hayter, on the other hand, attempted to calculate costs: he estimated that a family of five could be sent to the colonies at an expense no greater than that required to keep them in a workhouse for a year. He went on to anticipate possible objections. The likelihood that emigrants would return home he quite rightly dismissed as slim; the problem that parishes would have in raising money he did not see as insurmountable. On the fundamental question of compulsion his attitude was at once more humane and more realistic than that of Torrens. If necessary, Torrens favoured compulsion; those who refused to emigrate could be denied parish relief. Hayter was opposed: 'it would be an act of too arbitrary power' and, in fact, would not be called for because the government would have no difficulty in finding volunteers. This was the point of view

[7] ii. 304–5.
[8] Robert Torrens, 'A Paper on the Means of Reducing the Poor's Rates', *The Pamphleteer*, x, no. 20, 1817; W. G. Hayter, *Proposals for the Redemption of the Poor's Rates by means of Emigration* (London, 1817); C.O. 48/40, Hayter to Bathurst, 15 July 1819. On Torrens's paper see R. D. Collison Black, *Economic Thought and the Irish Question* (Cambridge, 1960), pp. 204–5.

that was to prevail amongst serious advocates of government-assisted emigration.

One other feature of Hayter's plan deserves mention. Like Colquhoun and others who submitted colonization plans to the Colonial Office during the following year, Hayter thought that the most eligible places for settlement were at the Cape.[9] Even before the Dutch colony had fallen into British hands, Englishmen stopping there briefly on their way to the east had eulogized its moderate climate, exotic fruits and flowers, and its appearance of prosperity. It was 'the finest colony in the world', a far happier destination than the frozen shores of Canada. Travellers enjoying an idyllic rest at the mid-point of a long ocean voyage may well have looked at the Cape with less than perfect judgement.[10] Very few Englishmen had yet contended with the formidable problems of settlement there. Impressions of the colony were idealized and incomplete and unrealistic expectations were held of its potential.

The Report of the 1817 Select Committee on the Poor Laws, the Committee to which Torrens and Hayter submitted their papers, included a passing reference only to the advisability of removing 'obstacles' that prevented the movement of labour to the colonies.[11] This was a very mild endorsement of the emigration remedy, but it was a marked advance from the attitudes of the past. The Committee saw emigration in a positive light and that was significant. In response to the rising cost of poor relief and to recent Luddite riots, objections to emigration were falling away. By 1819, the Poor Law Committee of that year was speaking not merely of removing 'obstacles' but actually of giving 'encouragement and facilities'.[12]

The Colonial Office, however, was inclined against pauper emigration. In May 1820, Under-Secretary Goulburn advised the Treasury that a measure that sent indigent people to Canada might hide the suffering of those people from their countrymen but would serve no other purpose;[13] the emigrants would probably find themselves in worse circumstances and the colony would be burdened with their care. Although Henry Goulburn was not an imaginative individual,

[9] He believed that the area adjacent to Mossel Bay, Plattenburg Bay, and Algoa Bay could be colonized by 40,000 or 50,000 paupers within a five-year period.

[10] This is suggested by John Barrow writing about the Cape in the *Quarterly Review*, Nov. 1819, p. 205.

[11] *Parl. Pap.* 1817, vi (462), 20.

[12] *Parl. Pap.* 1819, ii (529), 10.

[13] C.O. 43/59, Goulburn to Harrison, 15 May 1820.

he possessed qualities that his colleagues prized more highly: he was steady, confident, attentive to detail, and indefatigable. As a strictly departmental man he did not attempt to enlarge the sphere of his own desk. In this he stands in contrast to his successor, R. J. Wilmot Horton. Goulburn saw emigration as an aspect of colonial rather than domestic policy. He was more aware of the problems that pauper emigration would create in the colonies than of the benefits it would produce at home.

On this subject it is not easy to separate the opinions of the Colonial Secretary, Lord Bathurst, from those of his Under-Secretary. By comparing the handwriting on the turned-down corners of incoming letters and dispatches, Helen Taft Manning has concluded that Goulburn carried a much greater burden of work within the Office.[14] That is not to say that Bathurst was an ineffective chief. One well-placed observer in the 1820s expressed the opinion that Bathurst was one of four members of an inner cabinet which ran the government and called upon other ministers only to ratify decisions already made.[15] Within the Colonial Office Bathurst devoted a great deal of personal attention to the colonies he considered most important: Gibraltar, Malta, the Ionian Islands, and St. Helena.[16] The strategic and political significance of these possessions made them most worthy of his time. Although he reserved final word on all questions of policy, he took a very distant interest in the plantation colonies and the colonies of settlement. With respect to these he relied heavily on the industry and judgement of his Under-Secretary. As a result, Goulburn's assumptions about British North America or New South Wales tended to become those of the Colonial Office.

If there was one aspect of British North American affairs that Bathurst did not find tedious, it was colonial defence. The war in North America began one week after he became Colonial Secretary and lasted through the first thirty months of his administration. Bathurst understood the precarious position of British commanders in Upper Canada. He knew that the loyalty of the bulk of the population had never been a certainty; that the government could not

---

[14] *British Colonial Government After the American Revolution* (New Haven, 1933), p. 481.

[15] C. W. W. Wynn cited in W. R. Brock, *Lord Liverpool and Liberal Torysim*, 1820–7 (Cambridge, 1941), p. 73.

[16] This becomes apparent on examination of Bathurst's correspondence in B.M. Loan 57.

depend on 'ill disposed and disaffected settlers of American origin'.[17] If the colony was to be defensible in another war, the American influence would have to be checked. Shortly after the peace treaty was signed Bathurst ordered Canadian authorities to withhold grants of land from American citizens and to make every effort to prevent them from settling in either of the Canadas.[18] The effect of this policy was dramatic. The influx of Americans came to a halt. Undoubtedly the opening up of Indiana and Illinois after the collapse of Tecumseh's confederacy contributed more than marginally to the diversion of settlers from Upper Canada. Nevertheless, Robert Gourlay believed that the policy of discouraging American immigrants was the prime cause of the stagnation that established itself in Upper Canada after the war.[19]

While discouraging Americans Bathurst wished to encourage British emigrants to go to the Canadas. The possibility of giving free passages and grants of land occurred to him as early as 1813. Six months after the American attack on York and one year after Brock's death at Queenston he suggested to the commander-in-chief in Canada that an infusion of Highland settlers might bolster the militia of Upper Canada. He received an enthusiastic response in the affirmative.[20] Lieutenant-General Sir Gordon Drummond, the Administrator of Upper Canada, stressed the value of a settlement near Kingston to strengthen the weakest link in the defences of Upper Canada. By cutting off communications between Kingston and Montreal Americans could isolate and stop all supplies to the British forces in the inland province.[21] When they had possessed naval superiority on Lake Ontario in 1813 they had been turned away from this objective only by faulty intelligence. Successive commanders in Upper Canada reached the same conclusion: if the province was to be defended, a larger settlement at the eastern end of Lake Ontario was imperative.

Lord Bathurst had not made such a precise assessment of the need for a policy of assisted emigration. He had no specific location in

[17] C.O. 42/355, Drummond to Bathurst, 12 July 1814.
[18] George C. Patterson, *Land Settlement in Upper Canada 1783–1840* (Toronto, 1921), p. 112.
[19] *A Statistical Account of Upper Canada*, ii (London, 1822), 423.
[20] C.O. 43/23, Bathurst to Prevost, 29 Oct. 1813; C.O. 42/355, Drummond to Bathurst, 12 July 1814.
[21] G. M. Craig, *Upper Canada: The Formative Years* (Toronto 1963), p. 76; G. S. Graham, 'Views of General Murray on the Defence of Upper Canada, 1815', *C.H.R.*, June 1953, pp. 158–65; and A. R. M. Lower, 'Immigration and Settlement in Canada, 1812–1820', *C.H.R.*, March 1922, pp. 38–9.

mind when he first invited opinions, and when it was decided to carry out the project, he left the placing of the settlement to the local authorities. He acted simply in the belief that immigration to Canada was preferable to immigration to the United States. He expected the old pattern of emigration to reassert itself as soon as peace permitted. If the government did nothing, population that could buttress the British North American colonies would be lost to a rival power. On the other hand if the government intervened, it could achieve a double objective, at once strengthening Canada while diverting potential strength from the United States. Of the two, the latter may well have figured more prominently in Bathurst's considerations.

The Colonial Secretary would not have initiated any steps if he had not anticipated a large and spontaneous emigration. It is significant that plans for recruitment were directed mainly to Northern Ireland and Scotland, the regions in which the spirit of emigration ran the strongest. Robert Peel, the Irish Secretary, shared views in common with those of Bathurst and Goulburn. As he explained to a subordinate, the government did not propose to place a premium on emigration: 'we assume that Emigration will take place and we say to those who are about to Emigrate that they shall have a bounty on importation into Canada.'[22] Peel found it difficult to choose between Derry and Dublin as the residence for an emigration agent. He realized that most of the agent's business would be in Ulster and that any attempt to locate him outside that province would only add to the expense of his work. On the other hand, 'If we fixed on Derry or Belfast, would it not appear as if *we wished* to deport the Northerners and were glad to get rid of them?' Peel regretted the departure of Protestant Ulstermen; the country could better afford to be deprived of some of its 'Catholic Millions'.[23] Yet the enthusiasm for emigration in the Northern Counties could not be ignored. If Ireland's loss could be turned to Canada's gain it would be some consolation. Goulburn agreed: a programme of sponsored emigration was justified as a measure beneficial to Canada alone.[24]

The Colonial Office tried to attract immigrants to Upper Canada without drawing criticism for promoting emigration from Great Britain. In 1815 the desire to conserve population was stronger than the fear of pauperism. Shortly after the government's intention to

[22] Add. MSS. 40288, Peel to Hill, 29 Jan. 1815.
[23] Add. MSS. 40288, Peel to Enniskillen, 29 Jan. 1815.
[24] Add. MSS. 40242, Goulburn to Peel, 21 Jan. 1815.

assist emigrants was advertised in Scottish papers, the ministry was obliged to deny that it wished to excite the Scots with a desire to leave. Francis Horner, the respected member for St. Mawes, raised the matter in the Commons, and characterized the promotion of emigration as a 'pernicious' enterprise.[25] Goulburn did not challenge this description, but replied that it was government policy not to encourage but to divert. The government did not wish to see an increase in emigration but only a redirection of it to the British provinces in North America.

The advertised terms of the government's offer demonstrate the truth of this statement.[26] While the offer was generous, it could not have been accepted by a majority of those who would have been interested. Applicants who qualified would receive free passages to Quebec and provisions during the voyage. On arrival they would be given 100 acres of land and six months of rations would be supplied at low prices. To qualify for this assistance, applicants would be required to deposit £16 for each male of seventeen and over and two guineas for each married woman. This deposit would be forfeited if a settler abandoned his grant of land to skip over the border into the United States. The government was not going to risk the humiliating possibility of subsidizing emigration to the wrong country. In deciding on such a substantial deposit Goulburn and Bathurst ensured that no one could obtain a free passage who could not have afforded to pay the fare himself. Paupers could not take advantage of the offer. Even a tradesman earning £25 a year would find it difficult to raise the £16 or £18 that was demanded. Indeed, Robert Peel was afraid that insistence on a deposit of this size would seriously inhibit recruitment in Ireland.[27]

Goulburn was well aware that thousands of applications would be withdrawn when the terms of the government's offer were explained. It must be assumed that he welcomed this result. His department was interested only in the emigrant who could help himself. This was the emigrant who would go to the United States if no inducements were held out to him and this was the emigrant who would make the best settler in Canada. Because the Colonial Office had

[25] *Hansard*, 1815, xxx, col. 52.

[26] The announcement of the government's offer included a disclaimer of any intention to increase emigration. See C.O. 42/165, Campbell to Goulburn, 23 Mar. 1815, and the *Caledonian Mercury*, 27 Mar. 1815.

[27] Add. MSS. 40288, Peel to Gregory, 11 Mar. 1815, Peel to Bathurst, 2 Apr. 1815, and Peel to Gregory, 3 Apr. 1815.

no other objective than to turn to Canada's advantage what was viewed as an unfortunate emigration of valuable British subjects, it made sense to offer assistance on terms that could not be universally accepted.

In the spring of 1815 the Colonial Office planned to send to Canada 2,000 emigrants from Scotland, 2,000 from Ireland, and a small number from England.[28] This was a bold start. With the exception of the founding of Halifax three generations earlier, there were no precedents for officials to follow. The government was assuming responsibility in an area in which its role had traditionally been passive or even negative. In 1815, however, it was relatively easy to take this step. Not only were the lessons of the War of 1812 freshly in mind, but also some of the administrative consequences of that war made it opportune to act.[29] The Transport Office would be sending shipping to Quebec to bring back 20,000 of the troops who had been involved in the defence of Canada. Because the transports would otherwise be empty during their westerly crossing of the Atlantic, it would be economical to provide passages for 4,000 settlers. In addition, the reduction of the British naval forces on the North American and West Indies stations left a large store of provisions at Bermuda and Halifax; these provisions could be made available to settlers in Canada. Finally, some British regular troops serving in Canada were being demobilized and placed on land in the County of Glengarry, on the Rideau River, and at the head of the Bay of Quinte in Upper Canada and on the River St. Francis in Lower Canada. The establishment created to administer these military settlements could be given responsibility for civilian immigrants as well. Such an arrangement would enable Bathurst to pay the expenses of his settlers from the military chest and thus avoid asking Parliament for money.

These considerations made an ambitious project seem feasible. Unfortunately, the favourable moment was too fleeting to grasp. Until the American Senate ratified the Treaty of Ghent, until peace was a certainty in North America, the Colonial Office hesitated to authorize any expenditure.[30] As a consequence, an emigration agent

[28] C.O. 42/164, Transport Office to Goulburn, 13 Mar. 1815; C.O. 43/23, Bathurst to Drummond, 20 Mar. 1815.

[29] C.O. 43/23, Bathurst to Drummond, 20 Mar. 1815; C.O. 42/164, Transport Office to Goulburn, 23 and 29 Mar. 1815, and Treasury to Goulburn, 19 Apr. 1815.

[30] On the reasons for delay: Add. MSS. 40288, Peel to Enniskillen, 29 Jan. 1815. On the appointment of an agent in Scotland; C.O. 42/165, Campbell to Bathurst, 24 Feb. 1815 and 11 Mar. 1815. On the advertising in England and Ireland: C.O. 42/165, Campbell to Goulburn, 20 Mar. 1815.

for Scotland was not appointed until 6 March. Transports to take settlers from the Clyde and from Irish ports were not requested until 13 March. Although advertisements of the government's offer appeared, perhaps prematurely, in Scottish papers in late February, no notice was given in England or Ireland at this time or in early March. An emigration agent for Ireland had not been named at the end of March. By this date it was too late. On 1 March Napoleon had escaped from Elba and twenty days later he entered Paris. The British nation found itself in a renewed state of war. Troop withdrawal from North America was now a matter of urgent necessity; and transports appropriated for this service could not waste time taking on emigrants in Britain. On 1 April they were ordered to sail to Quebec and Halifax without delay.[31] Any expectation that a large number of emigrants could be sent out that year had to be abandoned.

Yet the process of recruiting emigrants had been set in motion and the government could not ignore its obligation to those who had accepted its offer.[32] In early May Goulburn ordered John Campbell, the emigration agent for Scotland, not to accept any more applicants. Campbell had already received deposits from over seventy families, many of whom had given up their possessions and houses and had come down to Glasgow to wait. In subsequent weeks many more families arrived in Glasgow from remote areas, having sold all they owned in the belief that they would qualify for free passages. Campbell's lists continued to grow; while Lord Bathurst cancelled most of the arrangements for a government-sponsored emigration in 1815, he realized that he would have to make good his promises in the case of 100 or 150 families.

About thirty families, probably from the north of England, had been scheduled to embark at Deptford.[33] They were the first to sail; most of the transports were fitted out at Deptford and it was possible to embark there with a minimum of delay. The settlers who had congregated at Glasgow were not so fortunate. Not until Napoleon's Hundred Days had run their course were transports available for them. During the long wait many families exhausted their savings; the government recognized its responsibility by providing a daily

[31] C.O. 43/52, Goulburn to Transport Office, 1 Apr. 1815.

[32] C.O. 42/165, Campbell to Goulburn, 6 May 1815, and Campbell to Bathurst, 4 Mar. 1815, 3 Apr. 1815, 25 Apr. 1815. C.O. 43/23, Bathurst to Drummond, 13 June 1815; *Caledonian Mercury*, 4 May 1815; *Hansard*, 1815, xxxi, col. 917.

[33] C.O. 42/165, Campbell to Goulburn, 24 Mar. 1815; C.O. 43/52, Goulburn to Transport Office, 7 Apr. 1815, and 14 Apr. 1815.

allowance of 9*d*. per man and 6*d*. per woman.[34] The most serious loss, however, was irretrievable. The auspicious season for sailing had slipped away; the settlers would be arriving in Canada too late in the year to be able to look after themselves.

One week after Paris fell to the allies transports were anchored in the Clyde. Between 11 July and 3 August all of the settlers embarked. There were 699 of them, far short of the 4,000 that Bathurst had originally intended to send.[35] The crossing was slow; not until late September did the fourth and last transport reach Quebec. It was with some dismay that the Canadian authorities greeted the arriving settlers.[36] Beyond Quebec lay an arduous journey inland to Upper Canada. Time would not allow the settlers to reach their destinations and to build shelters before winter. Instead, they were taken to Brockville, Fort Wellington, and Cornwall and kept in barracks which had recently been vacated by troops returning to Europe.[37] By spring of 1816, when they were at length located in the townships near the Rideau Lakes, they had been fed at government expense for a year. A crop failure that autumn and in each of the next two years compelled the government to continue assistance to some families until 1819.

Lord Bathurst urged Sir Gordon Drummond, the Canadian Governor-in-Chief, to do everything possible to make the settlers comfortable. The letters they sent home, he predicated, would do more to create a preference for Canada over the United States than any encouragement that the government could give.[38] If the small number of Scots who had come to Canada in 1815 were well treated, larger numbers of volunteer emigrants would follow them in the future. The history of the Rideau Settlement and of Upper Canada shows that this expectation was not disappointed.[39] In this sense, the the experiment was a success. On the other hand, the expense of maintaining settlers for a prolonged period of time taught officials in the Colonial Office to approach the subject of assisted emigration with increased caution in the future.

When Lord Bathurst first advised his Governor-in-Chief in

[34] C.O. 42/165, Campbell to Bathurst, 24 May 1815; C.O. 43/52, Goulburn to Transport Office, 29 May 1815.
[35] C.O. 385/2.
[36] C.O. 42/163, Drummond to Bathurst, 23 and 27 Sept. 1815.
[37] E. C. Guillet, *The Great Migration* (Toronto, 1963), p. 167; G. F. Playter, 'An Account of the Founding of Three Military Settlements in Eastern Canada—Perth, Lanark and Richmond, 1815–20', *O.H.S.P.R.* xx (1923), p. 98.
[38] C.O. 43/23, Bathurst to Drummond, 13 June 1815.
[39] H. I. Cowan, *British Emigration to British North America* (Toronto, 1961), pp. 63–4.

Rothes ● Banff ● Lonmay
Glenelg ●
Glenshiel ● ● Fort Augustus
Knoydart ●   Primrose ●
S c o t l a n d
● Ardgour
                Carie ● Fernan
        Finlarig ● ● Lawers   St. Vigeans ●
Craignure ● Killin   Dundee ●
                ● Callander
Craighouse ●   Kinglassie ●
        Old Kilpatrick   Fintry ●   ● Inverkeithing
        Barrowfield ● Glasgow ● Corstorphine ● ● Edinburgh
        Paisley ●   Anderston ●   ● Leith   ● Cockburnspath
            ● Beith   West Calder ●
    West Kilbride ●   Carnwath ●
        ● Kilmarnock
                ● Muirkirk
                        ● Redfordgreen
        Dunscore ● ● Lochmaben
        Torthorwald ●
    Wigtown ●   ● Tundergarth
                        Newcastle ●

I r e l a n d

                                    ● Kilburn

                    ● Blackburn   ● Spaldington
            Howick ●
                        ● Wakefield ● Waterside
                ● Hulton   ● Moorhouse
            ● Liverpool

                E n g l a n d

MAP 1. Home Localities of the Assisted Emigrants of 1815.

Canada that the planned emigration would not be carried out fully he referred to the decision as a deferment rather than a cancellation. The possibility that a large body of emigrants would be sent out in 1816 remained open.[40] In March 1816, however, the House of Commons rejected a motion by the Chancellor of the Exchequer to continue the property tax. This was a special tax which had been imposed in wartime and which the Commons were unwilling to see preserved in peace. As a result, Vansittart lost an important item of revenue and all departments were asked to economize. A tight budget had already forced a reduction of administrative staff; the office of the Secretary of State for War and the Colonies had lost seven clerks, one précis-writer, one interpreter, and an under-secretary.[41] There was no chance that such a novel enterprise as a scheme of assisted emigration would survive the budget cuts. In April John Campbell was advised that the plan had been abandoned.[42]

This decision did not represent a reassessment of objectives. While Bathurst and Goulburn came to believe that the scale of assistance given in 1815 had been too lavish, they still wanted to encourage capable settlers to go to Canada instead of to the United States. In January 1817, for example, Bathurst asked for funds to pay part of the expense of passages and three months rations for a group of settlers from the Isle of Skye, but was refused by the Treasury.[43] The concession of assistance to a small number of Scottish and English emigrants in 1815 had raised hopes in all parts of the British Isles. Welshmen, claiming to be as 'Loyal and Service-able' as the Scots, asked for equal encouragement to stay within the Empire. The volume of correspondence on emigration that the Colonial Office received, and continued to receive, stretched the capacity of its staff. As long as extreme parsimony ruled the Treasury, little expectation of help could be held out to those who wanted to settle in the North American colonies. Throughout 1816 and 1817 petitioners were told that the government could offer no more than a grant of land in proportion to the means of the settler.[44] Because

---

[40] C.O. 42/165, Campbell to Bathurst, 14 Oct. 1815; Add. MSS. 40249, Goulburn to Peel, 28 Nov. 1815.

[41] *Hansard*, 1816, xxxiii, col. 480.

[42] C.O. 43/53, Goulburn to Campbell, 15 Apr. 1816.

[43] C.O. 43/54, Bathurst to Vansittart, 4 Jan. 1817, and Goulburn to McCrummen, 23 Jan. 1817.

[44] For example see C.O. 43/53, Goulburn to Beckett, 11 May 1816, and C.O. 43/54, Goulburn to McClay, 31 Dec. 1816.

a grant could not be obtained without the payment of substantial fees, the offer was empty.

While the Treasury would not provide settlers with free passages from Britain, it agreed to a modest expenditure to redirect them to Canada from New York. James Buchanan, the British consul at New York, reported that a great number of emigrants were disappointed with the conditions they had encountered in the United States and had applied for grants of land in Canada.[45] Many of these emigrants came from Ulster. In Ireland Canada was little known, and then imperfectly, while ties with the United States were of long standing and had recently been publicized by several of the exiles of 1798. If Ulstermen were settled in Canada, this situation might be altered and the stream of Irish emigrants turned away from the United States. Buchanan thought that an attempt should be made to attract to Upper Canada those of the emigrants who were loyal, industrious, and 'comparatively wealthy'. Unless some inducement were held out they would not go.

For these reasons and in response to a request from the Colonial Office, the Foreign Office authorized Buchanan to spend up to ten dollars for each British subject who landed at New York and decided to settle in Canada.[46] In 1817 Buchanan forwarded over 1,600 emigrants at a cost of scarcely two dollars per head. These people were allotted land in Upper Canada in two newly surveyed townships named Monaghan and Cavan after the counties in Northern Ireland from which many of them had come.[47] Their arrival marked the beginnings of Irish settlement in a province which was eventually to acquire a pronounced Orange character. The established residents were not entirely happy with this development. Nevertheless, Buchanan carried on his work. By the end of 1820 he had sent about 7,000 persons to Upper Canada 'without spending that much in shillings'.[48] This was a significant contribution to a population which had numbered only 100,000 in 1815.

[45] F.O. 5/116, Buchanan to Castlereagh, 4 Dec. 1816; F.O. 5/125, Buchanan to Hamilton, 15 Mar. 1817; C.O. 42/167, Sherbrooke to Bathurst, 22 Aug. 1816.

[46] C.O. 43/24, Bathurst to Sherbrooke, 10 Jan. 1817; C.O. 43/54, Goulburn to Hamilton, 21 Nov. 1816; F.O. 5/116, Hamilton to Buchanan, 4 Dec. 1816.

[47] F.O. 5/125, Buchanan to Castlereagh, 5 Nov. 1817 (enclosure); John Strachan, *Remarks on Emigration from the United Kingdom Addressed to Robert Wilmot Horton Esq. M.P.* (London, 1827), p. 51; *Parl. Pap.* 1826, iv (404), 167–8; Edith G. Firth, ed., *The Town of York, 1815–1834* (Toronto, 1966), p. 39.

[48] James Buchanan, *Project for the Formation of a Depot in Upper Canada to Receive*

The value of Buchanan's efforts was diminished as soon as the ports of British North America assumed a larger role in the trans-atlantic-emigrants trade, and that happened within a very short period of time. In 1817, in response to the demands of Northern Irish shipping interests, Parliament altered the passenger regulations to permit vessels sailing to British North America to carry one passenger for every 1½ tons while vessels sailing to the United States were held to the old ratio of one passenger for every 5 tons.[49] The Colonial Office had no hand in framing this legislation; nor did it appear to be aware of the implications of the change that was made. In 1816, when uniform legislation had prevailed, 9,022 people had left the United Kingdom for the United States and 3,360 for British North America.[50] Under the new legislation the cost of a passage to Quebec was reduced to about one-half of the fare to New York. As the number of timber ships involved in the trade with North America increased, the cost fell further. Emigrants were influenced immediately by the difference; in 1817, 10,280 of them sailed to the United States and 9,979 to British North America. By 1819 almost 70 per cent of the emigrant trade was directed towards the colonial ports; 10,674 sailed to the United States and 23,543 to British North America. The revised passenger legislation had effectively shifted the course of a swelling stream of emigrants.

The greatest number of those who disembarked in British North America disappeared across the American border. The route that emigrants were taking had changed, but their destination remained the same, as the sudden importance of the port of St. Andrew's made abundantly clear. St. Andrew's, New Brunswick, was remarkable for its proximity to the border of Maine. Through it passed emigrants to the United States who took advantage of the cheaper fares to British North America. The number of Ulstermen who chose this route is suggested by the figures for the first six months of 1819.[51] Of thirty-nine emigrant vessels sailing from Belfast in this period, fourteen were headed for Quebec, thirteen for St. Andrew's, two for other ports in British North America, and ten for ports in the United

---

the *Whole Pauper Population of England* (New York, 1834), p. 9; C.O. 42/186, Buchanan to Goulburn, 6 July 1820, (enclosure); *Parl. Pap.* 1817, xiii (319), 5.

[49] Jones, 'Transatlantic Emigrant Trade', pp. 66–7.

[50] Cowan, Appendix B, p. 288.

[51] See Jones, pp. 47–8, 84–8. Destinations of vessels leaving Belfast from January to July are given in the *Evening Mail*, 19–21 July 1819.

States. Emigrants who could afford to sail directly to the United States travelled in relative comfort in vessels carrying forty or fifty passengers. Those who took the indirect route shared the confined space of a single vessel with 150 or 200 others. Over 2,500 Ulstermen from Belfast landed at St. Andrew's while no more than 437 disembarked at New York, Baltimore, and Philadelphia. For the Irish St. Andrew's had become a major port of entry into the United States.

Quebec shared this experience, but on a larger scale. No immigrant-port in North America was busier than Quebec in the years after 1817. About 40 per cent of all British emigrants landed there in 1819, and Quebec consistently received more than 10,000 emigrants in a year.[52] Yet this great demand on her facilities contributed surprisingly little to the settlement of the Canadas. W. B. Felton, a well-informed legislative councillor in Lower Canada, estimated that for every 8,000 emigrants who proceeded from Quebec to the United States, only 500 stayed in Lower Canada and no more than 1,500 went to Upper Canada.[53] There were superior opportunities in the republic and they were better known and advertised. Emigrants arrived at Quebec with a firm intention to cross the border. Either they followed the Richelieu River and Lake Champlain to New York State and New England, or, more frequently, they went by way of the St. Lawrence and Great Lakes to Upper New York State, Ohio, Indiana, and Illinois.[54] For the most part, the emigrants who remained in Quebec were the sick, the dying, and the destitute. The new pattern of emigration produced by the passenger legislation of 1817 created problems for the colonial government without adding much to the colonial population.

The Colonial Office did not foresee the large numbers of emigrants that would be passing through British North America under the altered passenger regulations. It was in this state of ignorance that Bathurst considered the renewal of assisted emigration in 1817. His interest now included settlement at the Cape as well as in British North America. At this time no tradition existed of British emigration to South Africa. The Cape of Good Hope had been taken from the Dutch eleven years earlier, and the British position there had

[52] Cowan, p. 288; and figures from the Port of Quebec exchange books cited by N. Gould, *Emigration, Practical Advice to Emigrants* (London, 1834), p. 118.

[53] *Parl. Pap.* 1826, iv (404), 101.

[54] Jones, p. 84.

been confirmed by treaty for less than two years. Although officials at the Cape had requested British settlers as early as 1813, Lord Bathurst had not replied until some time after the status of the colony was decided.[55] In July 1817 he introduced the idea as if it were a new one. He advised Lord Charles Somerset, the Governor at the Cape, that a great many individuals had applied for help to emigrate and that more than one of them wanted to go to South Africa; he asked Somerset whether or not an extensive British settlement could be established at the Cape and what arrangements would be the most practical to follow.

Somerset saw emigration as a means to strengthen defences in the region of the Great Fish Fiver, the formal boundary between the colony and the Bantu territories. In the early years of the century Xhosa tribesmen had moved into the frontier district in large numbers and their murders and robberies had become such a menace to Dutch settlers that by 1811 only one family remained east of Uitenhage.[56] In 1812 the Xhosa had been cleared out of the region west of the Great Fish, but since then Somerset had been obliged to keep a military force on the frontier. In 1817 the number of troops at the Cape had been reduced from 4,000 to 2,400 as part of a general measure of economy. Somerset was anxious to withdraw his frontier forces and he believed that he would be able to do so if that area were well populated. Xhosa raids could then be contained by the settlers themselves.

Bathurst suggested two methods of disposing of land to emigrants: large grants to men of means or small grants to individual settlers. In his reply of December 1817 Somerset declared for the former.[57] If land were granted only to capitalists who brought out labourers, a struggling settlement would automatically be provided with the leadership that Somerset believed would be essential. Settlers would need to be ready to protect their livestock and property from the Xhosa. A major proprietor would be less exposed to plunder than an individual farmer. Without the co-operative action that a large landholder could enforce upon his tenants or servants, a colony in the Zuurveld would be less than secure.

[55] C.O. 48/29, Somerset to Bathurst, 20 Jan. 1815; C.O. 49/12, Bathurst to Somerset, 28 July 1817.
[56] Ibid., 3 Apr. 1815; *Records of Cape Colony*, xi, Somerset to Bathurst, 24 Apr. 1817: C.O. 48/76, Somerset to Bathurst, 18 Dec. 1817; G. M. Theal, *History of South Africa*, v (Capetown, 1964), 249–64; G. E. Corry, *The Rise of South Africa*, i (London, 1913), 220–50.
[57] C.O. 48/76, Somerset to Bathurst, 18 Dec. 1817.

These were not the reasons which convinced the Colonial Secretary that large grants would produce the best results both at the Cape and in Canada. Bathurst wished to restrict as well as to encourage the movement of people to the colonies. Immigrants were not always desirable. Bathurst believed that the established policy of giving at least 100 acres of land to each British subject who applied in Canada led the wrong class of people to immigrate. A minimum capital requirement might prevent an unwanted influx of paupers. This thinking produced a plan which was presented to the Treasury for approval in December 1817.[58] Grants of crown land would be reserved for men with enough capital to employ and settle permanently at least ten families. An applicant would require at least £20 per adult male in his party to qualify. One-half of this money would be demanded in advance to be repaid once he had fulfilled his contract. The advantages of these regulations, as Goulburn saw them, were: first, that they would promote concentrated settlement; second, that they would ensure proper use of capital; and third, that they would protect the colonies from an inundation of idle persons. To induce men with capital to emigrate on these terms Goulburn asked the Treasury to sanction free passages. In comparison with the assistance that had been given in 1815, this would be a modest concession.

The plan was drawn up before Somerset's opinion was available. His dispatch advocating the colonization of the Zuurveld did not arrive in London until February 1818.[59] By then circulars describing terms of assistance to emigrants were in print and, in a few instances, already distributed. The Colonial Office acted on its own initiative and without any specific regard for the problem of policing the Kaffir frontier. One consideration figured pre-eminently in 1818 as in 1815: it was desirable to send to the colonies superior emigrants who might otherwise go to the United States. This consideration led the Colonial Office to offer uniform terms to emigrants going either to the Cape or to the North American provinces.

The scheme is interesting as an illustration of Colonial Office intentions rather than as an example of effective policy. Lord

[58] C.O. 43/24, Bathurst to Sherbrooke, 10 Nov. 1817; C.O. 43/56, Goulburn to Treasury, 6 Dec. 1817.

[59] The dispatch dated 18 Dec. 1817 was received 9 Feb. 1818. A circular was sent to Richard Talbot on 7 Feb. 1818. See E. A. Talbot, *Five Years Residence in the Canadas*, i (London, 1824), 9, and C.O. 384/3, Talbot to Goulburn, 7 Mar. 1818. For the full text of the circular see *Parl. Pap.* 1819, ii (529), 25.

Bathurst and his Treasury colleagues did not propose to support emigration in a liberal way. The offer of free passages was not advertised and potential emigrants were advised of it only if they wrote to the Colonial Office for information. Few people applied and fewer received official approval. Only four parties were given assistance in the first year: two of fifty or sixty people from Alston, Cumberland; a third of about 170 people, all Protestants, from Cloghjordan, Tipperary; and a fourth of over 300 from Breadalbane, Perthshire.[60] With the exception of some members of the Scottish party who went to Prince Edward Island, all of the assisted emigrants settled in Upper Canada. Some of them were quite well off. In the Irish party at least one settler was worth £300; no less than six possessed £100, and many had a minimum of £40 or £50.[61] Most of the emigrants were tenant farmers who were able to muster enough money to meet the terms of the government's offer.

Altogether, between 600 and 700 emigrants were sent to Canada in 1818 at a cost to the government of about £4,000, a sum smaller than Bathurst's annual salary.[62] This effort was dwarfed by the 10,000 voluntary emigrants who reached British North American ports in 1817 and the 14,500 who came in 1818. It became apparent that unassisted emigrants travelling under the new passenger regulations were going to continue to arrive at Quebec in large numbers. The most unfortunate consequence would be the dumping of hundreds of paupers on the towns of Quebec and Montreal. Emigrants with money could afford the journey to New York State or Illinois. Those who disembarked without a penny became a burden upon the colonials. In the winter of 1819–20 about 500 pauper emigrants were supported by public charity in Quebec and Montreal and there were many others distributed throughout the province.[63] By encouraging a few large parties of selected emigrants

[60] Cowan, pp. 44–7. For the correspondence of the party leaders, Milburn, Leathart, Robertson, and Talbot, with the Colonial Office and for Navy Office replies to requests for transports: C.O. 384/1, 3, 4. For Colonial Office instructions to Navy Office and to Canadian government: C.O. 43/24, 56, 57. For a record of deposits by individuals in Robertson's party: A.O. 1–2131/3 and 5. On the Talbot party; Talbot, *Five Years Residence in the Canadas.*

[61] Talbot, ii. 197–8.

[62] Statement of expenses for passages from Whitehaven, Cork, and Greenock: C.O. 42/183, Navy Office to Goulburn, 16 Feb. 1819; salaries of Colonial Office personnel; D. M. Young, *The Colonial Office in the Early Nineteenth Century* (London, 1961), p. 274.

[63] C.O. 42/182, Monk to Bathurst, 8 Nov. 1819 and enclosure; Talbot, ii. 214; C.O. 42/183, Treasury to Goulburn, 23 Mar. 1819.

the Colonial Office was not controlling the influx of paupers as it had hoped to do.

With respect to the Cape the offer of free passages was of no significance at all. Emigrants usually followed a beaten path and South Africa would have attracted them only if the government's scheme had been advertised. In the absence of any public announcement there were only a handful of inquiries and just one acceptable application.[64] The last involved a party of nineteen families which sailed near the end of the spring of 1819. During the same season a small party bound for Upper Canada embarked at Hull. This was the last group to sail to Quebec on the terms set out in 1818.[65] Bathurst and Goulburn were either unwilling or unable to carry out a vigorous test of their ideas. By the autumn of 1818 they had lost interest in the experiment and by the spring of 1819 they were telling new correspondents that free passages could not be expected in the future. 'You have been misinformed,' Goulburn wrote in June to a group of prospective emigrants to the Cape; 'no assistance is given to Settlers beyond a grant of land on their Arrival in the Colony.[66]

The Colonial Office abandoned its programme of sponsored emigration just as the Cabinet and Parliament became convinced of the domestic value of such a measure. In July 1819 Nicholas Vansittart, the Chancellor of the Exchequer, proposed a grant of £50,000 to send unemployed workmen to the Cape. He not only received the approval that he expected, but was 'hailed with applause from every part of the House'.[67] In the atmosphere of crisis that prevailed in 1819 the idea of pauper emigration was remarkably popular and Cabinet ministers were prepared to promote it in a partial way. The initiative now came from outside the Colonial Office. In sanctioning assistance to indigent emigrants Parliament ignored the priorities the

[64] I. E. Edwards, *The 1820 Settlers in South Africa* (London, 1934), pp. 47-9. See correspondence with Atkinson, Beale, and Tait: C.O. 48/38 and 49/11.

[65] See Spilsbury correspondence: C.O. 384/3 and 5; and C.O. 43/24, Bathurst to Richmond, 8 Mar. 1819.

[66] CO. 49/11, Goulburn to Matheson, 5 June 1819. For some time Goulburn had been advising people who inquired independently that no assistance was given to individuals. The point here is that he denies that there is a policy of encouraging groups. In the same volume of correspondence there is a curious letter from Goulburn to G. Banks, 8 June 1819, suggesting to Banks that the Cape would be a better place in which to settle than British North America. Goulburn, however, does not offer transportation; settlers must 'convey themselves'.

[67] [John Barrow], 'The Cape of Good Hope', *Quarterly Review*, xxii, Nov. 1819, pp. 208-9.

Colonial Office had observed since 1815. It had never been the intention of that department to encourage people to emigrate who otherwise would have stayed in Britain. The traditional view of population as a national asset dictated the thinking of the Colonial Secretary and his Under-Secretary. They revealed no appreciation of the emigration ideas advanced by Torrens, Hayter, and Colquhoun. Their objective in sponsoring emigration was to strengthen British possessions overseas. They wanted self-sufficient emigrants not paupers. The terms on which they granted assistance were designed to disqualify the indigent and the near indigent. They acted without reference to growing public concern about unemployment and over-population. Their measures were justified as valuable to the colonies but of no consequence to the home country. In this way, the emigration experiments of 1815 and 1818–19, which were conceived entirely within the Colonial Office, stand apart from those that followed.

III

ASSISTED EMIGRATION TO UPPER CANADA
AND THE CAPE OF GOOD HOPE, 1819–1821

IN 1819 and 1820 the reservations of the Colonial Office about
pauper emigration were superseded by other considerations. Fear of
working-class disturbances moved Parliament to vote £50,000 for a
project of emigration to the Cape and subsequently led the Prime
Minister and the Chancellor of the Exchequer to agree to help
Scottish weavers to go to Upper Canada. While the decision in each
case did not arise in exactly the same way, the circumstances were
comparable; the government responded to similar alarms and
apprehensions and the two experiments were, in a sense, parts of the
same story. Together they present a uniform picture.

This picture lies outside the vision of Isobel Eirlys Edwards, who,
in her book on the emigration to South Africa in 1820, says that the
government's real objective should be sought 'in considerations of
imperial defence' and particularly 'in the urgent appeals of Lord
Somerset'.[1] Miss Edwards builds her argument on her interpretation
of two principal items of evidence. First, she cites Somerset's
dispatches of 24 April and 18 December 1817 to prove that he inspired the decision to send settlers to the Cape. He was under
pressure to find an economical way to protect the colony's eastern
frontier against the Xhosa; his answer lay in bolstering the frontier
population. To make the Zuurveld sound attractive to settlers 'his
fertile imagination conjured up a picture of land flowing with milk
and honey'. Miss Edwards believes that the government's offer of
assistance to emigrants in 1818 came as a response and that, when
the Commons voted £50,000 in July 1819, it simply permitted the
extension of a decision that had been worked out eighteen months
earlier.

The Chancellor of the Exchequer, Miss Edwards says, was too

---

[1] *The 1820 Settlers in South Africa*, pp. 42 and 43–53. Miss Edwards attempts to
revise the earlier judgements of G. M. Theal, G. E. Corry, E. Walker, W. M. Macmillan,
and others.

astute to make any reference to the strategic purpose of the proposed settlement. Recruiting of emigrants would suffer if members of the government spoke too frankly. For that reason he obscured the government's intention to plant the settlement 'in the vicinity of the hostile and advancing Kaffir tribes'. Miss Edwards holds a very low opinion of Vansittart and his colleagues; she attributes to them the guile to seduce unsuspecting emigrants into a dangerous situation and the stupidity to believe that a military settlement so created could be effective. Nevertheless, her apparent scholarship has convinced those who have written subsequently on this subject; her contention that the government deliberately disguised a measure of colonial defence as an experiment in pauper emigration is now generally accepted.[2]

Miss Edward's thesis depends upon a strained reading of the documents. Although Somerset did tell Bathurst on 24 April 1817 that he could safely remove troops from the Great Fish River if the population of the Zuurveld were greater, he did not then recommend, suggest, or even mention British emigration.[3] It was already his policy to encourage Boer colonists to settle in the Zuurveld and he was optimistic that by this means the area would be quickly reoccupied. Somerset did not press for the establishment of a British settlement on the frontier until Bathurst expressed an interest in sponsoring emigrants. Even then, Somerset's opinion carried no influence; the Colonial Office proceeded to offer free passages without waiting for his reply.[4] In 1818 Bathurst and Goulburn were not concerned with the Cape alone; the system of assisted emigration that they adopted was designed primarily for the British North American colonies. The Cape was included as an afterthought; no weight was given to the consideration that British settlers could strengthen the colony's eastern border.

Of course, once they had seen Somerset's dispatch of 18 December 1817, Bathurst and Goulburn were aware that he attached importance to the settlement of the Zuurveld. This knowledge made little difference. Miss Edwards has not been able to cite a single dispatch in which either Bathurst or Goulburn admitted or discussed strategic reasons for sending settlers to South Africa. Moreover, the officials

[2] For example see T. R. H. Davenport, 'The Consolidation of a New Society: The Cape Colony', M. Wilson and L. Thompson, eds., *The Oxford History of South Africa* (Oxford, 1969), pp. 278–9.

[3] *Records of Cape Colony*, xi. 306–8.

[4] See pp. 27–8.

of the colonial department made no great effort to recruit emigrants for the Cape in 1818 or during the first six months of 1819; only one small party received assistance. If, in advance of July 1819, they planned to send several thousand settlers to the Zuurveld, they did so without leaving any evidence in the surviving correspondence. Instead, in June 1819, they informed applicants that the government no longer granted free passages.

The evidence that does exist indicates that the decision to sponsor a large contingent of emigrants to South Africa came in haste. That was how one Cabinet minister later remembered it; the measure, he wrote, 'which was pressed upon the government by the House of Commons upon a particular emergency, was necessarily undertaken in a great hurry without much time for previous preparation'.[5] This explanation makes it easier to understand why the authorities at the Cape received no hint of the government's intention until October 1819. The vote of £50,000 caught Bathurst by surprise. He did not have time to consult Somerset, but wrote simply to advise him that the emigrants were coming.[6] His letter reached Somerset only a few weeks before the first emigrants embarked.

Two points in this letter suggest that the Colonial Secretary did not give foremost consideration to the settlement of the frontier district. The Governor at the Cape was instructed to make the landdros 'of each district in which settlers may be placed' responsible for their welfare. Bathurst expected that settlers would be located in more than one district; he did not assign any priority to the Zuurveld. It occurred to him that craftsmen might find more profitable employment in Cape Town than in a new settlement. These people, he told Somerset, could be allowed to go anywhere in the colony provided they were not tied down by contracts with their party leaders. Bathurst wanted to see the settlers achieve independence and self-sufficiency without delay. This was his first concern. If he also wanted to strengthen the line of defence along the Great Fish River, it was an objective of secondary importance and one to which he did not refer.

Clearly, the emergency that motivated the British government did not spring from the activities of the tribesmen of Bantuland. It is easy to exaggerate the threat posed by the Xhosa. Although they

[5] B. M. Loan 57/23, F. J. Robinson's memorandum on emigration and corn.
[6] C.O. 49/12, Bathurst to Somerset, 20 July 1819; C.O. 48/39, Somerset to Bathurst, 6 Nov. 1819.

periodically invaded the Zuurveld in strength, they could be contained by a relatively small number of troops. When several thousand
Xhosa attacked Grahamstown in April 1819, they were driven back
by a force of only 250 men.[7] News of this Fifth Kaffir War, it should
be remarked, did not reach Britain until about 20 August, too late to
be considered the inspiration of the motion to send settlers to South
Africa. The number of people who were exposed to the menace of
the Xhosa was not great; in the whole of the Zuurveld in 1816 there
were no more than 145 families. The constant fear in which the
Boers on the frontier lived should not be underestimated. The
incessant plundering of Xhosa raiders rendered their position precarious and in 1816–17 at least ninety families were forced to leave.[8]
On the other hand, the problem of protecting the cattle of a handful
of Dutch farmers was not one of great national significance.

The emergency which prompted the Cabinet to sponsor a project
of emigration in 1819 was domestic, not colonial. Since the spring
the political reform movement had been gaining energy in the manufacturing districts of Northern England and Scotland. It fed on the
despair of workmen who felt the impact of a poor harvest in 1818 and
a glut in the textile market.[9] Fifteen years earlier a hand-loom weaver
in Glasgow had earned 25s. a week. His self-respect had been considerable. He had not been affected by the competition of power
looms because so many of his fellow tradesmen had been recruited
to fight in the Napoleonic Wars. With the demobilization of the army
his weekly earnings fell to 10s. He reacted by working fourteen hours
a day and succeeded only in depressing the value of finished materials.
An importation of surplus quantities of raw cotton, silk, and wool led
him to over-produce at such a rate that by 1819 he was working
night and day to earn only 5s. a week. He expected help from the
government; Radicals counted on his disappointment to bring him
to their side.

---

[7] 'Life was dangerous for those who chose to farm on the frontier,' writes W. M.
Macmillan, 'but their troubles and difficulties were not a matter of life and death for the
Colony as a whole; as late as the twenties even frontier Grahamstown was almost more
concerned about the Cape struggle for political life than with the Bantu in their neigh-
bourhood.' See *Bantu, Boer, and Briton* (Oxford, 1963), p. 43. For the encounter at
Grahamstown see Theal, *South Africa*, v 337–8; C.O. 48/51, pp. 24–5. Somerset wrote
to Bathurst on 22 May 1819 (C.O. 48/39) to describe the incident but his letter was not
received until 2 Sept. 1819, long after arrangements for the settlers had been made. The
incident was reported in the British press in late August; see the *Courier*, 20 Aug. 1819.

[8] *Records of Cape Colony*, xi. 306.

[9] *Hansard*, 1819, xli, col. 892–3, 922; *Parl. Pap.* 1818, v (400), 216.

Through a network of informants Lord Sidmouth, the Home Secretary, followed the events of 1819 with mounting alarm. As the summer advanced, the activity and confidence of the Radicals increased. Great outdoor meetings were held at Glasgow, Stockport, Leeds, and elsewhere. To Sidmouth all signs pointed to one conclusion: 'the disaffected in the North of England' were planning an insurrection.[10] On 7 July Sidmouth wrote to the Lord-Lieutenants of all of the counties in the vicinity of the Reform meetings to advise them to place their Yeomanry Cavalry in a state of readiness. On 13 July, when the Prince Regent dismissed Parliament, he emphasized his determination to suppress the traitorous designs of those who would 'subvert our happy constitution, under the pretence of Reform'.[11] The country was ripe for the kind of panic reaction by local authorities that produced the 'massacre of Peterloo' five weeks later.

This was the atmosphere on 12 July, the last business day of the session, when Parliament decided to encourage emigration to South Africa. In meeting the radical threat the government's first inclination was to use force. Yet it was realized that the principal source of discontent was economic and not political. As soon as there was an improvement in trade, the crisis would subside. In the meantime, the attitude of the unemployed was of critical importance. Magistrates were urged to do everything possible to prevent 'the disloyal from influencing the conduct of the distressed'.[12] At this moment a token offer of assistance could be expected to have more than token value.

In Scotland and to a lesser extent in northern England, there was evidence amongst weavers of a strong desire to emigrate; a development which did not meet the approval of Radicals. On 16 June 1819 a meeting was called in Glasgow to petition the Prince Regent for the means to go to the colonies and 35,000 or 40,000 people attended. Radical speakers insisted that emigration was not the answer. Low wages were not caused by redundant population but by misrepresentation in Parliament. The only people who should emigrate were the 'borough monger, sinecurists, and 150,000 of the clergy'.[13] A choice

[10] H.O. 41/4, Hobhouse to Silvester, Wright, etc., 3 July 1819, and Sidmouth to Derby, 7 July 1819. Sidmouth's letter to the Lord-Lieutenant of Chester was published in the public press; for example see the *Morning Herald*, 20 July 1819, or the *Caledonian Mercury*, 22 July 1819.

[11] *Courier*, 14 July 1819.

[12] Hobhouse to Silvester, etc., 3 July 1819.

[13] *Caledonian Mercury*, 21 June 1819. See R. J. White, *Waterloo to Peterloo* (London, 1963), p. 179.

lay in front of the unemployed weavers: they could join those who were petitioning for assistance to emigrate, or they could join those who were agitating for political reform. This was a choice that the government wished to influence and it could do so only by showing itself to be responsive to the petitioners' demands.

In 1819 members of the Cabinet did not believe that the government should bear much responsibility for the welfare of the unemployed. Their concept of the function of government did not go far beyond the preservation of law and order. Lord Liverpool, the Prime Minister, spoke for most public men when he opposed in principle the use of national resources to alleviate local distress.[14] He was not generous in the grants he sanctioned for the relief of the poor in the manufacturing districts. Nor was he prepared to spend a very large sum on emigration. The money allocated for this purpose did not exceed the annual income offered to Queen Caroline in 1820. Liverpool did not envisage emigration on a scale sufficient to reduce unemployment except in a very minor way. His objective was political rather than humanitarian. While he waited for an improvement in the textile trade, he wanted to give hope to those who might otherwise fall into the Radical camp. No time was lost in thoroughly advertising the decision to promote emigration.[15] For the government's purposes the announcement of this decision was more important than its subsequent execution.

The offer of assistance to emigrants was welcomed in Parliament and in the press.[16] No one expressed surprise that the emigrants should be directed to South Africa. The Cape was generally believed to be an ideal colony for settlement. On 18 June, 1819 in an article calling for state-supported emigration, *The Times* had declared that the Cape of Good Hope had the finest soil and climate in the world. The colony could be described only in superlatives; it produced in unequalled abundance all of the necessities and all of the luxuries of life; it commanded the commerce of the globe; it was 'the key to India', 'the bridle of America', and it could take the place of the whole of Europe as a supplier of materials to Britain. As a resident of Cape Colony observed, many writers and speakers attributed to the

[14] C. D. Yonge, *The Life and Administration of Robert Banks, Second Earl of Liverpool, K.G.*, ii (London, 1868), 438.

[15] For example, advertisements first appeared in the *Morning Post*, 17 July; the *Courier*, 17 July; the *Evening Mail*, 16–19 July; the *Morning Chronicle*, 19 July; the *Morning Herald*, 19 July; *Caledonian Mercury*, 22 July.

[16] See the *Morning Post*, 13 July; the *Courier*, 13 July; *The Times*, 29 July.

Cape 'a climate and a fertility known only in romance'.[17] This conviction of the superiority of the Cape had already led several
prominent individuals to propose the development of settlements at
Saldanha Bay or along the coastal strip between Plattenburg Bay
and the Great Fish River, but their plans had not received the
approval of the Colonial Office. Members of the Select Committee
on the Poor Laws had responded to prevailing opinion when they
listened to evidence on the Cape on 28 June 1819, before recommending that every reasonable facility should be given to those who
wished to emigrate.

Henry Goulburn himself believed that a settler possessed a better
chance to succeed in South Africa than in Canada.[18] There were no
forests to clear and no winter to contend with. A settler could plough
the land without preparation and he could grow more than one crop
in a year. While a pauper emigrant in Canada would depend on
rations for twelve months or more, in South Africa he could be
expected to support himself almost immediately. Goulburn had
never been convinced that the emigration of paupers to Canada was
desirable. The paupers who were sailing unassisted to Quebec were
a sufficient problem for the Canadian authorities. Consequently,
when the Cabinet decided to encourage emigration, the choice of
South Africa as the place of settlement was clear.

Public curiosity about South Africa was stimulated by the govern-
ment's decision; travellers and pamphleteers hastened to issue new
books and new editions. Among the publications that appeared in
1819 were William Burchell's *Hints on Emigration to the Cape of
Good Hope*, a third edition of R. B. Fisher's *The Importance of the
Cape of Good Hope as a Colony to Great Britain*, the Reverend C. J.
Latrobe's *Journal of a Visit to South Africa* in 1815 and 1816,
G. Ross's *Cape of Good Hope Calendar and Agricultural Guide*, and
John Wilson's *The Emigrant's Guide to the Cape of Good Hope*. In
addition, there were long articles on South Africa in *Blackwood's*
and in the *Quarterly Review*.[19] Much of this literature was inaccurate,
but it served to fan the excitement created by the government's offer.
At least 80,000 people wanted to take advantage of that offer;

[17] [W. Wilberforce Bird], *State of the Cape of Good Hope in 1822* (London, 1823),
p. 233.

[18] C.O. 49/11, Goulburn to Banks, 8 June 1819.

[19] [John Barrow], 'The Cape of Good Hope', *Quarterly Review*, Nov. 1819; 'Emigration to the Cape of Good Hope', *Blackwood's* Oct. 1819.

Downing Street was crowded daily by those who waited for the results of their applications.[20]

The administrative burden fell entirely on the Colonial Office. Although the size of the undertaking warranted the appointment of two or three special officers with a secretary and an office, this step was not taken. By dealing only with men who would organize and lead parties of emigrants the Colonial Office attempted to keep its work to manageable proportions. Even so, it was pressed beyond capacity. The government did not intend to give assistance to more than 5,000 emigrants. In selecting those who were to go, Goulburn acted without any discernible system. The methods of the Colonial Office were so chaotic that it was possible for one man's application to be accepted on the basis of a letter of reference written for another.[21] In September Goulburn confessed that he could not be certain that even one of the party leaders was a man of responsible character. He had no knowledge of them except from their correspondence and that had not told him much.

The party leaders who had been so casually chosen were entrusted with the task of recruiting the bulk of the emigrants. The only interest that the Colonial Office took in the matter was to insist, for the sake of information, that it be sent the names of those who were enrolled. Emigrant parties were offered assistance on the same terms as were available in 1818 with the added provision that parishes could deposit money on behalf of paupers.[22] Parties of three types were organized: parish paupers who were to receive 100 acres per family on arrival; individuals who had paid their own deposits and who were also to be granted separate lots; and indentured servants whose employer-leader was to receive a large block of land. The Colonial Office made no attempt to safeguard the rights of the emigrants who composed those parties and several leaders used their positions to impose special conditions. The seeds of the dissension that broke up a great many parties after they reached South Africa were present from the beginning.

The weavers of Glasgow experienced little of the excitement generated in England by the government's offer of free passages to the Cape of Good Hope. As soon as the offer had been publicized,

[20] A. K. Millar, *Plantagenet in South Africa, Lord Charles Somerset* (London, 1965), p. 121.

[21] C.O. 49/13, Goulburn to Powell, 20 Oct. 1819, and Goulburn to W. R. Cartwright, 8 Sept. 1819. See also Corry, *The Rise of South Africa* ii. 15–17.

[22] C.O. 48/76, Bathurst to Somerset, 20 July 1819 (enclosure).

a number of them had drafted a letter to Bathurst expressing their disappointment.[23] There were two reasons for this reaction. First, the deposit required by the government presented a serious obstacle. The Scottish Poor Law placed no obligation on local authorities to provide relief for those who were capable of working. While English parishes might be willing to pay the deposits of their pauper emigrants in order to get them off the poor roll, the same incentive did not exist in Scotland. Even if charitable organizations were willing to raise deposits for them, the weavers did not want to go to South Africa. They already knew families from communities in the Glasgow area who had been given generous assistance to go to Upper Canada in 1815. They had some idea of what they might expect to encounter there. The climate, people, and geography of South Africa were altogether too exotic; 'our hearts can never lye to the Cape of Good Hope.'

Within months many of those who did sail to South Africa would agree. The first ships to embark left the Thames in early December 1819; on 17 March their passengers sighted Table Mountain. By the end of June about 3,500 emigrants had arrived either at Table Bay or at Simon's Bay. Most of them sailed on up the eastern coast to Algoa Bay where they disembarked and then proceeded inland 150 miles by wagon to their settlement in the Zuurveld. It had been no secret that this was their most likely destination.[24] No other district in the colony contained as much unclaimed accessible and usable land. Everything that the settlers had read led them to expect an area of high fertility; they were not disappointed by what they first saw. 'I have a beautiful Stream of water before the House, the farm has the appearance of a fine level down, but the grass is equal to the richest in Wales,' Thomas Philipps wrote in early June.[25] As soon as a plough arrived he could start to work; he had no undergrowth to dig up and no trees to remove. The soil, he reported, was excellent.

Philipps's optimism would have been tempered if he had understood the meaning of Zuurveld; sour fields. The soil was acidic and deficient in phosphates; the sources of water were frequently dry and in many of the brooks and springs the water was too brackish to

[23] C.O. 384/4, Cannon to Bathurst, 16 July 1819. On the subject of the Scottish Poor Laws see *Parl. Pap.* 1818, v (400), 100, and 'The Causes and Cure of Pauperism', *The Edinburgh Review*, Mar. 1817, p. 3.

[24] See *The Times*, 29 July 1819.

[25] Arthur Keppel-Jones ed., *Phillips, 1820 Settler* (Pietermaritzburg, 1960), p. 70.

drink.[26] In occasional patches there were such high concentrations of salts in the soil that nothing could grow. Because the streams ran through deep and broad ravines, no simple system of irrigation was possible. With manure good gardens could be developed, but the absence of periodic rain meant that in many years crops would be a total loss. The Boers who lived in the Zuurveld knew that the region was valuable only for grazing, that it was unsuitable for sheep, and that cattle had to range over a wide area for nourishment. Boer farms usually included about 6,000 acres. To the British settlers, the government was granting only 100 acres per family. They were expected to become cultivators, not herdsmen. They quickly discovered that this was impossible.

Although the officials in Cape Town had grossly overestimated the fertility of the Zuurveld, they realized that this district could not accommodate all of the emigrants who were arriving from Britain. Sir Rufane Donkin, the Acting Governor while Lord Charles Somerset was on leave, doubted the existence of sufficient supplies of food to keep such a large number of people until they could harvest their first crops.[27] He decided to send some parties to other parts of the colony. Lord Bathurst had already suggested that the emigrants from the three parts of Great Britain should be located separately.[28] Consequently, a small party of Scots led by Thomas Pringle, once editor of the *Scots Magazine*, were taken from Algoa Bay to the valley of the Baviaans River, far inland from the Zuurveld. The Irish, who numbered about 350, were disembarked at Saldanha Bay on the west coast and located in the District of Clanwilliam. In addition, four parties were given land on the Sonderend River within 60 miles of Cape Town and one party of fishermen settled at the mouth of the Swartkops River on Algoa Bay.

Within weeks of their arrival Pringle's settlers realized that they could not manage on the land that they had been granted.[29] Ten

[26] For descriptions of the Zuurveld in the 1820s: Thomas Pringle, *Narrative of a Residence in South Africa* (London, 1835), pp. 107–9; Pringle, *Some Account of the Present State of the English Settlers in Albany, South Africa* (London, 1824), pp. 15–20; [Bird], *State of the Cape of Good Hope*, p. 180; and C.O. 48/76, Report of the Commissioners of Inquiry, 25 May 1825, p. 19. On the size of the grants see C.O. 48/76, Statement of the British Settlers, 10 Mar. 1823; and Corry, *Rise of South Africa*, ii. 61.

[27] C.O. 48/49, Donkin to Bathurst, 24 Apr. 1820.

[28] C.O. 49/12, Bathurst to Somerset, 6 Nov. 1819; H. E. Hockly, *The Story of the British Settlers of 1820 in South Africa* (Cape Town, 1948), pp. 46–7, 62–3.

[29] Pringle was recommended to the Colonial Office by Sir Walter Scott. See A. M. L. Robinson, 'Thomas Pringle and Sir Walter Scott', *Quarterly Bulletin of the South*

times their initial allotment would not be enough. In September 1820 they were allowed to draw their boundary three miles further down the valley and by a further extension nine months later their holdings were increased from 1,100 acres to 20,000 acres. With these concessions they were able to hold on through the drought and blight of 1821 until by the end of 1822 they could consider the worst of their difficulties behind them.

In Clanwilliam the Irish found themselves in a more serious predicament. They were located in an arid valley dominated by a chain of rugged mountains. Their farms were rock and sand in which grew parched and stunted bushes. A few small springs offered no water beyond the needs of the Boers who already lived there. In the judgement of the land-surveyor there were less than 10 acres of arable land available for each settler. Of all this the officials at Cape Town were painfully ignorant. It was amazing, a commission of inquiry later reported, that the colonial government should have known so little about Clanwilliam and that it should have done so little to find out more.[30] The sole preparatory investigation by the Cape Government Secretary, Colonel Christopher Bird, took the form of a casual conversation with a magistrate who had served in that district twelve years earlier. William Parker, a former mayor of Cork, who had been advised by John Barrow and other British authorities on the Cape to seek a grant at Knysna on the east coast, was understandably disappointed when he was sent to Clanwilliam.[31] When he learned that the Governor's chief administrative officer, Colonel Bird, was a Roman Catholic, he decided that it was all a Jesuit plot.

Months passed before the colonial government could be convinced of the magnitude of its error. Eventually the Irish were offered land in the Zuurveld with the government providing them with transportation to get there. Many agreed to go; they were

---

African Library, Dec. 1951, pp. 52–3; L. J. Jennings, ed., *The Croker Papers*, i (London, 1884), 147–8; C.O. 323/144, Lockhart to Hay, 30 Oct. 1826. On Pringle's party: Pringle, *Some Account of the Present State of the English Settlers*, pp. 106–8; Pringle, *Narrative of a Residence in South Africa*, pp. 1–167, 355–6.

[30] C.O. 48/88, Report of Commissioners of Inquiry, 17–18 June 1825. For Secretary Bird's version: Sir Rufane Donkin, *A Letter on the Government of the Cape* (London, 1827), p. 120. See also Corry, ii. 71–2.

[31] William Parker, *Proofs of the Delusions of His Majesty's Representative at the Cape of Good Hope* (Cork, 1826), p. 12; Parker, *The Jesuits Unmasked; Being an Illustration of the Existing Evils of Popery in a Protestant Government* (London, 1823). See C.O. 48/87, pp. 145 and 388.

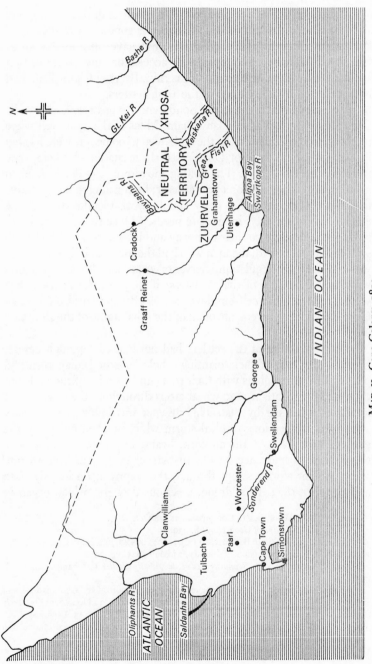

Map II. Cape Colony, 1819.

motivated as much by the prospect of free rations during the journey as by any hope that they would find better conditions at the end.[32] Parker bought land at Saldanha Bay, but gave up after his crops failed and launched a campaign of accusation and recrimination against those whom he blamed for his ruin. By 1824 Clanwilliam had been deserted by all but one of the Irish settlers.

The parties that went to the Sonderend River discovered conditions almost as bad as in Clanwilliam. Most of them, as well, were removed to the Zuurveld. In the end, over 3,700 people were located in this district in spite of Donkin's early hesitation.[33] There, they were compelled to stay. The Acting Governor was determined to prevent any dispersion for a year at least; he considered it imperative that those who came as a party should work together to produce enough wheat for their immediate needs.[34] Once this was achieved, settlers could safely go their own way and labourers could be free to seek employment with the men who had the most capital. This policy was enforced by regulation. Servants were not allowed passports without the consent of their masters; if they left the district, they were arrested. When self-employed settlers began to drift off towards Cape Town, the movements of all of the inhabitants of the Zuurveld were restricted.

A large number of the settlers had never used a plough before. Stories were told of their planting whole cobs of Indian corn and putting in young onions with their roots up.[35] Yet ineptitude was not their undoing. Late in 1820 wheat crops throughout the colony were attacked in full ear by rust. This disaster was followed in January 1821 by a tremendous tropical storm which washed out all of the gardens and fields of Indian corn, beans, and potatoes. Nor were these solitary occurrences.[36] The rust struck every year from 1820 to 1825; violent storms swept through the colony again in July 1822 and October 1823. In addition, a serious drought, which began in

[32] C.O. 48/88, Woodcock to Commissioners, 20 Oct. 1824.

[33] Bird, *State of Cape of Good Hope*, p. 239.

[34] C.O. 48/49, Donkin to Bathurst, 20 July 1820; C.O. 48/76, Bird to Cuyler, 22 Mar. 1820; Report of Commissioners of Inquiry, 25 May 1825, pp. 20–2.

[35] H. H. Dugmore, *The Reminiscences of an Albany Settler* (Grahamstown, 1958), p. 27.

[36] For contemporary accounts of the crop failures: Report of the Commissioners of Inquiry, 25 May 1825, p. 37; C.O. 48/49, Donkin to Bathurst, 30 Dec. 1820; *Quarterly Review*, July 1821, p. 460; the *South African Commercial Advertiser*, 14 Apr. 1824; C.O. 325/33, Details of circumstances which have led to the present distressed State of the Cape of Good Hope, 1826.

1825, persisted until the middle of 1826. Instead of rapidly achieving a position of self-support, the settlers were dependent on public and private charity.

Nature alone was a formidable enemy; the settlers also had to contend with an ill-disposed colonial government. According to Henry Ellis, Under-Secretary at the Cape, the colonial government was not greatly concerned about the fate of the new settlement. Secretary Bird was sympathetic to the way of life of the Dutch colonists and he was attached to the existing system of arbitrary government.[37] He regarded the British settlers as intruders whose political aspirations would be an inevitable source of trouble. The policy of encouraging emigration from Britain was one that he regretted. His attitude was very early apparent to the settlers. As a consequence, Ellis observed, their actual suffering was aggravated by a belief that they were being neglected.

While he was Acting Governor, Sir Rufane Donkin conscientiously tried to support the efforts of the settlers, but Lord Charles Somerset, who returned in 1821, reacted in a very different way. As a result of an incident involving his son, Somerset's dislike of Donkin ran high. His antipathy to the settlers worked in combination with his inclination to contradict everything that Donkin had done.[38] The landdros of the Zuurveld or Albany District, who had been appointed by Donkin and who was popular with the settlers, was dismissed and replaced by a man whom they found intolerable. The town of Bathurst, which Donkin had established in a central location for the convenience of the settlers, was abandoned and the residence of the landdros and seat of magistracy were moved to Grahamstown. The soldiers, whom Donkin had stationed on the Fish and Baviaans Rivers and at Fredericksburg in the neutral territory to cover the Zuurveld, were withdrawn. And the enlargement of the original grants, which Donkin realized was necessary and of which Lord Bathurst approved, was refused.

In Somerset's opinion the settlers were exaggerating their difficulties in order to create trouble. A majority of them, he was convinced, were Radicals and their chief objective was to oppose authority. They were lazy and would exert themselves only to 'promote and sow the seeds of discontent wherever their baneful

[37] W.H.P. Ellis to Horton, 23 Oct. 1822 and 27 Mar. 1827.
[38] Corry, ii. 131–4; Donkin, *A Letter on the Government of the Cape of Good Hope*; Pringle, *Narrative*; p. 219; W.H.P., Bigge to Horton, 25 Sept. 1823.

influence can extend'.[39] The wheat blight and other disasters had worked to their advantage, giving them additional means to foment antagonism against the government. He suspected the worst when Pigot, Campbell, Phillips, Moodie, and some of the other principal settlers wanted to hold public meetings to bring their plight to his attention. His answer was to ban such meetings. When they petitioned him for permission to meet legally, he denied it to them. It was not surprising that the appeals of the settlers to the home government became 'loud and importunate'.

In March 1823 a statement of grievances addressed to Lord Bathurst was signed by 374 settlers.[40] All of the ways in which the colonial government had been unhelpful or obstructive were listed, but the grievance that was described as most pressing and insupportable concerned the defencelessness of the settlers against the Xhosa. During the first eighteen months that they spent in the Zuurveld, the frontier had been quiet. The Xhosa were attracted by large numbers of cattle and small numbers of men. In the beginning the settlers had little livestock, but by 1821 had acquired a considerable amount and in September they were stunned to learn of a brazen raid in which an English herdsboy was murdered and forty-eight head of cattle driven off. It was later discovered that Gaika, the paramount chief of the Xhosa, had himself appropriated some of the cattle. During subsequent raids there were several more murders. In 1822 the Xhosa stole 2,591 head of cattle, horses, and oxen. Only 778 were recovered. In a few months the settlers lost most of their livestock.

While officials in the Colonial Office did not dismiss the settlers' misfortunes with the insensibility that Somerset displayed, they were not anxious to do anything that could be construed as a direct admission of error on their part. The whole matter was referred to the commissioners of inquiry who had been sent in 1823 to investigate conditions at the Cape and Mauritius. Their report, while reasonably fair and objective, was not finished until May 1925.[41] In unofficial circles there was a more immediate response. A society for the relief of the British settlers was formed in Cape Town; through this organization, £7,000 were raised in the United Kingdom and India and another £3,000 in the colony; the money was distributed to the settlers in January 1825.[42]

The recipients of this charity were just a remnant of the emigrants

---

[39] Corry, ii. 150.   [40] C.O., 48/76, p. 121.   [41] Ibid., p. 1.
[42] Corry, ii. 163–4; Pringle, *Narrative*, pp. 222–3.

who first came to the Zuurveld. After crops failed in three successive years, the colonial government made no attempt to stop settlers from leaving their locations. Those who could went to Cape Town, Graaf-Reinet, Grahamstown, and Uitenhage and found work as clerks, shopkeepers, labourers, or craftsmen. A census of May 1823 showed about one-half of the settlers still on the land.[43] Among them were a majority of the upper and middle-class people who had come out as party leaders. Their condition, according to Thomas Pringle, was the most desperate. Their capital was gone; their land was unproductive; they owed large sums to the government for rations; and there was no suitable employment for them in the colony. Yet Pringle, in 1824, believed that success was still possible.[44] Within the following two years events began to prove him right.

After 1824 the blight that had attacked the wheat crops occurred less frequently. In the same year the colonial government recognized the limits imposed on agriculture in the Zuurveld and the necessity of an enlargement of the original grants of land. Conditions on the frontier improved when trade was legalized between the colonists and the tribesmen; a relative quiet prevailed until 1834.[45] In the spring of 1825 Lord Charles Somerset went to see the Zuurveld for the first time. He found the settlers suitably deferential and he became more appreciative of their difficulties. As a consequence he suggested that their debts to the government be remitted and Bathurst agreed. In Somerset's opinion the principal handicap the settlers suffered was a shortage of labourers, and he moved to redress this situation by allowing them to hire natives. He also dismissed Rivers, the unpopular landdros. Shortly afterwards Somerset's own tour of duty came to an end. Early in 1826 he was ordered to return to Britain to answer accusations that had been made by the settlers and to account for irregularities in the expenditures of his government.[46] Somerset's departure opened the way for the reforms of 1828 which conceded freedom of the press and granted a charter of justice that amended the colony's entire legal system and made English

[43] [Bird], *State of the Cape of Good Hope*, p. 239; Report of Commissioners of Inquiry, 25 May 1825, p. 45; Pringle, *Some Account*, pp. 30–4.

[44] Pringle, *Some Account*, pp. 35–8.

[45] Edwards, *1820 Settlers*, pp. 123–5; J. C. Chase, *The Cape of Good Hope and the Eastern Province of Algoa Bay* (London, 1843), p. 84.

[46] See Millar, *Plantagenet in South Africa*, pp. 221–50, and Edwards, pp. 117–55, for contrasting accounts of Somerset's recall. See also C.O. 323/144, Plasket to Hay, 1 Mar. 1826 for an inside judgement on Somerset's regime.

the official language. In the late 1820s the British settlers found both nature and the government to be more hospitable than during the first ruinous years.

The project of assisted emigration to the Cape had been hastily conceived, and, while it was not a complete failure, it proved to be a poor advertisement for settlement in South Africa. The Chancellor of the Exchequer had described it as an experiment, but the government did not attempt to follow it up. This was not surprising. Even if the emigrants had met with greater success, a repetition would have been far from certain. The original decision had been very much a consequence of the tensions of 1819. The Cabinet was unlikely to act except under similar pressure.

In the spring of 1820 such pressure was evident but localized in Glasgow. Throughout the autumn and winter of 1819–20 Glasgow weavers had been agitating for assistance to emigrate.[47] They had rejected the government's offer of passages to the Cape of Good Hope because they would not gamble on the totally unfamiliar, but they had continued to plead for help to go to Canada. Their petitions had been refused by the Colonial Office which might have welcomed applications from Highlanders but considered paupers from a manufacturing area to be poor risks as settlers in British North America. Goulburn did not believe that the weavers possessed the character and aptitude needed to meet the harsh conditions they would encounter in Upper Canada. Although the weavers found support for their petitions among local nobles and gentlemen, they received no encouragement from the Colonial Office.

While a deaf ear was turned to the weavers who wished to emigrate, the closest attention was paid to those who preached radical reform. In the autumn of 1819 reform activity appeared more threatening in Glasgow than in any other centre in Great Britain.[48] The city contained between 10,000 and 15,000 individuals

---

[47] C.O. 384/4, Cannon to Bathurst, 16 July 1819, and R. Hamilton to Bathurst, 18 Sept. 1819; C.O. 384/6, Petition of the Operative Manufacturers and others in the Town and Vicinity of Paisley, May 1820, and Note in Behalf of the Emigrant Societies in Lanarkshire, 27 Apr. 1820; C.O. 43/59, Goulburn to Vansittart, 17 Apr. 1820, and Goulburn to Harrison, 15 May 1820; H.O. 102/30 Bannatyre to Feeling, 14 Sept. 1819.

[48] Liverpool to Canning, 23 Sept. 1819, and Liverpool to Grenville, 14 Nov. 1819, cited by Yonge, *Robert Banks, Second Earl of Liverpool*, ii. 408, 431; *Hansard*, 1819, xli, cols. 922–3, 938; H.O. 102/30, Melville to Sidmouth, 1 Aug. 1819, Rae to Sidmouth, 3 Aug. 1819, Monteith to Sidmouth, 13 Aug. 1819, Finlay to Sidmouth, 14 Sept. 1819,

dependent upon charity. A nervous town council brought in cavalry and used it frequently to clear the thoroughfares of refractory crowds of unemployed. In this atmosphere the reformers seemed dangerously well organized. There were disciplined meetings of 5,000, 10,000, and even 30,000; on 1 November and on 15 November, simultaneous meetings were held in Glasgow, Paisley, and elsewhere. It was believed that Radicals were drilling by night and government forces stood ready to meet 'an army much talked of but never seen'.[49]

The authorities wanted a show-down; towards the end of March 1820 there were indications that they would have their way. For some time ash trees, suitable for the manufacture of pikes, had been disappearing from plantations in the vicinity of Glasgow. The Radicals behaved with increasing confidence and daring, and the Lord Provost of Glasgow predicted that matters would come to a head on the first day of April.[50] His information was almost accurate. On Sunday morning 2 April the citizens of Glasgow, Paisley, and all of the manufacturing towns and villages for twelve miles around found an incitement to revolt posted in the streets.[51] Workmen were called upon to strike and, if resisted, to use force to overthrow the existing government and to establish a provisional one. It was rumoured that uprisings had already taken place in England and that 50,000 troops had embarked from France. On Monday the strike began. All of the weavers, the spinners, the colliers, and some of the machine-shop employees obeyed the Radical order. Word had spread that ammunition was on the way and that its arrival would signal the beginning of the insurrection.

By nightfall Monday the troops in Glasgow were reinforced by the Dunbartonshire and the Ayrshire Yeomanry Cavalry and a detachment of infantry from Edinburgh. The government wanted provocation, but the insurgents proved to be more voluble than violent. Although there were minor disturbances in Glasgow, Paisley, and Greenock, the most serious clash occurred on Wednesday when the Radicals sent an armed contingent of thirty or forty to seize

---

Melville to Sidmouth, 20 Sept. 1819; George Eyre-Todd, *History of Glasgow*, iii (Glasgow, 1934), 453.

[49] George S. Pryde, *Scotland from 1603 to the Present Day* (London, 1962), p. 126.

[50] H.O. 102/32, Monteith to Sidmouth, 26 Mar. 1820, Fulton to Glasgow, 31 Mar. 1820, Blantyre to Sidmouth, 31 Mar. 1820.

[51] *Glasgow Herald*, 3 and 7 Apr. 1820; H.O. 102/32 Monteith to Sidmouth, 2 Apr. 1820.

the Carron Iron Works, a great cannon foundry.[52] On the road to Falkirk this contingent was dispersed after firing on a small detachment of the Hussars and the Kilsyth Yeomanry. On Thursday there were no major incidents; by Friday the strikers were throwing away their pikes and some of them were returning to work. In the aftermath of this Radical War twenty-four sentences of death were passed and three hangings actually carried out. Officials were disappointed that their opponents had not shown more strength. The Radicals were frightened, the Lord Advocate of Scotland reported to the Home Secretary; there would be no opportunity to administer the punishment 'which I came here in the hope of seeing inflicted'.[53]

The ineffectiveness of the revolutionaries in no way lessened the apprehensions of the gentry and nobility. A decisive encounter had been desired, one that would have demonstrated the hopelessness of any further rising. It was feared that, as soon as the troops and cavalry from other counties were withdrawn, Radical threats and harassment would recommence. There was no inclination to underrate the crisis that had passed; 'enough has been brought to light', wrote one observer, 'to convince us that we were in great danger'.[54] At the conclusion of the strike the leaders of the communities in the Glasgow area were highly motivated to support any measure that could be expected to reduce tension. When the local members of Parliament went up to London at the end of the month for the first session in the reign of George IV they were determined to obtain government assistance for the weavers who wanted to emigrate.

At the first opportunity during the debate on the opening day one of the members for Lanarkshire, Lord Archibald Hamilton, took the floor. Hamilton was a man of liberal views and an outspoken critic of the Liverpool Administration; his speech reflected his political outlook. From the spirit and temper of the Cabinet ministers, he asserted, it was evident that they had not given much consideration to the miserable state of the poor in his part of the country. In their opinion the main cause of the uprising had been disaffection rather than distress; they had used force to suppress disturbances which could have been stopped more effectively by providing the means of subsistence. Last year, Hamilton recalled, the Commons had voted £50,000 for the promotion of emigration to the Cape of Good Hope;

---

[52] *Caledonian Mercury*, 10 Apr. 1820.
[53] H.O. 102/32, Rae to Sidmouth, 6 Apr. 1820.
[54] Ibid., unsigned, 7 Apr. 1820.

'the object of the grant was, undoubtedly, that which the House and His majesty's ministers ought to have in view . . . the alleviation of distress',[55] but there was no perceptible reason why the government should be more willing to encourage emigration to South Africa than to any other quarter of the globe. The government's policy was especially difficult to understand in light of the powerful reasons which Scottish people had for preferring the British colonies in North America.

The Chancellor of the Exchequer, Nicholas Vansittart, replied for the government. He offered no likelihood of help for the weavers. The Cabinet, he said, was not averse to giving assistance to pauper emigrants, 'but such a measure should not be hastily or prematurely adopted'. Already, the parliamentary grant had been considerably exceeded in sending settlers to South Africa. Most of these people were still in the course of their passage out. It would be premature to dispatch a second wave of emigrants to the Cape before learning of the success of the first. On the other hand, to promote emigration in North America would be most unwise. Under prevailing conditions in the United States new arrivals would encounter great privation; in the British provinces, also, there was such an excess of emigrants that the strongest remonstrances had been made by the Canadian government.

Vansittart was being evasive; yet his arguments had some foundation. In November of the previous year Sir James Monk, the Administrator of Lower Canada, had advised Lord Bathurst that the presence of large numbers of sick and destitute emigrants was placing insupportable pressures upon the residents of the colonial ports.[56] He doubted the colony's ability to absorb an extensive and unregulated immigration. At the same time, there was reason to believe that Americans were equally concerned about the same problem. In 1819 the Secretary of State, John Quincy Adams, had published throughout Europe a paper apparently designed to discourage immigration, and the American Passenger Act of that year imposed standards far beyond the means of most emigrants.[57] Although Vansittart exaggerated the misgivings of Canadian officials as well as the difficulties faced by emigrants who landed at New York, he did not invent them. His statement was not altogether misleading.

The question of assistance to the weavers, however, was not to be

---

[55] *Hansard*, 1820, i, cols. 40–2.   [56] C.O. 42/182, Monk to Bathurst, 8 Nov. 1819.

[57] Max J. Kohler, *An Important European Mission to Investigate American Immigration Conditions and John Quincy Adams' Relatives thereto* (Chicago, 1919), p. 22; J. G. Malcolm, *An Enquiry into the Expediency of Emigration as it respects the British North American Colonies* (London, 1828), pp. 29–31.

dismissed. From the government side of the House, Kirkman Finlay, one time Lord Provost of Glasgow, supported Hamilton; he had also received communications from a large number of people who wanted to emigrate but did not have any money and could not have raised the deposit required of settlers going to the Cape. In deference to the strong feelings of the Scottish members, the government quickly and quietly gave in. Hamilton and Finlay spoke on Friday 28 April. By Tuesday 2 May a delegation which included Hamilton and the Lord Advocate of Scotland, Sir William Rae, was meeting with the Prime Minister and the Chancellor of the Exchequer to consider the petitions of five emigration societies. These societies represented 1,100 people from Glasgow and Lanarkshire who asked for free passages and government help costing an estimated £11,000 which they promised to repay within a limited time.[58]

The Prime Minister agreed to an arrangement of this nature. The government would provide transportation from Quebec to Upper Canada at no charge, grant each family 100 acres free of fees, and supply seed corn and implements at prime cost. Moreover, to carry the settlers through their first year the government would advance them £10 in four instalments on the condition that they clear the debt within ten years.[59] The weavers, however, were called upon to provide their own transportation from Greenock to Quebec. In a sense, the terms under which emigrants went to the Cape were reversed. Instead of requiring the weavers to raise capital to purchase supplies after they landed, the government asked them to find their own passage money. This scheme was no less difficult for the emigrants but it did cut down the administrative responsibilities of the Colonial Office.

The Colonial Office had not been represented at the meeting on 2 April; the decision to send out the weavers was not made by Bathurst and Goulburn and they chose to interpret its implications as narrowly as possible. The government's concessions had been granted specifically to petitioners from Lanarkshire; Goulburn refused to extend the help to any other people. Weavers from Renfrewshire and Paisley who asked for the same advantages as their neighbours in Lanarkshire and Glasgow were turned down.[60] In

[58] *Glasgow Herald*, 8 May 1820; C.O. 384/6, p. 1573.

[59] C.O. 43/41, Bathurst to Maitland, 6 May 1820.

[60] C.O. 384/6, Ritchie to Blantyre, no date; C.O. 43/59, Bathurst to Vansittart, 23 June 1820, and Goulburn to Treasury, 10 June 1820.

June John Maxwell, a member of Parliament for Renfrewshire, introduced a petition from the weavers from his constituency with the warning that it was 'politically prudent as well as humane to pay attention to their distress'.[61] Other notables from his county intervened as well; by the end of the summer they had extracted a pledge of government assistance for a further emigration from western Scotland in the spring of 1821.

The departure of the Lanarkshire petitioners was organized by a special committee of interested gentlemen.[62] Money was raised by subscription in the county and in Glasgow to defray part of the cost of passage. The committee contributed £1 per individual; the emigrants had to find another £3 or £4 themselves. In early June 1820 over 600 members of the five Lanarkshire emigration societies embarked at Greenock and Grangemouth, leaving behind 600 who could not pay any part of the cost of passage. A special appeal to private charity produced enough money to commission one more ship which sailed in July with 176 passengers who had been chosen by ballot. Four hundred members of the Lanarkshire societies remained to be transported in the following season.

At the end of July Kirkman Finlay advised Goulburn that the emigration of over 800 individuals had helped considerably to restore tranquillity to the Glasgow area.[63] He wanted to know whether or not the government would repeat the experiment. Before the first reports were received from Canada, his committee was overwhelmed by the applications of thirty-two societies representing 6,281 individuals who wanted to go to Canada in 1821. The government, committed to the 400 who had been disappointed in 1820 and besieged by petitions from Renfrew and other counties, agreed to look after a maximum of 1,800 persons.[64] In October 1820 the Glasgow Committee instructed the various societies to begin the painful task of cutting their lists, and after a winter of ruthless pruning they struck off more than two-thirds of the names. In the spring of 1821 four

[61] *Hansard*, 1820, i, col. 744; C.O. 384/6, Mure to Sidmouth, 28 Sept. 1820.

[62] Robert Lamond, 'A Narrative on the Rise and Progress of Emigration from the Counties of Lanark and Renfrew (Glasgow, 1821)', California State Library, Sato Branch, *Occasional Papers*, No. 12; C.O. 384/6, Finlay to Goulburn, 2, 3, and 10 June.

[63] C.O. 384/6, Finlay to Goulburn, 21 July 1820; C.O. 43/60, Goulburn to Finlay, 4 Sept. 1820; Lamond, p. 12.

[64] C.O. 384/6, Finlay to Goulburn, 10 Aug. 1820, Hamilton to Bathurst, 11 Sept. 1820, Macfarlane to Bathurst, 16 Oct. 1820, and Finlay to Goulburn, 2 Dec. 1820; C.O. 384/7, McCallum to Bathurst, 9 Feb. 1821, and Finlay to Goulburn, 2 Mar. 1821; C.O. 43/60, Bathurst to Hopetown, 29 Jan. 1821.

vessels carried 1,883 persons to Quebec. Altogether, in 1820 and 1821 the Glasgow committee sent out 2,716 emigrants.[65]

The weavers had asked for land near the Rideau Settlement where the Scottish settlers of 1815 had been located; they were taken to Lanark, Dalhousie, Ramsay, and North Sherbrooke townships which lay between the Rideau Lakes and the Ottawa River. Millions of acres of better land were available in the western half of the province, but the Canadian government found it advantageous to give the weavers the location they had requested. In the village of Perth a military establishment already existed to administer the settlement of reduced officers. Because the expenses involved in settling the weavers in Upper Canada were paid out of the military chest, it was convenient to put them under the supervision of Colonel William Marshall, the responsible officer at Perth. As a consequence, the weavers were placed on what they later described as 'the worst tract of land on which any extensive settlement was ever attempted in Upper Canada'.[66]

The area in which they were located was pressed against the Canadian Shield. There were scraps of useful land but most of the surface was rock, sand, or swamp. About fifty families settled on a fertile strip running through the eastern part of Ramsay, but the remainder chose lots which should never have been cleared: lots so broken by rocky outcroppings that there were few places where an acre of arable soil could be found.[67] How the weavers were persuaded to take such worthless land can be explained in part by their lack of energy and spirit at the end of a five-day journey by wagon from Prescott, preceded by five days of travel on the St. Lawrence by steamship then by bateaux, all of which came after a six-week crossing from Greenock to Quebec. By the time they reached their destination they were glad to pick any spot. As tradesmen who had seen little outside the limits of Glasgow and its surrounding towns

---

[65] The cost to the Committee was about £6,800 and to the government £31,200. This was economical in comparison with the £111,000 spent by the British and Colonial governments on approximately 3,500 emigrants to South Africa. For expenditures on the emigration to Upper Canada: *Parl. Pap.* 1826, iv (404), 217–18, 223, 225; *Parl. Pap.* 1826–7, v (550), 90, 96; C.O. 42/222, Marshall to Couper, 8 Mar. 1829; C.O. 42/187, Dalhousie to Bathurst, 14 June 1821; A.O. 1/2131, rolls 7 and 8. For expenditures on the emigration to the Cape: *Parl. Pap.* 1821 xiv (45); Bird, *State of Cape of Good Hope*, p. 144.

[66] C.O. 42/393, Colborne to Goderich, 17 Apr. 1831 (enclosure).

[67] C.O. 42/419, Colborne to Stanley, 10 Oct. 1833 (enclosure); C.O. 42/425, Colborne to Spring Rice, 3 Jan. 1835 (enclosure).

they had no idea what they should look for and the appearance of the country was deceptive even to those who did. The tree cover, predominantly maple, beech, and elm, indicated good soil; not until the trees were removed did settlers discover that they could not get ploughs through because there were so many boulders.

The weavers held on to the profitless land they had been given with the tenacity of those who had learned to make the most of very little. The American border was only 40 miles away and less timid people might have run away from their debts to the British government. Instead, the weavers stayed, scratching out enough to live on and no more. Of 569 heads of families who occupied lots in 1820–21, 544 remained in 1829 and 403 were still there in 1834.[68] In the space of twelve or thirteen years, seventy-three had died; fifty-one had gone elsewhere in the province and only forty-two had left the country. In the early years of their settlement the weavers apparently thought themselves well off. They had no means of saving the £30 or £40 per family that they were obliged to pay to the government;[69] but in the primitive economy of Upper Canada their level of existence compared reasonably well with that of their neighbours. Only when markets began to develop for agricultural produce, did their situation become unacceptable. In the 1840s, as a consequence, they began to desert Lanark and Dalhousie townships, many of them moving to the excellent land in the Huron Tract which the Canada Company was offering on easy terms of purchase.

The expectations of the weavers were low and the accounts that they sent back to Glasgow were cheerful. In the summer of 1827 the *Glasgow Chronicle* and the *Glasgow Herald* printed a series of letters which contained warm descriptions of the success that the weavers had made as settlers: they were better dressed than they had ever been in Scotland; their tables were laden with good food; they gave meat to their cats and dogs that they once would have been happy to eat themselves; and they could never bear to return to the poverty at home.[70] From the beginning the settlers had written to their relatives with optimism. William Miller's letter to his father in the autumn of 1820 was published by the secretary of the Glasgow Emigration Committee as representative of many others. 'Let my

---

[68] Colborne to Spring Rice, 3 Jan. 1835 (enclosure).
[69] In 1836 the Colonial Secretary agreed to wipe the slate clean. Cowan, p. 63.
[70] *Glasgow Chronicle*, June 1827, J.S. to editor: see C.O. 42/382, Marshall to Horton, 21 June 1827 (enclosed clippings), and extracts in *Glasgow Herald*, 4 June 1827.

brothers, Robert, James, and Andrew know that I wish they would come,' he urged his father, 'let Robert A. and his mother and sisters know that there are farms to buy . . . I have nothing more to say, but that I never thought such a country was here and I wish I had been some years sooner.'[71]

Letters like this one provoked a continued spirit of emigration amongst the weavers of Glasgow. Throughout the 1820s they pleaded with the government for a repetition of the assistance given in 1820 and in 1821. Kirkman Finlay, however, had supported the arrangements in 1820–1 in spite of a conviction that the desire to emigrate should be limited and restrained as much as possible. He saw the project very much as a special answer to a temporary situation. Once quiet had been established, he did not believe that further encouragement to emigrants was warranted. In June 1821, on behalf of the Glasgow Emigration Committee, he advised the Colonial Office that the measure had served its purpose.[72] Although the weavers protested that their trade had not revived, but in fact had declined, the government showed no disposition to help them once the Glasgow Committee was satisfied that it was unnecessary.

The projects of assisted emigration to the Cape in 1819–20 and to Upper Canada were analogous in two respects: they were inspired by domestic rather than colonial considerations, and they were undertaken on the initiative of senior members of the Cabinet rather than on the initiative of the Colonial Secretary alone. Lord Liverpool and his colleagues were willing to exploit the idea that pauper emigration might be desirable, even if they gave little thought to a permanent system. They called the emigration to the Cape an experiment, a word that suggested an intention to promote emigration on a more extensive scale in the future, but they acted only when social order was threatened, and they lost interest as soon as the danger was diminished. No attempt was made to assess the emigration projects in retrospect. The settlers had experienced unnecessary hardship and disappointment, but those who were responsible were never compelled to digest their own mistakes.

---

[71] Lamond, p. 63.
[72] C.O. 384/7, Finlay to Goulburn, 2 Mar. and 18 June 1821, and Petition of Operative Manufacturers in Paisley, 20 Oct. 1821; C.O. 42/189. Minutes of Glasgow Committee on Emigration, 1 June 1821.

IV

WILMOT HORTON

IN 1815 Henry Goulburn defended the recruitment of settlers with the explanation that the government did not intend to stimulate emigration but wished only to direct it into new channels. He believed that assisted emigration could not be justified except as a measure beneficial to the colonies; as a consequence, he did not want to encourage the emigration of people who had no resources of their own. While attitudes changed remarkably after 1815, Goulburn was not the kind of man who adjusted rapidly to new ideas. He supervised the arrangements for the settlers at the Cape and for the Glasgow weavers without committing himself to the principle of pauper emigration. He did not become a warm advocate of similar experiments for the future.

After ten years as Parliamentary Under-Secretary in the Colonial Office, Goulburn was promoted to the post of Irish Secretary. In December 1821 he was replaced by Robert John Wilmot, a Derbyshire gentleman who had represented Newcastle under Lyme since 1818. This appointment opened the way for a marked change in the organization and outlook of the Colonial Office. Wilmot came without any administrative experience and without any background in colonial affairs, but he brought an innovative spirit, a great deal of energy, and no small amount of ambition. He was as anxious to influence policy as he was to achieve high office. Rather mistakenly, as events proved for him, he thought that he could do both, that if he rose above the routine business of his department to play a conspicuous role in larger affairs he could ensure his own advancement. Instead, through his publications on the Catholic question, he made himself unacceptable for the Irish secretaryship which he wanted badly.[1]

Wilmot was married to an exceptionally attractive woman with a modest inheritance. (Byron, his cousin, wrote the lines 'She walks in

---

[1] See Wilmot's biography, E. G. Jones, 'Sir R. J. Wilmot Horton, Bart., Politician and Pamphleteer' (M.A. Thesis, Bristol, 1936), pp. 78–9; and Hatherton Correspondence, Horton to Littleton, 22 Nov. 1827 and 24 Sept. 1834.

beauty, like the night . . .' after meeting her.) The price of Mrs. Wilmot's inheritance was a change of name, and in 1823 Wilmot became Wilmot Horton in acceptance of the terms of his father-in-law's will; it is most convenient to refer to him by that name.

Even with income from his wife's properties Wilmot Horton was far from wealthy. A political life was barely within his means. The constituency he represented contained a large number of voters and was an expensive one in which to campaign.[2] His inability to face the costs of repeated elections was a severe handicap. One of the attractions of the position of Under-Secretary of State for the Colonies was that the office did not 'vacate'; a new occupant was not required to resign his seat to seek immediate re-election. Lord Bathurst realized that this was an important consideration and he drew Horton's attention to it when he offered him the appointment.[3]

Horton had earned an invitation to take office through his performance in the House of Commons. Although he protested that he was not a party man and that he did not belong to any faction or group, Horton had sought the quickest route to promotion by loyally supporting the government.[4] During his first four years in the Commons he spoke effectively on the government side on several occasions. In April 1820 Castlereagh asked him to second the address on the Speech from the Throne and in the wake of the disturbances in the north of England and most recently in Glasgow Wilmot Horton took a strong stand against parliamentary reform. The Tories saw him as a reasonable and amiable young man; John Cam Hobhouse characterized him as 'one of those who were in the habit of eulogizing things as they are.'[5]

Long before he became a parliamentarian, Horton embarked on a strenuous course of reading in political economy in preparation for his later career. The respect that he entertained for this new science set

---

[2] Jones, pp. 25–9; S. M. Hardy and R. C. Bailey, 'The Downfall of the Gower Interest in the Staffordshire Burroughs, 1800–30', *Collections for a History of Staffordshire* (1954), pp. 267–77.

[3] On Horton's appointment: Jones, p. 32; W.H.P., Bathurst to Horton, 29 Nov. 1821 and 9 Dec. 1821; B.M. Loan 57/13, Goulburn to Bathurst, 28 and 30 Nov. 1821; and Harrowby to Bathurst, 1 Dec. 1821.

[4] For his declaration of independence of party: *Hansard*, 1819, xxxix, col. 588. For his major speeches; *Hansard*, 1819, xl, col. 1478; 1820, i, col. 33; and 1821, v, cols. 391 and 758.

[5] *Hansard*, 1821, v, col. 395. For a Tory opinion: Francis Bamford and the Seventh Duke of Wellington, eds., *The Journal of Mrs. Arbuthnot, 1820–1832*, i (London, 1950), 130.

him apart from old-school Tories like Lord Bathurst. His advocacy of Catholic emancipation had the same effect. Horton's views conformed most closely to those of the Canningites, a loose grouping of liberal Tories led by George Canning, William Huskisson, and Frederick Robinson. Yet Horton denied that he was attached to Canning.[6] If they travelled the same path, it was simply because their objectives were coincidental. When he looked for support for his greatest project, he could not find it with Canning or Huskisson, although Goderich was more sympathetic.

Even on the Catholic question Horton was less disposed to follow Canning than to pursue an independent course. As a young man he had been advised by Reginald Heber, later Bishop of Calcutta, to adopt the tone of a reformer but to maintain an aristocratic prejudice; to incline secretly to the Tory side, but to take an ostentatious position just to the other.[7] Such tactics came naturally to Wilmot Horton and he pursued them to the confusion of allies and opponents alike. He was more likely to turn to an elaborate position than to a simple one. In part, this tendency was attributable to his restless nature; he wanted immediate answers and he sought them in complicated compromises. Always there was a desire to produce a solution which could be identified as his own. For a man who wanted to bring about compromise on the great issues of the day, he was remarkably incapable of accommodating other opinions.

Horton was driven by financial considerations to try for early success; his natural impatience made him strive for a large reputation while he still held a junior office; his wilfulness and energy led him to push vigorously for measures of his own conception. When Horton entered the Colonial Office, he was ready to take up a cause; he found it in emigration. The subject had already attracted parliamentary attention and it had been discussed in the periodicals and in several pamphlets. Considerable interest existed in the possibilities of pauper emigration before Horton entered the picture. After he seized upon the idea, however, he monopolized it. Its advancement became his central purpose—'mania' was the word that he used—and he came to be known primarily as an emigration propagandist.

Before he took office, Horton did not devote much thought to the

---

[6] W.H.P., Horton's statement explaining his political conduct, 6 July 1829.

[7] W.H.P., Heber to Wilmot, 5 Nov. 1816. After Heber's death Wilmot wrote that 'he was one of the dearest friends I had in the world. He was also a clergyman with whom I had no political differences of opinion.' W.H.P., Horton to Blake, 22 June 1827.

subject that was subsequently to absorb so much of his time. He did refer to it in passing in July 1819, when he replied to Sir Francis Burdett's motion for a reform of Parliament.[8] Reform, Horton had said, would not reduce the suffering of the poor; it would instead act as a lever by which the force of the lower classes could be used to overthrow all that was stable and salutary in the state. If the nation wished to provide real relief, he had stated, there were two remedies. The first would be a radical alteration in the system of Poor Laws and the second a policy of encouraging emigration. Eleven years later, when he re-read this speech, he was pleased to discover that he had supported emigration at such an early date. Yet he had not given it the same emphasis in 1819 as he was to after 1822. As a champion of the emigration remedy Horton reversed priorities: he put the establishment of a system of emigration ahead of an amendment of the Poor Laws.

According to Horton, his engrossment in the topic of emigration began with a concern for the development and defence of the North American colonies. He became aware of the weakness of these colonies soon after he assumed his place in the Colonial Office; he identified the problem as a shortage of population and decided that, unless the colonies could gain population faster than the natural rate of increase would allow, they would continue to be backward.[9] Like Bathurst and Goulburn, Horton regretted the loss of thousands of emigrants to the United States; while this movement might be advantageous to Great Britain in time of peace, it contributed to the power of the United States in time of war. In 1822 Horton produced a plan by which redundant labour, 'the curse of the mother country', could become 'the active labour and blessing of the colonies'. At this time, he offered little in the way of justification for such a measure, assuming that it was necessary and showing how it could be carried out. The arguments that he elaborated on labour, wage rates, and population were published subsequently when he saw that he would have to convince the government of the value of his project. In effect, he started with a remedy and went on to make a diagnosis.

The chain of reasoning that Horton eventually worked out rested on the principle that every able-bodied labourer for whom there was

---

[8] *Hansard*, 1819, xl, col. 1479.

[9] W.H.P., Horton to Malthus (1827); R. J. W. Horton, *An Inquiry into the Causes and Remedies of Pauperism. First Series. Containing Correspondence with C. Poulett Thomson* (London, 1830), p. 34.

no productive work was redundant and a tax upon the community.[10] He believed that the redundant population of England, Ireland, and Scotland was less than two million. A country with extensive unemployment was over-populated, but this term was to be understood in a relative rather than in an absolute sense. The condition of the working class depended upon the ratio between their numbers and the demand for their labour. From this point followed two conclusions, each of which suggested that emigration could produce practical benefits. First, over-population could be seen as a temporary phenomenon; the country could conceivably support a much larger population when greater capital resources allowed an increased demand for labour; in the meantime, emigration could provide immediate relief. Second, a slight excess in numbers could depress the wages of the entire working class; consequently, the emigration of a few paupers would improve conditions for a great many more; it would not be necessary to transport every pauper in order to eliminate pauperism.

Horton adopted Malthus's statement that wartime spending had stimulated the birth-rate and that emigration offered the best means of adjusting the balance between labour and capital in the short run. Yet he rejected the fundamental Malthusian proposition that population must inevitably rise beyond the level of subsistence. He did not believe that an improved standard of living would necessarily encourage earlier marriages and larger families.[11] This was an argument used against emigration; if a few families were removed from a locality and wages went up in response, the effect would be rapidly obliterated as people began to have more children. To this Horton replied that there were three states of society: in the first one found an indefinite extent of fertile land, a greater temptation to clear new land than to work for someone else, high wages, and a conviction among the lower classes that children were a source of wealth as well as enjoyment; in the second the supply of labour and capital were in balance and people with a comfortable way of life were likely to keep the families small; in the third there was a scarcity of good land, an excess of labour, and a feeling of hopelessness which led to reckless

[10] *Causes and Remedies of Pauperism. Second Series. Containing Correspondence with C. Poulett Thomson with a Preface*, p. 28; R. J. W. Horton, *Lecture X. Delivered at the London Mechanics' Institution* (London, 1831), p. 7; R. J. W. Horton, *A Letter to Sir Francis Burdett* (London, 1826), p. 23; *Parl. Pap.* 1826–7, v (550), 16; W.H.P., Horton to Place, Sept. 1830.

[11] Ibid., pp. 35–6; W.H.P., Horton's answers to Lord Palmerston's Question, 12 Dec. 1829, and Horton to Place, Sept. 1830.

marriages and a high-birth rate. It was evident to Horton that any improvement in the condition of the poor would serve to check rather than to stimulate further population growth.

Because Horton did not think that hunger discouraged sexual indulgence, he did not believe that poor relief encouraged paupers to have children. He was not an apologist for the existing Poor Law system. The parish practice of supplementing wages permitted farmers to hire labour cheaply and tended to depress the level of wages generally. Horton supported Poor Law reform that would eliminate this practice, but he did not accept the idea that parish assistance ought to be withheld entirely from the able-bodied poor.[12] The parish should provide the unemployed with work that was not competitive with that of other labourers. This was a consistent position for Horton to take; emigration was merely another form of poor relief and his plan presupposed the existence of a parish rate which could be used to settle paupers in the colonies instead of maintaining them at home.

In the long run, Horton conceded, the benefits of an amendment of the Poor Laws might be great, but it would not answer the present problem. If the measure was to succeed, it would have to be introduced in conjunction with a large-scale system of emigration. This could be supplemented by a programme of public works; Poor Law reform, public works, and emigration constituted the complete Horton system.[13] Horton denied that minimum wage legislation, tax reduction, or cheap corn could do any good. Current economic thought taught him that wages were paid out of a fixed fund; unless the capital supply were increased or the labour supply diminished, there could be no general improvement in wages. On the other hand, the same source of opinion endorsed the remission of taxes as well as free trade in corn. Ricardo and his disciples were convinced that the Corn Laws and the tax burden drove capital out of the country and depleted the wage fund. Horton looked at these questions in another light.

When there were large numbers of unemployed, Horton reasoned, the advantage of cheap corn would not be passed on to the working

[12] Horton, *Lecture IX*, p. 29; *Causes and Remedies of Pauperism. Fourth Series. Containing Letters to Lord John Russell*, pp. 13, 16, 19, 70; *Speech of the Right Honorable Robert Wilmot Horton, M.P., in the House of Commons, 9th March, 1830, on Moving for a Committee to Consider the State of the Poor of the United Kingdom* (London), pp. 11–17.

[13] W.H.P., Horton to Mahoney, 17 Jan. 1831.

classes.[14] Instead, master manufacturers in search of higher profits would lower wages in the knowledge that there were thousands of wretched people looking for employment. As long as there was an excess of labour, wages would not rise above the minimum required for food, clothing, and shelter; when that minimum fell, wages would fall also. Turning to tax reduction, Horton asked whether or not the money involved would be spent more productively by the individual or by the government.[15] If the wealthy had more money, would they use it to employ the poor or to purchase luxuries from abroad? What would happen if the government suddenly stopped spending money at a time when the labour market was already glutted? Horton insisted that the most effective way to combat pauperism was through public expenditure; he did not flinch at the prospect of sending 1,000,000 paupers to the colonies at a cost of £12,000,000.

Horton considered himself a student of political economy. He held a high regard for the classical economists, Ricardo, James Mill, and J. R. McCulloch. Yet his Tory instincts led him to argue that ideal solutions were not always practical in a real world.[16] The principles of political economy served as a guide, but allowance had to be made for friction and resistance. As a consequence, Horton could think of himself as a free trader while opposing a repeal of the Corn Laws. He insisted that his ideas were in keeping with 'the roundest views of Political economy' and that assisted emigration was justified by free-trade theory.[17] Labour, like any other commodity, should be allowed to go to the market where it was most valuable; workmen who were unemployed in Britain would be welcomed as settlers in the colonies; it was a question of supply and demand. The argument was tenuous. Horton did not propose to remove restraints on emigration; he wished to subsidize it. Furthermore, he intended to send emigrants to the colonies instead of to the country in which they could obtain the highest price for their labour.

Because Horton wrote at length under such titles as *The Causes and Remedies of Pauperism*, he exposed himself to the charge that he was primarily concerned with the internal problems of Great Britain

---

[14] B.M. Loan 57/17, Horton to Bathurst, 21 Oct. 1826; R. J. W. Horton, *A Letter to Dr. Birbeck, the president and members of the London Mechanics' Institute on the Subject of the Corn Laws* (Richmond, 1839), pp. 18–22.

[15] *Lecture I*, pp. 18–24.

[16] See *Hansard*, 1820, i, col. 720.

[17] *Causes and Remedies of Pauperism. First Series*, p. 33.

and that he was engaged in a process of 'shovelling out paupers'. Yet Horton's emigration projects were closely bound up with his belief in the value of colonial possessions.[18] If peace were perpetual, colonies would be superfluous; Britain could bring down her tariff barriers and trade on an equal basis with all states. But peace was not perpetual; colonies contributed to British power and colonial trade deserved to be protected. Horton wished to build up the colonies, not to burden them with the failures of British society. He kept his purpose firmly in mind. It was not enough simply to invite paupers to leave; their movement should be regulated by legislation and supported by capital. Nor did Horton feel that emigration was an equally appropriate remedy for all paupers. Artisans were not as likely to be successful as settlers; it was desirable that emigrants to the North American colonies should have some knowledge of agriculture.[19]

Horton drafted his original scheme with the rural poor of England in mind. In 1822 the agricultural population was suffering the effects of a fall in the price of wheat.[20] Between June 1817 and December 1821 the price had dropped from 113s. to 49s. per quarter. Abundant harvests of low-quality wheat had brought the price below the expenses of high-cost producers. All levels of rural society were affected. The House of Commons received a flood of petitions from landholders praying for a reduction of taxes; there were reports of labourers deliberately courting arrest in order to be lodged and fed in jail. In 1821 and again in 1822 the Commons appointed a Select Committee on Agricultural Distress. Horton first presented his plan to this committee.

For practical advice on the costs involved in transporting and settling emigrants Horton had turned to Colonel Thomas Talbot whom he interviewed several times in the spring of 1822. Talbot, an

[18] R. J. W. Horton, *Letters Containing Observations on Colonial Policy* (London, 1839), pp. 16–24; *A Letter to Sir Francis Burdett*, pp. 15–16; *Parl. Pap.* 1825, viii (129), 18.

[19] In 1822 Horton described his plan as 'perfectly applicable' for redundant population from manufacturing districts, although he saw that this class of people would be 'least suited for the experiment'. *Parl. Pap.* 1823, vi (361), 172. He subsequently came to believe that, with the exception of weavers from the region of Glasgow or Manchester, artisans would not be successful. *Causes and Remedies of Pauperism. Fourth Series. Explanations of Mr. Wilmot Horton's Bill in a letter and Queries addressed to N. W. Senior*, p. 83. See also *Lecture VI*, p. 9.

[20] A. D. Gayer, W. W. Rostow, A. J. Swartz, *The Growth and Fluctuations of the British Economy, 1790–1850* (Oxford, 1953), pp. 156–7; L. P. Adams, *Agricultural Depression and Farm Relief in England, 1813–1852* (London, 1932), pp. 97–109; *Hansard*, 1822, vi, col. 454.

Anglo-Irish aristocrat, ruled with lead pencil and eraser over 12,000 inhabitants of the north shore of Lake Erie.[21] He had come to London to impress upon Horton and Lord Bathurst his claims for special financial concessions and he left in April with much of what he had demanded. Since 1800 Talbot had devoted all of his energy to the settlement of the western region of Upper Canada; he had succeeded remarkably in compelling those who received land in his townships to develop their lots and to open their road allowances. The names of his settlers were recorded in pencil in his register; an eraser always lay at hand to obliterate those who did not meet their obligations. Talbot was applauded for effectively populating his townships while the provincial government allowed vast tracts of alienated land to remain unoccupied. He was warmly interested in Horton's plan and ready to volunteer his services to carry it out.

Talbot suggested that, in addition to transportation and land, each emigrant family should be given a cow, a temporary shelter, implements, and twelve months of rations.[22] Taking into consideration such expenses as clothing, bedding during the voyage, and agents to meet the emigrants at various points along the route, Talbot estimated the total cost at £88 per family of four or £102 per family of five. In comparison, the Lanarkshire weavers had received between £67 and £75 in assistance per family of five. Horton, however, relied on Talbot's information rather than on the evidence of previous experience. Several years later Talbot rather curiously described Horton's emigration experiments as extravagant although his own figures had not been exceeded. 'All Govt. undertakings are made jobs of,' Talbot observed.[23] He was perhaps disappointed that he had not been given a chance to make a job of assisted emigration himself.

In prescribing the method by which pauper emigration should be financed, Horton was influenced by the ideas of the economists who were opposed to a large outlay by the national government for a measure of this nature. The acceptable alternative which Horton advocated was to enable parishes to raise the money that would be required. This form of expenditure was less objectionable because it could be directly related to local needs and interests. The idea was

[21] F. C. Hamil, *Lake Erie Baron* (Toronto, 1955), p. 106.
[22] *Parl. Pap.* 1823, vi (361), 171.
[23] W. H. G. Armytage, 'Thomas Talbot and Lord Wharncliffe: Some New Letters Hitherto Unpublished', *Ontario History*, Sept. 1953, p. 193.

by no means novel.[24] It had been advanced by Hayter in 1817 and discussed in an article in the *Monthly Review* in 1820. For several years a number of parishes in Cumberland had been shipping off their poor, although in a most callous manner; emigrants were given only £3 each so that they would not have enough money to get back home.

Horton appreciated the inhumanity and short-sightedness of any measure which dumped penniless emigrants at North American ports. His plan was conceived with the problems of the parish, the welfare of the emigrants, and the interests of the colonists in mind. The government should advance money to the parishes on the security of the poor rates. If the parishes repaid the money by a terminal annuity calculated at 4 per cent, they would be able to give each emigrant £35 and still reduce their yearly expenditure on poor relief. The calculation was mathematically correct but, none the less, imprecise.[25] Horton did not know how many paupers there were in England or how much it cost to maintain them. If most paupers were on relief for only part of the year then the figures he presented were misleading. In addition, there was a danger that a parish might suffer a second wave of unemployment after going into debt to get rid of its paupers. If this happened, parish revenue might not answer the demand upon it.

During the winter of 1822–3, Horton obtained written opinions of his plan from at least thirty-five individuals of whom the most prominent were: Robert Peel, the Home Secretary; Frederick Robinson, President of the Board of Trade; C. W. W. Wynn, President of the Board of Control; Henry Hobhouse, Under-Secretary of State for the Home Department; John Barrow, Second Secretary of the Admiralty; William Sturges Bourne, chairman of the Select Committee on the Poor Laws in 1819; Thomas Chalmers, Scottish theologian and administrator of the pauper fund in his parish of St. John's Glasgow; David Ricardo, the economist; T. P. Courtenay, a member of Parliament and author of *A Treatise on the Poor Laws* published in 1818; the Duke of Somerset, a progressive landlord; the Bishop of Limerick; John Beverley Robinson, the Attorney-General of Upper Canada; Robert Southey, the Poet Laureate and author of a masterly

[24] *Monthly Review*, Dec. 1820, p. 385. On the emigrants from Cumberland see: W.H.P., Southey to Wynn, 19 and 28 Apr. 1823.

[25] *Parl. Pap.* 1823, vi (361), 171, and 1825, viii (129), 16–17; *A Letter to Sir Francis Burdett*, pp. 19, 23.

article on the poor in the *Quarterly*; and Sir Robert Inglis, formerly private secretary to Lord Sidmouth.[26]

Courtenay and three or four other gentlemen objected to the proposal in principle. Others criticized details: the amount of assistance that was suggested, the assumption that paupers would be willing to emigrate, the involvement of the national government in the financial arrangements, the size of the grant of land, the lack of any provision to guarantee the good character of the emigrant, and the likelihood that parishes would refuse to pay a long-term annuity after getting rid of their paupers. Yet a majority of those whom Horton consulted agreed with his broad objectives. He was encouraged by the evidence of considerable support for some measure of assisted emigration.

Most important were the reactions of the ministers.[27] Wynn's criticisms were minor and his interest positive. Bathurst was tolerant although apprehensive lest parishes use Horton's plan to get rid of their most incapable paupers. Robert Peel also thought that it would be unwise to leave the selection of the emigrants in the hands of the parishes. Peel, who had become Home Secretary shortly after Horton took office, had advocated assisted emigration more than once when he was Irish Secretary. He remained friendly to the idea but had

[26] Estimations of the plan were also given by E. J. Littleton, M.P. for Staffordshire and a close friend of Horton; Col. John Ready, a member of the executive council of Lower Canada; Lt.-General William Dyott, a Staffordshire magistrate; John Galt, the Scottish novelist who was also agent for the inhabitants of Upper Canada with military claims against the government; George Vernon, the son of Lord Vernon; Thomas Fisher, rector of Roche, Cornwall; Dr. Edward Copleston, Provost of Oriel College, Oxford; Stephen Peter Rigaud, Savilian Professor of Geometry, Oxford; J. Lowe, author of *The Present State of England*, published in 1822; George William Chad, Secretary of the British Embassy in Brussels and a property owner in Norfolk; John Davenport of Burslem, Stafford, later an M.P.; George Chetwynd, M.P. for Staffordshire and a supporter of the Poor Removal Bill; Michael Nolan, M.P. for Barnstaple and an opponent of the Poor Removal Bill; Richard Hart Davis, M.P. for Bristol; Thomas Babington, a former M.P. for Leicester; G. Tren. Goodenough, who had been Tax Office Commissioner twenty years earlier; Charles Forster, the domestic chaplain to the Bishop of Limerick; T. G. Buchnall Estcourt, M.P. for Devizes and a nephew to Lord Sidmouth; Thomas Gisborne, curate of Barton-under-Needwood, an abolitionist and an intimate friend of Wilberforce; Kirkman Finlay, a former M.P. for Glasgow who organized the emigration of weavers in 1820–1; and W. S. Kinnersley, Horton's fellow M.P. representing Newcastle under Lyme. Dyott, Estcourt, Davenport, and Littleton expressed the most hostile criticism. See W.H.P., especially Horton's précis of the letters and opinions he received.

[27] W.H.P., Horton's précis, Peel to Horton, 11 Apr. 1823, F. Robinson to Horton, 6 Feb. 1823, Southey to Wynn, 28 Apr. 1823. Goulburn Papers, Box 11/13, Peel to Goulburn, 7 Feb. 1815.

reservations about the project that Horton outlined. Frederick Robinson believed that the question deserved serious study; if the government decided not to do anything, it should be prepared to show why. He suggested to Horton that a House of Commons committee on emigration might be worth while.

When Robinson looked at the emigration plan, he was in the process of surrendering his duties at the Board of Trade to Huskisson and moving to replace Vansittart as Chancellor of the Exchequer. As a consequence, Horton could expect a fair hearing from three key figures: the Colonial Secretary, the Home Secretary, and the Chancellor of the Exchequer. The atmosphere was sufficiently favourable to give confidence to a man of Horton's temperament. He knew that there were recent precedents for government involvement in pauper emigration. In 1819 Parliament had greeted such a step with warmth and most of the members whom Horton questioned in 1822 had given their approval. For Horton the odds that he could accomplish something were good enough; he took the bit in his teeth.

V

EXPERIMENTS IN IRISH EMIGRATION

HORTON was not familiar with any of the more acutely distressed areas of the British Isles. He approached the question of pauper emigration as a political economist, not as a philanthropist or a spokesman for a particular region or constituency. The problem was for him an abstract one. While he began with a plan for the parish poor in England, he responded enthusiastically when Robert Peel suggested emigration from Ireland. Peel, who was four years younger than Horton, had become Home Secretary in 1822 at the age of thirty-four and was already a powerful Cabinet figure. He was an unmistakable Tory, but on economic questions he paid attention to Ricardo and was attracted to the policies of Huskisson. To Peel, more than to anyone, Horton looked for eventual support in making an extensive system of emigration a reality. For his part, Peel withheld approval while managing to give encouragement. When he proposed a small emigration from Ireland, he did not endorse Horton's views, but he did offer a means to test them.

Peel brought to the Home Office a greater knowledge of Ireland and Irish affairs than any of his predecessors in the period since the union.[1] He was bound to follow events attentively and to direct Irish policy with a firm hand. Because his close friend, Henry Goulburn, was a new and inexperienced Irish Secretary, Peel guided him step by step. Goulburn did not object; the crisis that he faced in 1822–3 was the worst that Ireland had seen in twenty years.[2] Incessant rain in 1821 had spoiled the potato crop. In the south of Ireland, where the whole population lived mainly on potatoes, thousands were reduced to one meal of oatmeal a day. Cork, Kerry, Limerick, Galway, Mayo, Sligo, Leitrim, Roscommon, Clare, and Tipperary were all areas of acute distress. In the spring of 1822, half of the population of half of Ireland was destitute.

[1] Norman Gash, *Mr. Secretary Peel, The Life of Sir Robert Peel to 1830* (London, 1961), p. 369.
[2] *Hansard*, 1824, xi, cols. 452 and 1822, vii, col. 107; *Parl. Pap.* 1823, vi (561), 3–4; Gash, pp. 375–6.

Hunger was accompanied by violence. While the government hesitated to supply food, there was no doubt of its responsibility to uphold the law. In February 1822 Parliament passed the Insurrection Act and the Irish Habeas Corpus Suspension Act. 'The ignorant classes are in rebellion,' Castlereagh told the Commons.[3] Yet there was no political purpose in the terrorism of the 'Whiteboys' and 'Ribbonmen', the secret societies supported by the Irish tenantry. Land was the issue. Cattle-maiming, arson, and murder were the acts of those deprived of their leasehold. Church property and farms from which tenants had been evicted were the usual objects of attack. No reform-inspired uprising could have been as difficult to suppress as this anarchic rebellion.

For a while the suspension of normal legal processes seemed effective in restoring order. After a turbulent spring the summer and early autumn of 1822 were comparatively quiet. The harvest was always a signal for trouble; tithe corn and hay went up in smoke; but the yield of potatoes was adequate. In January 1823 conditions were much better than they had been during the previous winter.[4] Except for a few incidents in Clare and Tipperary, disturbances were confined to a few districts on the north-western boundary of County Cork. Lord Wellesley, the Lord-Lieutenant of Ireland, expected that the special provisions of the Insurrection Act would not be needed much longer.

March brought disappointment. In the first week the police magistrate of Cork reported seventeen separate instances of terrorism.[5] Scarcely a night passed in which some property was not put to fire. To a lesser extent, Limerick, Clare, Westmeath, Queens, and the other counties in Munster experienced an increase in violence. This was the time of year in which leases terminated. It was usually a period of unrest; in 1823 it witnessed a regeneration of all the brutality that had been manifested in 1822. Members of the propertied class were more alarmed than ever. A year earlier they had placed some faith in the Insurrection Act; now that measure had proved inadequate.[6]

Not until he received a dispatch from Lord Wellesley in mid-April, was Robert Peel fully aware of the situation. One of his first

---

[3] *Hansard*, 1822, vi, col. 111.
[4] H.O. 100/208, Wellesley to Peel, 29 Jan. 1823.
[5] Ibid., 8 Apr. 1823.
[6] *Hansard*, 1823, ix, col. 1150.

concerns was to seek a renewal of the Insurrection Act. At the same time he decided that this was a proper moment for the government to offer to remove surplus population. Within a week of drafting a reply to Lord Wellesley, Peel had arranged for Horton and Goulburn to discuss a plan of assisted emigration.[7] Peel made two specifications: first, the emigrants should be recruited in Southern Ireland; second, the measure should be financed entirely by the government with no expectation of reimbursement from local assessment. Frederick Robinson, the Chancellor of the Exchequer, was consulted and he approved a small experiment. The plan was put before the Prime Minister, Lord Liverpool, and one week after Peel had suggested it, it was agreed upon.

County Cork was the centre of trouble; it was singled out as the place to start.[8] Goulburn and Horton met three of the members of Parliament from Cork and several other Irish gentlemen to explain the government's proposal. These men became Horton's liaison with Ireland. Although Peel had expected that the Irish government would co-operate with the Colonial Office, Goulburn was actively involved only at the onset. He was happy to leave the matter in Horton's eager hands. Nor did he bother to advise the Lord-Lieutenant of the British government's intentions. Lord Wellesley remained in the dark until Peter Robinson, the government's agent, arrived in Ireland and began to recruit settlers. Wellesley was understandably annoyed.[9] How could penal measures work, he asked, if the punishment of the guilty became the reward of the innocent? How could he achieve anything by transporting convicts to Bermuda and Australia if Mr. Robinson tramped up and down the country advertising the advantages of emigration?

This protest was ignored; Wellesley's government was bypassed. For advice and assistance Horton depended on the representatives from Cork, Lord Ennismore, W. W. Becher, and Sir Nicholas Colthurst, and landlords such as Lord Doneraile, Lord Mount Cashell, and Lord Kingston.[10] These men were responsible for the decision

[7] Goulburn Papers, Peel to Goulburn, 30 Apr. 1823; W.H.P., Peel to Wilmot, 30 Apr. 1823; Add. MSS., F. Robinson to Liverpool, 6 May 1823. At this time the number of emigrants leaving Southern Ireland was not great. In 1817 only seven ships left Dublin for Quebec; in 1826 twenty-seven ships left with 2,555 people. Annual emigration from Sligo, Galway, and Limerick was about 1,000 in 1822 and 2,000 in 1826. Cork, Waterford, and New Ross sent out 1,500 or 1,900 emigrants annually. See Jones, 'Transatlantic Emigrant Trade', p. 74.

[8] Parl. Pap. 1823, vi (561), 168-9.   [9] W.H.P., Forster to Inglis, 30 June 1823.

[10] Parl. Pap. 1823, vi (561), 179.

to take most of the settlers for Upper Canada from Mallow and Fermoy, the most disturbed baronies of Cork. They introduced Horton's agent to local magistrates and officials; they helped to recruit; and they influenced the final selection of emigrants. Inevitably, charges of favouritism arose. There was little to prevent Ennismore, Becher, and the others from clearing tenants from their own estates first. It was a temptation they could not completely resist.

Fifteen thousand pounds were allocated for emigration from Cork. The money was spent on two separate projects.[11] Two-thirds of it was used to send settlers to Upper Canada; the remainder to assist labourers to go to the Cape of Good Hope. Horton was more interested in the Upper Canadian than the South African experiment, but in each case he had long-term objectives. At the Cape a shortage of labour kept wages at a high level. Capitalists might be encouraged to bring in indentured labour; an initial priming of the pump might set in motion a subsequent emigration at no further government expense. Canada was a different proposition. While this colony could absorb far more emigrants than the Cape, it could not take them as labourers for hire. In Canada paupers would have to be placed on land. The government offered free transportation, land, implements, and rations for 500 people to settle in Upper Canada. If the experiment succeeded, it could be repeated on a more extensive scale in the following years.

The vision of a privately sponsored movement of labour to South Africa was founded on a shaky understanding of the situation there. It was true that capitalists in Cape Town and in the Zuurveld or Albany District were handicapped by the cost of manpower.[12] Labourers receiving 3s. a day were much better paid than their counterparts in Great Britain. Mechanics and tradesmen, particularly tailors, shoemakers, saddlers, bricklayers, upholsterers, coopers, sawyers, carpenters, and blacksmiths, were able to demand as much as 6s. a day, and the immigration of 400 or 500 labourers annually would probably not have altered the prevailing rate of wages. But much of the work that was available was occasional; employers could not afford to engage men continuously. Many of the gentlemen settlers who had been located in the Albany district could not manage without hired labour; nor could they manage with it. Those who kept

---

[11] *Parl. Pap.* 1823, vi (561), 180.

[12] Ibid. 1826, iv (404), 228, 877–902, and 1826–7, v (550), 145; C.O. 48/79, Report of Commissioners of Inquiry, 1 June 1825.

servants had been employing them at a loss for three years; the prices obtained for the District's limited exports were too low to permit a profitable return on a large farming operation. These men wanted cheaper labour but could not afford to bring it out from Britain. Even if their capital had not been depleted, they would have been deterred by the high cost of transportation from Britain to the Cape. Only with a government subsidy did traffic in indentured servants become profitable.

In the mistaken belief that, once the way was shown, private capital would act alone, such a subsidy was granted to John Ingram, a one-time Cork merchant and a settler at the Cape of Good Hope. Under the great government scheme of 1820 Ingram had gone to the Cape at the head of a party of sixty-eight persons from Cork. Since then he had returned to Britain to bring out his own family and another fifty labourers and he had applied to the Colonial Office for assistance to take out a larger number. He came to Horton with the backing of Lord Ennismore and Sir Nicholas Colthurst.[13] Ingram represented himself as a settler who needed agricultural servants for himself and who was willing to supervise the emigration of several hundred people for the public good. In fact, he was a speculator bent on making government money work for himself. Along with the other Irish settlers in 1820 Ingram had been placed on a hopeless grant of land in the District of Clanwilliam. He had no need for the servants that he brought out in 1820, but extricated himself from this position in fine style, leasing his grant and allowing his servants to buy back their contracts. They were anxious to do so because they could earn much better wages in Cape Town than from Ingram. On the basis of this experience Ingram realized that any man who held a large number of cheaply paid servants under contract in South Africa could make money quickly.

The contract that Ingram made with the government required him to take fifty labourers at his own expense because that had been his expressed intention from the beginning. The government would allow him £14 per person, the cost of a passage, for another 350.[14] All of the emigrants recruited by Ingram were indentured to him,

[13] C.O. 48/79, Ennismore to Wilmot, 26 Mar. 1823, and Colthurst to Wilmot, 10 May 1823; C.O. 49/16, Horton to Commissioners of Inquiry, 11 Feb. 1824; Report of Commissioners of Inquiry, 1 June 1825; *Parl. Pap.* 1823, vi (561), 180.

[14] C.O. 48/79, Terms of Ingram's Indenture, and Ingram to Horton, 14, 16, and 20 May 1823; C.O. 49/16, Bathurst to Somerset, 20 July 1823; C.O. 49/15, Horton to Ingram, 25 June 1823, and Horton to Treasury, May 1823.

adults for three years and children for seven. He was bound to pay men at least 1s. a day and women 6d. and to provide lodging, medical treatment, and provisions on the same scale as were issued to H.M. troops. These wages were well below the standard rates in South Africa. Ingram did not advertise the fact that he was spending government money; he was afraid that, if the emigrants knew, they would try to evade their contracts after they reached the colony. For publicly assisted emigrants it was a poor bargain to be legally tied to a private speculator.

When Ingram arrived at Cape Town late in 1823 he landed only 347 persons, not one of whom he had assisted from his own pocket.[15] With reports of the failure of the 1820 settlers circulating Ireland, it had not been easy to find a shipload of emigrants. In the end he had recruited most of his emigrants from the roughest element of the seaport population of the city of Cork, but his passenger list was still short of the fifty he was supposed to take on his own account.

After disembarkation Ingram encouraged his people to find work with other masters. As a price for release Ingram demanded from each man, woman, and child £30, £20, and £15 respectively.[16] Within a few months most of the emigrants were transferred to other employers. Mechanics and tradesmen were able to earn from 6s. to 8s. a day, while common labourers got as much as 4s. None of the emigrants would admit to being better off than if he had been given employment in Ireland. Although the labourers' rate of pay was high, their work was irregular and they were in competition with slave and free coloured labour which cost only £2 a month plus provision and lodging. Most of all they complained of the cost of obtaining quittance from Ingram. In this matter Ingram insisted on all of his legal rights.

Through the sale of indentures Ingram obtained at least £5,710, a handsome return when one remembers that he invested nothing but his time. This was not clear profit. A hard core of fifty alcoholics and misfits remained on his hands.[17] If he had financed the venture himself, he would have been in the red. As it was he had made a small fortune. In 1825 the Commissioners of Inquiry, Major Macbean

[15] Report of Commissioners, 1 June 1825. On Ingram's difficulties before embarkation: C.O. 48/79, Lewis to Horton, 4 Sept. 1823; C.O. 49/15, Horton to Treasury, 7 Sept. 1823; Horton to Lewis, 28 Aug. 1823, Horton to Ingram, 20 Sept. 1823; C.O. 384/17, Ingram to Horton, 5 Oct. 1827. See Corry, pp. 159–60.

[16] Report of Commissioners, 1 June 1825.

[17] C.O. 384/17, Ingram to Horton, 5 Oct. 1827.

George Colebrooke and Mr. John T. Bigge, produced a report on Ingram as they did on almost everything else during their interminable investigation of the affairs of Cape Colony. The Commissioners recommended a repetition of the experiment, but on terms more favourable to the emigrants. Ingram, they declared, would have been amply compensated for his efforts if he had received £1 per person, or £347 altogether.

As William Parker observed, Ingram could not be blamed for taking advantage of the 'susceptibility to delusion' that he found in the Colonial Office.[18] Horton had sanctioned a project, the operation of which he clearly did not understand. Yet no great harm was done. The emigrants found employment; Ingram banked some money; and there the matter ended. Critics of the Colonial Office missed this opportunity to raise embarrassing questions. Horton continued to advocate the emigration of labourers to the Cape of Good Hope; to support his point of view he published an extract of the Commissioners' Report in an appendix to the Report of the Select Committee on Emigration in 1826.[19] Yet he realized that the full story of the Ingram experiment cast little credit on himself and he made no attempt to bring Ingram as a witness before the Emigration Committee of 1826 or its successor of 1827.

Horton did not allow the same omission with respect to Peter Robinson, the superintendent of the parallel emigration to Upper Canada. This experiment, Horton believed, was a success; he presented its results in full detail, appearing himself as a witness before parliamentary committees in 1823 and in 1825, and sending Robinson to testify before the House of Lords Committee on Disturbances in Ireland in 1824, and the Commons Committee on Emigration in 1827. It has been suggested that this last Committee was first appointed in 1826 to defend the government's action in assisting Irish emigration to Canada. The ease with which Horton passed over the questions surrounding Ingram's experiment suggests very strongly that he could have avoided any discussion of the money spent by Robinson if he had thought it desirable. But Horton was prepared to argue that the emigration to Canada had proved the correctness of his theories; for that reason, he wished to advertise the findings.

In 1822 Peter Robinson, an honorary member of the executive

---

[18] C.O. 48/87, p. 424: Paper drawn up by William Parker 11 Feb., 1824.
[19] *Parl. Pap.* 1826, iv (404), 283.

council of Upper Canada and a member of the legislative assembly, had come to London with his brother John Beverley Robinson, Attorney-General of that province. The Robinsons were central figures in the Family Compact, the Upper Canadian ruling clique. They were the sons of an aristrocratic Virginia family which had chosen the wrong side in 1776; they had been raised in the home of the first Anglican missionary in Upper Canada; and John Beverley had received his grammar-school education from Dr. John Strachan who was, in many respects, the architect of the Family Compact.[20] This background was reflected in an attitude of conservative and unapologetic intolerance. Few English statesmen defended the Church of England so resolutely or looked upon democracy with such distaste. John Beverley, the younger but abler brother, was first appointed Attorney-General at the age of eighteen before he was called to the bar; eventually, in 1829, he became Chief Justice, a position which he held in addition to membership in the executive council and speakership of the legislative council. His influence in the government of Upper Canada was already considerable in 1822.

John Beverley Robinson had been sent to London to represent the interests of his province in a dispute with Lower Canada over the division of customs duties collected at Quebec. After his arrival he became involved in an abortive effort by Horton to legislate a union of the two Canadas; this business kept Robinson in London through the winter of 1822–3. He was available for consultation by Horton when the experiment in Irish emigration was launched. At first thought the idea was repugnant. He knew that the Irish gentry wanted to get rid of the young and unemployed who 'hung loose upon society' and were 'the ready actors in all disturbances'.[21] Violence and religious bigotry were native products of Ireland which Robinson did not wish to import to Upper Canada. Yet he was prepared to believe that the behaviour of the Irish was not ingrained and that, in the calmer atmosphere of a colony in which they were given equal footing with their neighbours, old quarrels could be forgotten. He decided that he would be happier to accept Catholics from the South of Ireland than Protestants from the North; Ulstermen might be more intelligent and less violent, but they were also more republican. Robinson preferred the 'ignorant, poor and priest

[20] C. W. Robinson, *The Life of Sir John Beverley Robinson* (Edinburgh, 1904), p. x.
[21] C.O. 384/12, J. Robinson to Horton, 14 June 1825; Add. MSS. 38294, J. Robinson to Horton 5 May 1823.

ridden' to those 'who think for themselves in matters of Government and religion, and too often think wrong'.[22] The desirability of a scheme of government colonization for sparsely populated, land-rich Upper Canada was manifest and nothing could be more welcome to an Upper Canadian than the spending that such a programme would entail. Robinson favoured Irish immigration, but not at such a rate than they might become a majority in the province; 'then they would have the law in their own hands' and there would be no stopping their shooting and burning.

On Tuesday 29 April Peel opened the question of Irish emigration; on Saturday 10 May the Robinsons intended to embark for Canada. In that short period Peter Robinson was persuaded to stay behind to superintend the project. It was through John Beverley that Horton approached Peter; John Beverley could think of no one 'more likely to do justice to such a trust than my brother'.[23] Moreover, Peter was there, in Britain, and available. Colonel Thomas Talbot, who knew Ireland as Robinson did not, and who possessed long experience in colonization, would have been an obvious and willing candidate; but Talbot was in Canada and Horton needed a man immediately.[24] Peter Robinson was ready to take the job. He saw an opportunity to gain credit by carrying out a measure of importance both to Britain and the colony; but he was afraid that this credit would be tarnished unless the entire management on both sides of the Atlantic were placed in his hands. He insisted on an overall superintendence in which he would be held directly accountable only to the British government. This condition was acceptable to Horton; Robinson undertook a task singlehandedly which would have been accomplished with greater efficiency if he had been assisted by the authorities in Canada.

At the end of May 1823 Peter Robinson found himself crossing the Irish Sea instead of returning to Upper Canada with his brother. During the first week of June he visited all of the principal towns in the northern part of Cork, appointing in each a person to make a list of those who wished to emigrate.[25] These lists were subsequently

[22] C.O. 384/12, J. Robinson to Horton, 19 Feb. 1824.
[23] J. Robinson to Horton, 5 May 1823.
[24] On 14 Feb. 1823, Talbot wrote to Horton: 'I . . . hope that you have not abandoned your scheme for encouraging Emigration . . . should a Bill on your plan be carried into operation I offer my humble services . . . in undertaking any portion of the superintendence.' See W.H.P.
[25] C.O. 384/12, P. Robinson to Horton, 2 and 9 June 1823; Cowan, p. 70.

combed by magistrates who marked the names of suspected trouble-makers who were most eligible to go. The Irish peasants were under-standably suspicious of an invitation that smacked so much of deportation. Like Lord Wellesley, they could not appreciate the subtle difference between transporting the convicted for their crimes and the unconvicted for their poverty.

In this respect, the appointment of a foreigner as a recruiting agent in Ireland was fortunate. While local magistrates were not trusted, Robinson himself was very successful in encouraging volun-teers.[26] By the end of June he had distributed embarkation tickets to 600 persons. During the first two days of July 571 boarded two vessels provided by the Transport Office. A majority of the men were labourers; a few were unemployed and homeless; a small number were landless farmers. To the best of Robinson's knowledge, which under the circumstances could not be perfect, all were penni-less. Robinson asked no questions of the past conduct of his pas-sengers. Although he allowed the magistrates to pick out their least wanted citizens, no man was sent against his will. The law-abiding went with the lawless. As an Upper Canadian Robinson might have been expected to give preference to those who had no criminal back-ground. His impartiality was based on a belief that if men were given the responsibility of owning land, they would become peaceful citi-zens. This belief was not held universally; the project was a social experiment and something of a gamble.

In the course of an eight-week crossing Robinson discovered that the Irish stomach tolerated a very restricted diet. The emigrants were issued with a minimum allowance of navy rations. Men received a pound of salt pork, a pound of ship's biscuit, and almost half a pint of spirits daily; women were given half a pound of salt pork, a pound of biscuit, and tea and sugar. Cocoa was provided for breakfast and plum pudding for Sunday dinner. The Irish were used to eating potatoes and herring; they normally had meat once in a season. When faced with inferior pork and alien food they lost appetite.[27] Meat was thrown overboard by the hundredweight, plum pudding refused by every man, woman, and child; only a few individuals would touch the cheese, and cocoa was turned aside until the ship's officers proved

[26] C.O. 384/12, P. Robinson to Horton, 9 June 1823, and 2 Apr. 1824, Becher to Horton, 1 July 1823; *Parl. Pap.* 1825, vii (200), 258.

[27] P. Robinson to Horton, 2 Apr. 1824; H. T. Pammett, 'Assisted Emigration from Ireland to Upper Canada under Peter Robinson in 1825', *O.H.S.P.R.*, 1936, p. 179; *Parl. Pap.* 1826-7, v (550), 347.

MAP III. Baronies in which the Irish Emigrants of 1823 were recruited.

it could be taken safely. Robinson was amazed to hear sick children crying for potatoes when they were offered arrowroot as a medicament. Yet he learned nothing from his observations. The emigrants were kept on similar rations for fifteen months after they arrived in Canada. Rather than eat food that they found disgusting, they traded a large part of it for whiskey, potatoes, and cows. If he had been more imaginative, Robinson might have provided the head of each family with a small sum and allowed him to make his own purchases.

In spite of the diet and the relatively slow crossing, the health of the emigrants was generally good. One woman and eight children died of smallpox, but these losses could not be blamed on the conditions on board ship.[28] The journey from Cork in Ireland to Prescott in Upper Canada was managed with admirable timing. At Quebec Robinson found steamboats waiting for him and was able to transfer his people to these vessels without landing. Conveyance was also ready for him at Montreal; with a minimum of delay he brought his party to Prescott on 15 September. Nearly 600 men, women, and children, travelling by steamboat, wagon, and bateaux, had been moved 320 miles in thirteen days.

The season was, nevertheless, advanced, and Robinson had not yet selected a tract of land. On 18 September he left the emigrants in Prescott while he surveyed half a dozen townships in or adjacent to the Rideau Military Settlement. After an absence of several days he returned to Prescott to move the Irish the last 60 miles to their destination. A majority were located in Ramsay Township behind concession lines occupied by some of the Glasgow weavers. The others were placed in adjacent townships which were partially occupied by military men and Scottish assisted emigrants of 1815 and 1820–1. From the beginning the Irish found themselves on poor terms with their neighbours. They were disliked equally for their Catholicism and their reputed lawlessness. Inevitably, the Scottish weavers compared the liberal assistance that the Irish were receiving with the help that they themselves had been given.[29] The weavers were required to repay £10 per head; but each Irish family received a log house, cow, blankets, farming implements, and provisions as outright gifts. Knowledge of this was a factor in the eventual failure of the Scots to return one farthing of their debt. In the meantime they and the other established settlers complained bitterly amongst

[28] P. Robinson to Horton, 2 Apr. 1824; Cowan, p. 71.
[29] C.O. 42/373, FitzGibbon to Hillier, 10 June 1824.

themselves that so much should be given to such inferior people. The annual muster of the local militia regiment in the following April sparked a brawl which roused the Irish to commit a subsequent act of vandalism.[30] A party led by the local deputy-sheriff, an Orangeman, marched out to the settlement to make arrests and fired on a building in which the men had gathered. One Irishman was killed and two were wounded. The exaggerated first reports of this incident alarmed authorities at York. John Beverley Robinson was ready to believe the worst; 'I am something staggered in my opinion of Irish Emigration,' he told Horton.[31] After reflection, and with more evidence before him, he took a saner view. It was evident that the Irish had received some provocation before their original outburst; an investigating officer charged the deputy-sheriff's party with a 'wanton and outrageous attack upon the lives of the new settlers'.[32] Any desire to seek blood for blood was checked by the restraint of the Irish in the ensuing months; this was the only occasion on which they were collectively on the wrong side of the law in Upper Canada.

Corrections were slow to catch up with first judgements. Long after J. B. Robinson had qualified his initial statement, he was quoted in the House of Commons in proof of a claim that attitudes in Upper Canada had hardened against further Irish immigration.[33] Although Robinson assured Horton that the provincial legislative assembly would welcome 100,000 Irish paupers if the Imperial government chose to send them, the unfavourable stories were never completely silenced. Prominent among those giving publicity to these stories was the Governor-General of Canada, Lord Dalhousie. His principal source of information was Lieutenant-Colonel William Marshall, superintendent of the Lanark and Rideau Settlements, a man prejudiced on the side of his own settlers and disgruntled by the creation of a new settlement under the supervision of a civilian. Dalhousie had predicted failure for Robinson's emigrants from the moment they were placed on the land; the tone of his dispatch enclosing Marshall's version of the disturbances in Ramsay Township was one

[30] J. K. Johnson, 'Colonel James FitzGibbon and the Suppression of Irish Riots in Upper Canada', *Ontario History*, Sept. 1966, p. 142.

[31] C.O. 384/12, J. Robinson to Horton, 10 May 1824.

[32] C.O. 42/373, FitzGibbon to Hillier, 10 June 1824. See also C.O. 384/12, J. Robinson to Horton, 14 June 1825.

[33] C.O. 384/12, Horton to J. Robinson, 14 June 1825. See also W.H.P., J. Robinson to Horton, 6 July 1830.

of satisfaction in having his doubts confirmed. The Irish would never be reconciled to their neighbours, he claimed, not even in small numbers. Most of them would abandon their land and become wandering beggars. Robinson's scheme should be stopped, he told Bathurst; it was 'a waste of Public monies and a most serious mischief done to the Canadas'.[34]

On this issue, Dalhousie and the Lieutenant-Governor of Upper Canada, Sir Peregrine Maitland, were diametrically opposed. Maitland applauded Peter Robinson's efforts and took a personal interest in the success of his experiment. To a certain extent, Maitland and Dalhousie reflected the separate problems of their provinces. Voluntary emigrants continued to arrive at Quebec at a rate of 10,000 a year. The destitute among them were still creating serious difficulties for the government of the Lower Province. Under these circumstances, Dalhousie was apprehensive about the encouragement of further pauper emigration. Quebec served as the principal port for both Canadian provinces, but the care of helpless, sick, and dying emigrants bound for Upper Canada and the United States became the responsibility of the government of Lower Canada alone. Upper Canadians did not entertain misgivings about pauper emigration because the worst of the human wreckage did not reach them.

An element of vanity influenced Dalhousie's opposition to the emigration conducted by Peter Robinson. The Governor-General had not been consulted, but had simply been informed after all of the arrangements had been made. He objected not so much to the principle involved as to the actual system that had been adopted.[35] First, he argued that the expense of transporting emigrants inland to Upper Canada was too great and that it would be impossible to prevent desertion from that province to the United States. Second, he did not think that Upper Canada required assisted emigration because considerable numbers went there at their own expense. Third, he thought that the Irish emigrants should be placed under strict control to make them work; he asserted that Peter Robinson and his subordinates were not competent to do this. As an alternative, Dalhousie favoured a settlement in his province, in the Gaspé, under the rigid supervision of military personnel.

In November 1825 Dalhousie reported to Horton on Lieutenant-

---

[34] C.O. 42/200, Dalhousie to Bathurst, 18 May 1824.
[35] C.O. 42/204, Dalhousie to Horton, 12 Nov. 1825.

Colonel Marshall's authority that half of the settlers who had come out in 1823 had run away. Maitland replied that this estimate was far from the truth. 'I cannot but regret,' he wrote to Horton, 'that Lord Dalhousie . . . should not have thought it a safer and better course, to have consulted the Government of this Province, as to the real situation of the Emigrants before he transmitted to you such erroneous and discouraging information.'[36] In May 1826 Maitland sent the results of an on-the-spot count. Of 182 heads of families brought out by Peter Robinson, eight had died; 121 were on their land; nine were known to have gone to the United States and one had returned to Ireland. Of the remaining forty-three, at least twenty-two were working in the immediate vicinity as farm labourers and tradesmen. Many of the others had found jobs in Kingston, Prescott, and Montreal, as rafters on the St. Lawrence, or as labourers on the Welland Canal. Some of them could be expected to return to their land after they had earned enough money to buy some stock. Predictions that a majority would slip over the American border at the first opportunity had proved to be without basis.

The emigration of 1823 was the first part of an experiment which was to be carried on for two or three years. Peel had advised Horton to think of an expenditure on the same scale or larger in the second year. The government, however, had been motivated by a siege of disorder in Ireland and its interest might lapse as soon as that siege were lifted. The country was fairly quiet during the winter of 1823–4; Horton held little expectation of a grant in that spring.[37] Peter Robinson was informed in a letter written late in February 1824 that his services would probably not be needed that year. On this occasion Horton misread his colleagues' intentions. Peel and Frederick Robinson conceded more than immediate value to the experiment. In April a formal request for a grant was submitted to Lord Liverpool and the Chancellor of the Exchequer; towards the end of May the government gave its consent. By that time the season in which the emigration should have been organized had passed. Horton's hesitation before seeking a grant and the Treasury's leisurely response had cost so many months that it became advisable

[36] W.H.P., Maitland to Horton, 9 Mar. 1826; C.O. 42/377, Maitland to Bathurst, 1 May 1826.

[37] W.H.P., Peel to Horton, 6 Aug. 1823; Add. MSS. 40356, Horton to Peel, 20 June 1823; Add. MSS. 40357, Horton to Peel, 2 Aug. 1823; C.O. 43/64, Horton to P. Robinson, 25 Feb., 21 May 1824, and Bathurst to Liverpool, 10 Apr. 1824; C.O. 384/12, P. Robinson to Horton, 16 Dec. 1823; H.O. 79/8, Peel to Goulburn, 4 Aug. 1824.

to postpone the project. Consequently, the Treasury and the Colonial Office agreed to take no action in 1824 but to ask Parliament for a double grant in the following year.

In August and September 1824 Peter Robinson spent six weeks in Ireland compiling a list of people who wanted to go to Canada. He encountered none of the suspicion and holding back on the part of the peasantry that had hindered him in 1823. Cheerful reports from Canada dispelled all doubts of the generosity of the government's offer; the problem now was not recruiting emigrants, but selecting them. Fifty thousand people applied for 1,500 places.[38] Most of the settlers were taken from the same part of Cork as in 1823 although half of the petitions came from other places in Ireland. Lord Kingston sent 400 tenants. A few nobles and gentlemen in Cork cleared their estates while nominations from other counties were passed over. Horton did not apologize for this favouritism. If the same number of emigrants had been collected in equable proportions from several counties, the expenses of the government would have been doubled. This measure, he maintained, although it might unfairly benefit particular districts, should be considered only as an experiment.[39]

Ruthless as he was in turning away applications, Peter Robinson was unable to keep his lists down to 1,500 names. In May 1825 six ships sailed from Cork carrying 2,024 persons. Robinson did not cross at the same time as the emigrants. On 24 May he left Cork for London where he settled some accounts with the Treasury and then left for Liverpool, whence he sailed on 19 June by the *Panther* bound for New York.[40] All but one of the emigrant ships had made short passages of under thirty-one days, but the *Panther* was less fortunate; Robinson, who travelled inland through New York State, did not reach Niagara until 28 July.

In Robinson's absence, the emigrants had been moved from Prescott to Kingston by bateaux and encamped in tents.[41] In 1825 July was an exceptionally hot month. The camp was located on low, swampy ground so there was no relief from the Upper Canadian humidity. Temperatures rose to 100°F. in the shade and the

---

[38] *Parl. Pap.* 1826–7, v (550), 344 and 1825, viii (129), 314; C. W. Robinson, *Sir John Beverley Robinson*, p. 168; Pammett, 'Assisted Emigration from Ireland', pp. 180–2.

[39] *Parl. Pap.* 1826–7, v (550), 444.

[40] C.O. 384/13, P. Robinson Memorandum, 15 Dec. 1824.

[41] Pammett, pp. 186–92; W.H.P., Maitland to Horton, 13 Feb. 1826; C.O. 342/95, Horton to J. Robinson, 18 Nov. 1825.

emigrants, already weakened by the crossing, fell ill with fever and dysentery. In one day, eleven were buried. When Robinson finally arrived in Kingston, he was received with jubilation by both the emigrants and the local officials. The first ship-load of emigrants had already spent a sweltering month in tents.

Robinson organized the movement of 500 emigrants from Kingston to Cobourg, but was obliged to take some time to repair a twelve-mile stretch of road.[42] Another eight days were lost while a boat was built to carry the emigrants twenty-four miles up the Otonabee River. Then Robinson went up the Otonabee with twenty local axemen and thirty of the healthiest of the emigrants to erect log shelters and to begin work on a depot. While all of these preparations were made, the bulk of the party remained in their tents by the lake. Although Robinson had known for twelve months that he would be bringing a large number of emigrants, his arrangements were haphazard and hurried. It was good fortune rather than good planning that allowed him to locate and shelter his people before winter.

When Wilmot Horton received from various sources reports that the emigrants were spending the summer under canvas, in a swamp, exposed to scorching sun, and were dying fast, his immediate fear was that this would put an end to all future experiments. He felt let down by the provincial government. He had not expected that the emigrants would be left in tents for five days, much less a month. Nothing, he said, that he had encountered since he entered the Colonial Office had annoyed him so much.[43] It was apprehension of bad publicity more than compassion for the emigrants that aroused him. Horton had already decided that assisted emigration was both possible and necessary; he viewed the experiments not as tests but as demonstrations of the correctness of his views. In his *Inquiry into the Causes and Remedies of Pauperism* Horton argued that the death-rate among the emigrants of 1825 was not alarming.[44] By means of dubious calculations he produced a ratio of one death in twenty-one; combining this ratio with one obtained for the emigrants in 1823 he arrived at a ratio of one in forty which, he observed triumphantly, was no worse than that for Carlisle, the healthiest place in England. Horton obtained the ratio of one in twenty-one by dividing the

[42] *Parl. Pap.*, 1826–7, v(550), 346.
[43] Horton to J. Robinson, 18 Nov. 1825.
[44] *Third Series*, pp. 79–84; C.O. 42/377, Maitland to Bathurst, 31 Mar. and 1 May 1826; Pammett, p. 210.

number of deaths up to March 1826 into the total number of emigrants. The actual ratio over the full year was one in eleven, a most disturbing statistic. To Horton, the sum of 192 deaths was simply a number which could be subjected to mathematical manipulation. He did not comprehend the story it represented of an exceptional Canadian summer, government mismanagement, and human misery.

The Irish themselves bore suffering without complaint. In their native country they had learned to treat officials and strangers warily. They appeared by force of habit to reply to questions with answers they thought were wanted rather than with answers they believed. It was difficult to discover their real feelings. When Captain Basil Hall interviewed a number of them during his tour of North America in 1827 none would admit having been destitute in Ireland; but, when asked if they appreciated what had been done for them, they spoke with animation of the change from their old life to 'their present happy conditions'.[45] Their replies perplexed more than they satisfied. Basil Hall thought it odd that he did not hear a murmur of dissatisfaction about the assistance provided by the government. Perhaps it did not occur to the emigrants to doubt the judiciousness of the arrangements that Peter Robinson had made on their behalf. They may have accepted their early trials as an unavoidable prelude to a better life. If they had any other feelings, they kept them to themselves.

In March 1826 Robinson took a census of his emigrants; 1,921 were found on their lots in the Newcastle and Bathurst Districts where they were receiving government rations.[46] Two men had met friends in Quebec and stayed there; twenty-six individuals were living in Montreal and two more in Kingston. By this time 102 emigrants had died; this loss had been partially redressed by the birth of thirty-three children in Canada. One family of four had disappeared at Cobourg and was presumed to have gone to the United States. The discovery of a high percentage of emigrants on the land at this stage did not prove that the experiment was a success. Lord Dalhousie predicted that they would stay for their twelve months' rations and then most of them would go away. Horton ordered another census after a two-year interval.[47] Un-

[45] Basil Hall, *Travels in North America in the Years 1827 and 1829*, i (Edinburgh 1829), 285–6.

[46] Maitland to Bathurst, 31 Mar. 1826.

[47] R. J. W. Horton, *Ireland and Canada : Supported by Local Evidence* (London, 1839), p. 68; W.H.P., P. Robinson to Horton, 1 Mar. 1829.

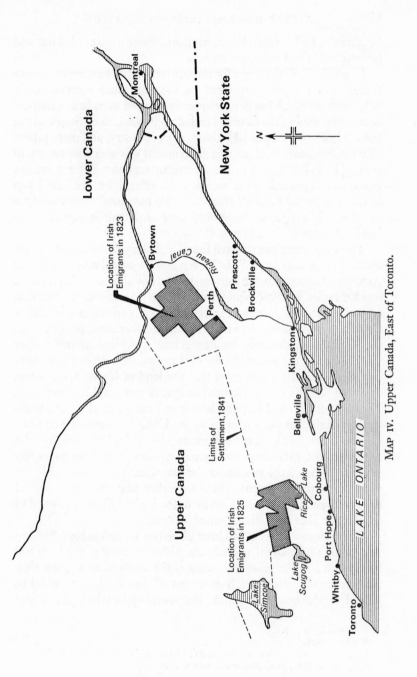

MAP IV. Upper Canada, East of Toronto.

fortunately, he left office before his instructions were carried out and he never obtained complete returns.

In reference to the grant for the emigration of 1823, a contributor to the *Monthly Review* expressed a conviction which was commonly held then and which has been frequently referred to by later writers.[48] Most emigrants to the Canadas ended up in the United States where there was more commercial activity, more industry, and more profitable employment. In effect, the government was spending money to convey British subjects to the American republic. After a second grant was approved, these words were echoed by William Lyon Mackenzie in the *Colonial Advocate*: 'To how much more useful a purpose might £30,000 have been expended than in recruiting in Ireland for the United States.'[49]

This scepticism was not well founded. Each year thousands of unassisted emigrants landed at Quebec and Montreal and crossed the American border, but the movement was not all in one direction. A much smaller but still significant number of emigrants were disembarking at New York and travelling directly to Niagara in Upper Canada. Furthermore, hundreds of native Americans, notably from the German settlements in Pennsylvania, were entering Upper Canada during the 1820s in spite of the province's Alien Act.[50] Anyone who worked the soil knew that the land of Upper Canada was endowed with as much potential as that of any neighbouring state. For a settler who had invested labour and energy in clearing a backwoods lot the temptation to go to the United States was resistible. On the other hand, recent emigrants who wished to work for hire were attracted to the republic by the opportunities there, especially while the Erie Canal was under construction. Those who criticized the Robinson experiments failed to realize that the procession of emigrants passing through Canada to the United States consisted of labourers rather than disappointed settlers.

The Glasgow weavers had been placed on worthless land, but had held on to it for more than a decade. Although some of the Irish had been located in the same townships as the weavers, as a group they received much better land. The success of their settlement might be judged by the results in Emily, the township in which the largest

[48] July 1823, p. 307.
[49] 8 Dec. 1825.
[50] A. C. Casselman, 'Pioneer Settlements', *Canada and Its Provinces*, xvii (Toronto, 1914), p. 49; W.H.P., A. C. Buchanan, minute 1826.

number of Irish were concentrated in 1825. There were 142 lots occupied by these people in November 1826. Eight years later eighty-one of the Irish settlers in Emily were recommended for their patents. Most of these people still held title to their land in 1841.[51] Between 1826 and 1834 43 per cent of the lots were abandoned. This figure does not include the desertions during the first year. It would probably be reasonable to say that 40 per cent of Robinson's emigrants settled permanently on their original grants. It would be wrong to assume that the others crossed the border; there were alternatives: setting up as tradesmen, working for other farmers, seeking employment in the towns of Upper and Lower Canada, and squatting on land elsewhere in the province.

Several Upper Canadians argued that Robinson had achieved his results at unnecessary cost. Horton was himself pleased that the expenses had been close to the estimate he had given to the 1823 Committee on Ireland. Omitting Peter Robinson's salary to make the figures come out the right way, Horton calculated the expenditure per person in 1823 at £22. 1s. 6d., and in 1825 at £21. 5s. 4d. Between £12 and £15 were spent after the emigrants' transports landed at Quebec.[52] According to Colonel Thomas Talbot, the emigrants had received twice as much as they needed. As a result they had been slow to clear their land, but quick to trade rations for whiskey.[53] Charles Rubidge, who assisted Robinson in placing some of the Irish on their land in 1825, thought that the settlers should have been given a shanty, five barrels of flour and one of pork, two axes and two hoes for a family of five, and then left to fend for themselves. They could have earned money in occasional employment to supplement their rations. As it was, the emigrants had been issued with about seven barrels of flour and four of meat over a period of twelve months. E. A. Talbot, maintained that a family could be shipped to Canada, located, and provided with two cows and a yoke of oxen for only £12 a head. In 1821 the Glasgow weavers had been settled at a cost to the government and the Glasgow Committee of about £16. 8s. 0d. It should be added that the weavers travelled

[51] Lillian F. Gates, *Land Policies of Upper Canada* (Toronto, 1968), pp. 92–3.

[52] C.O. 384/12, Horton to P. Robinson, 30 Dec. 1824; C.O. 324/97, Horton to Lewis, 13 Oct. 1827; *Parl. Pap.* 1826–7, v (550), 347, 349; A.O. 2/34 Account of Peter Robinson, 12 May 1823–31 Jan 1829, pp. 48–55.

[53] Armytage, 'Talbot and Wharncliffe', p. 193. For Rubidge see Horton, *Ireland and Canada*, pp. 58–60, and Hall, *Travels*, i. 336. For E. A. Talbot see *Five Years Residence in the Canadas*, ii. 213.

under more lenient passenger legislation at much less cost. Nevertheless, all of the evidence together suggests that Robinson's expenses were 20 to 30 per cent higher than necessary.

In his history of Irish emigration W. F. Adams concludes that the experiments under Peter Robinson, 'viewed from almost any angle', were failures.[54] This judgement is much too harsh. Although the Irish settlers had been exposed to misadventure through government incompetence, most of them stayed for some time in the districts in which they had been located and sent home reports that created great interest in further emigration to Canada. The experiments were insignificant when measured against the Irish poverty they were intended to relieve, but they were important events in the early history of Upper Canada. Robinson did not manage his business well. Yet one must acknowledge his triumph in creating a set of responsible farmers from the rejects of Irish society.

Yet in some ways the efforts of 1823 and 1825 left the government no wiser than before. Although Wilmot Horton might not have admitted it, he had not discovered an effective means of administering a scheme of emigration. Neither in the execution of the emigration to South Africa nor in the supervision of those to Canada did the Under-Secretary deserve much credit. Great as his interest was in these projects, he had not given them enough thought. Furthermore, the experiments did not answer two critical questions. First, how much money would landlords in Ireland be willing to contribute towards the resettlement of their emigrants? Second, how soon would the emigrants themselves be in a position to repay the Government for the assistance that had been given them? These were questions Horton sought to answer as chairman of the Select Committees on Emigration which met in 1826 and in 1827.

[54] *Ireland and Irish Emigration* (New Haven, 1932), p. 283.

VI

THE EMIGRATION COMMITTEES:
PARISHES AND LANDLORDS

In 1826 and 1827 the House of Commons appointed committees to
study the questions surrounding the subject of emigration. The
House had never before devoted an entire committee to this single
subject nor was it ever again to discuss it in such broad terms. The
legislative accomplishments of the Select Committees on Emigration,
like those of most parliamentary committees, were limited; in the
end they served to shelve rather than to advance the idea of a
national system of emigration. They were, nevertheless, an important agency for publicizing information about emigration and the
British colonies. Their reports were extensively discussed in the
press and knowledge of their activities reached not only the educated
classes, but also the poor and under-privileged. One negative consequence may have been to delay the departure of large numbers of
would-be emigrants who were encouraged to expect government
assistance in the near future. But if the short-term effect of the
Committees was to diminish emigration, the long-term effect must
have been to increase public awareness of the British Colonies and
to promote the movement of people there. The Committees raised a
colonial issue of wide public interest. In the past the problems of
distant and sparsely populated overseas possessions had been noticed
by only an interested few. The Committees provoked a controversy
which brought into sharp focus prevailing opinions about and
attitudes towards the colonies. Domestic and colonial questions were
associated in a way which attracted attention; economists, statesmen, and propagandists were impelled to put their ideas on colonies
and colonization into writing.

Emigration had been cursorily examined by the Poor Law Committees of 1817 and 1819 and the Irish Committees of 1823 and 1825.
After the Irish experiments Horton wished to have a full discussion
of the subject. The possible value of an emigration committee had
been suggested by Frederick Robinson in 1823; and in the spring of

1825 such a committee had been demanded by Henry Bright, the member for Bristol, who believed that emigration could be supported much more economically than Horton indicated.[1] The events of 1825 encouraged Cabinet ministers to view the question seriously. In the early months of 1825 came the end of a stock-exchange boom which had begun in 1822. By autumn the banking system was in danger and industry was contracting. Wages, which had been rising, now fell as the calendar moved towards 1826, a year of distress and working-class unrest unmatched since 1819. The moment was well chosen for Horton to bring his ideas forward. In November 1825 it was agreed that he should have a committee during the next session of Parliament.[2]

Horton became chairman and was the most active member of the Committees which subsequently met. His voice was the principal one heard in defence of the completed work. The role he played was so obvious and the results so meagre that he has emerged as a solitary figure of ridicule. In recent histories the other members of the Committees have been treated as ciphers who allowed Horton to ask almost all of the questions and to reach almost all of the conclusions, to dominate the Committees while being ignored by Parliament.[3] These judgements are not easy to accept when one examines the memberships of the Committees. They include an impressive number of rising politicians with five future prime ministers among them. Horton worked with able men. If his ideas were not considered important by the House, the subject of emigration certainly was.

The Cabinet was represented on the Committees by Peel and Goulburn.[4] Peel was the one member whose support was essential if any of the recommendations were to be acted upon. When he agreed to serve, it was understood that he could not attend regularly. He kept himself informed by reading the minutes day by day and he

[1] *Hansard*, 1825, xii, cols. 1358–61. For Robinson's suggestion: W.H.P., F. Robinson to Horton, 6 Feb. 1823.

[2] Add. MSS. 38301, Goulburn to Peel, 19 Nov. 1825.

[3] W. S. Shepperson, *British Emigration to British North* America (Minneapolis, 1957), p. 12; Adams, *Ireland and Irish Emigration*, p. 281.

[4] On the composition of the Committees: *Journals of the House of Commons*, 1826, lxxxi. 167, 184, 213, 246, 305, and 1826–7, lxxxii. 178, 343. Lists of the members of the Committee in 1827 can also be found in R. W. Horton, *The Causes and Remedies of Pauperism Considered*, Pt. 1 (London, 1829), pp. 10–11, and G. J.; Malcolm, *An Enquiry into the Expediency of Emigration as Respects the British North American Colonies* (London, 1828). The lists that Horton and Malcolm provide do not accord perfectly with the *Journals*.

followed the entire proceedings carefully.[5] Yet he was involved only at a distance and his attitude remained ambivalent. He agreed that emigration was a weighty subject, but he was critical of the measures proposed. In the end the Committees floundered in their efforts to put principles into practice because they could not answer his objections.

Aside from Horton, the work of the Committees was carried forward most energetically by Whig members, particularly E. G. Stanley and Thomas Spring Rice. Spring Rice, later Colonial Secretary in Melbourne's ministry, was an Irish landlord who had been clearing his estates of sub-tenants while expressing regret at leaving these people in wretchedness.[6] Nothing would have made him happier than to see the government step in to remove them. In his opinion it required only superficial knowledge of Ireland to convince the most stubborn opponent of emigration of its necessity. His assurances encouraged Horton to believe that a scheme for promoting emigration would have the support of Irish landlords. Yet Spring Rice did not see emigration as an exclusive remedy; he found fault with Horton who, he thought, undervalued other solutions which were 'more obtainable if not so important'.

Stanley, successor to the Earl of Derby, was a youthful member of Parliament marked for early advancement. In 1827–8 he replaced Horton as Colonial Under-Secretary; when the Whigs came to power in 1830, he went to Ireland as Chief Secretary; he was eventually to lead three Conservative ministries as Prime Minister. Stanley was talented and clear-sighted, if narrow in outlook; he made a valuable committee member. Although he was only twenty-seven, he better understood what emigration involved than most of his colleagues. Stanley owned property in Ireland, too little to give him a great vested interest in proposals for Irish emigration, but enough to allow him to appreciate the position of the Irish landlord.[7] In 1824 Stanley, in company with J. E. Denison, Henry Labouchere, and John Stuart Wortley, who were also to serve on the Emigration Committee, had visited Upper Canada. The four of them had been guests of Lieutenant-Governor Maitland for two weeks at his summer home near Niagara Falls. They met Colonel Talbot and

[5] W.H.P., Peel to Horton, 10 Mar. 1826; Add. MSS. 40392, Horton to Peel, 10 Mar. 1827; Add. MSS. 40393, Horton to Peel, 20 Mar. 1827.

[6] W.H.P., Spring Rice to Horton, 10 Sept. and 20 Oct. 1826, and Spring Rice to Horton, no date.

[7] W.H.P., Stanley to Horton, 14 Nov. 1825. On Stanley's Canadian visit: Armytage, 'Talbot and Wharncliffe', p. 190; Hamil, *Lake Erie Baron*, pp. 117–18.

spent some time with him at Port Talbot. As a consequence, Stanley knew something of the problems of settlement in the British North American colony.

Canada was not as attractive as the United States to most emigrants. Although the soil and climate of Upper Canada were favourable, the United States would continue to draw the largest number of people as long as it remained more civilized. Stanley recognized this fact. Yet he felt that immigration to Upper Canada was made unnecessarily difficult.[8] If the colony wanted settlers, it would have to find them among the lower classes of the United Kingdom. Thousands of Irish poor were arriving at Quebec without assistance. They were persuaded to go to the republic by the promise of good summer wages. If they had any desire to farm in Upper Canada, they were deterred by the expense of the journey inland and by the high fees charged for land there. Many landed without a penny and were stranded at Quebec. At the very time that Peter Robinson's emigrants were coming out, the Canadian government was giving destitute Irish emigrants help to return home. Stanley did not object to the system followed by Horton and Robinson but rather to the lack of any system at all.

There was a practical role that the government could play. Stanley suggested that a government scheme of emigration would be most valuable in gradually removing the evicted peasantry of Ireland. For this purpose the government should allocate an annual sum giving preference to tenants of landlords who paid all or part of the expense of passage. If private money carried emigrants across the Atlantic, public money could be used exclusively in transporting them inland from Quebec. It was in the last stage of the journey that assistance was most needed. Stanley imagined that emigrants could be located and established as settlers in the manner followed by Colonel Talbot. The government could encourage other large landholders to take on the same responsibilities. These ideas were tentative. Stanley wanted more information and he told Horton that the Committee should make a thorough study of evidence from Canada: 'unless it goes into the whole state of the new settled townships both in Upper and Lower Canada, it will do, in my mind, comparatively nothing.'[9]

[8] E. G. Stanley, *Journal of a Tour in America 1824–5* (privately printed, 1930), pp. 114–18; W.H.P., Stanley to Horton, 20 Apr., 7 Sept. 1825.

[9] Stanley to Horton, 20 Apr. 1825.

Two other working members of the Committee were Sir Henry Parnell and the Rt. Hon. Maurice Fitzgerald, also Irish landlords and opponents of the government. Parnell had been the principal spokesman for the Irish agricultural interest; in the late 1820s he achieved prominence as a Free Trader, financial reformer, and critic of the colonial connection. It was impossible for him to accept all of Horton's ideas, but he did believe that the English taxpayer might be persuaded to pay for Irish emigration. It was Parnell who wanted to call Malthus as a witness and who approached him and asked him to attend.[10] Fitzgerald, the Knight of Kerry, was one of Horton's staunchest allies; he provided unequivocal support in debate. His motives and those of his compatriots were not universally respected. As far as Frederick Robinson was concerned, if Irish landlords favoured government loans for emigration, there could be no better reason to offer opposition: 'It smells of a job in every part; and Spring Rice, the Knight of Kerry &c &c are all jobbers the worst because they affect purity.'[11]

At least one detractor charged that the Committees were made up mostly of Irish landlords.[12] This was not strictly true. With Spring Rice, Parnell, Fitzgerald, Charles Brownlow, Lord Castlereagh, and Lord Oxmantown among the members of the Committee of 1827, Ireland was well represented; but it was not over-represented. Of thirty-five members of this committee, twenty-three were English, seven Irish, and five Scottish. In all respects the Committee membership was well proportioned: between government and opposition, between front bench and back bench, and among the parts of the United Kingdom. The Committee included men who were known to be outspoken critics of government-assisted emigration. Of these, Joseph Hume was the principal figure. He attended the Committee of 1826 and, although this experience changed neither his opinions nor those of a majority of the Committee members, he was given an opportunity to probe witnesses for responses that were hostile to Horton's plan. In the beginning many of the members shared the attitude of Alexander Baring, the great London banker. Baring had little confidence in the idea that parishes could borrow money against poor rates.[13] On the other hand, he did think that many emigrants

[10] *Parl. Pap.* 1826–7, v (237), 167; W.H.P., Malthus to Horton, 8 Apr. 1827.

[11] W.H.P., F. Robinson to Horton, 25 Mar. 1826.

[12] J. R. Elmore, *Letters to the Right Hon. The Earl of Darnley on the State of Ireland* (London, 1828), p. 125.

[13] *Hansard*, 1827, xvi, col. 504, and 1828, xviii, col. 1555.

could be located in Canada with the aid of a small government outlay. It was to find the best way to accomplish this objective that
Baring entered the Committee.

Horton easily confused opposition to his own ideas with opposition to the broad principles of emigration. He became alarmed when
he heard a rumour that Peel and Baring had united to put down his
'wild and visionary schemes' and that they had succeeded in getting
the Committee to abandon them. Both men denied the story. Peel
assured Horton, 'the last thing I would do would be to concert with
others the means of defeating any suggestion of yours'.[14] Yet the
incident illustrated the peculiar dilemma in which those interested
in assisted emigration were placed. Horton's ardour and energy were
invaluable assets to the Committees yet his judgement was not
reliable and his mind was so set that he could not adjust to criticism.
Those who foresaw a useful role for government in sponsoring or
promoting emigration could only wait in the hope that the Committee
under Horton's guidance would arrive at a useful conclusion. Peel
and other involved Cabinet ministers followed a cautious course,
saying little to dampen the enthusiasm that pushed the work of the
Committees forward while taking care to avoid by implication any
government sanction for recommendations that in the end might
very likely prove impractical.

In her history of British emigration Helen Cowan describes the
final report of the Committee of 1827 as an emigration report in
name only. Its scope, she suggests, is much wider than the title
implies. Miss Cowan consciously follows Horton's assessment of the
work of the Committee; four-fifths of the evidence, he wrote, was
related to 'a specific inquiry into the condition of the Poor'.[15] On
this point one must read Horton sceptically. By representing the
Committees' procedures as a general study of pauperism leading to
the identification of emigration as a remedy, he was giving the report
more authority than it warranted. Colonization abroad, he claimed,
was for him a subordinate question. It was just "the best and cheapest
mode" of ridding the general market of superfluous labouring
population.[16] Horton wanted people to believe that he and the

[14] Add. MSS. 40392, Peel to Horton, 19 Mar. 1827. See also Add. MSS. 40392, Horton to Baring, 17 Mar. 1827, and Add. MSS. 40393, Baring to Horton, about 20 Mar. 1827.

[15] Cowan, p. 89; *Causes and Remedies of Pauperism. First Series*, pp. 27–8.

[16] *First Series*, pp. 22–3. After reading this passage R. C. Mills wrote that Horton
was interested in emigration merely as a means of removing redundant population. See
Mills, *The Colonization of Australia, 1829–42* (London, 1915), p. 31.

Emigration Committees had arrived at their conclusions through a process of elimination. The truth was that he was an emigration enthusiast first and foremost; the Committees undertook no more than to inquire whether or not the government should encourage emigrants and to determine what system might be followed.

During the two years that they sat the Committees spent about half of their time listening to witnesses from the colonies.[17] After reading the first two hundred pages of evidence, Peel admonished Horton for not examining more witnesses knowledgeable about English parishes.[18] When the Committees did call domestic witnesses, their members always kept their prime purpose in mind. The sequence of questions invariably ran: Are you aware of a surplus population in your parish? Would emigration be beneficial? How much does it cost to keep a family on the poor rate? Would your parish be willing to advance money to facilitate emigration? How much would it advance? If some paupers were removed, would their places be quickly filled up as the population increased? How would you prevent the population from increasing? Would labourers be willing to emigrate? The Committees did not invite witnesses to speculate on the steps that should be taken to eradicate pauperism. If that had been done, then a wide range of remedies might have been discussed. Instead, the Committees assiduously confined their questions to those exploring advantages of sponsored emigration.

The witnesses provided a fairly honest cross-section of opinion. Horton had little opportunity to choose only those who would promote his ideas. Men could not easily be called from the colonies or from the extremities of the United Kingdom. For that reason people were called who happened to be in London on other business. Almost anyone connected with the colonies who put his face into the Colonial Office in 1826 or 1827 was liable to be drafted as a witness. He could be a former governor or a radical colonial politician with a grievance to voice; in either case, he was sent to testify as an expert on colonization. Irish witnesses were recruited in equally haphazard fashion. In April 1827 Horton, to his annoyance, was forced to miss

---

[17] Horton observed that one-fifth of the witnesses were called from the colonies. The colonial witnesses, however, were examined much more thoroughly and at much greater length than most of the other witnesses. Of fifty-eight meetings of the Committee, nineteen were devoted exclusively to colonial witnesses, nineteen to witnesses from Great Britain and Ireland, and twenty were devoted exclusively neither to one class of witness nor to the other.

[18] Add. MSS. 40393, Horton to Peel, 20 Mar. 1827.

a meeting of the Emigration Committee in order to attend an Irish election committee. As a consequence, he met a land agent from Westmeath and four days later brought him before the Emigration Committee. Several other Irish witnesses were discovered in a similar manner. 'It . . . is impossible to have witnesses more unprejudiced more unprepared, or might I say, more accidental,' Horton boasted.[19]

Because the witnesses were not carefully selected, Horton inevitably placed some on the stand who stoutly contradicted him. Nevertheless, one cannot read the minutes of evidence without being aware that Horton was conducting his inquiry not as a judge but as an advocate. His questions and those of his colleagues (the questioners are not identified) were leading ones. If the desired answer was not obtained the question was re-phrased repeatedly until the witness made a concession. A contributor to *Blackwood's Magazine* illustrated the proceedings of the Committee of 1827 in the following passage:[20]

Mr. Strickland is sounded as to his views about emigration to the colonies, and at once declares himself point blank against any such thing. From question 3485 to 3495 they invite him in vain to a different declaration; he still insists it would be better to cultivate the waste lands at home; at length, anxious to have his suffrage for emigration, notwithstanding the waste lands to which he clings so firmly, they wish to know whether he does not think the population is so redundant as to afford sufficient 'candidates for emigration' in addition to those who might be employed on the waste lands. His direct answer is 'I do not.'
With a skill in the art of examination of which any learned gentlemen in Westminster Hall might well be proud, the witness is led away from this point on which he appears so inflexible and for sixty questions is not troubled about Emigration, but has to give general information concerning the state of the country; at length, however, the examiner draws him to the point again, in the following question, which we defy any lawyer to put more adroitly, supposing his purpose be the obtaining an answer favourable to emigration from one who had previously delivered a contrary opinion. Mr. Strickland having spoken of the wretched condition of the peasantry in his part of the country, he is asked, in question 3558 'Do you conceive that the most effective remedy for the evil which exists, would be the transfer of a great proportion of the pauper population to some other situation where they may be rendered comfortable and prosperous?' he

[19] W.H.P., Horton to Mahoney, 13 Aug. 1828.
[20] May 1828, p. 616.

answers 'Certainly, to other situations and improvements *in Ireland.*' Mr. Strickland is not asked a single question more.

From the beginning the Committee in 1826 and its successor in 1827 operated on the assumption that a direct parliamentary grant would not be available for emigration.[21] The Committees saw as their primary task the discovery of an alternative source of money. Horton believed that funds could be raised by means of long-term annuities which would be paid in the early years by landlords or parishes, and in the later years by the emigrants themselves. This conviction was set clearly before the Committee at the moment it first met. The objective of the inquiry became proof or disproof of the practicality of Horton's proposed system. As witness succeeded witness, Horton tenaciously pursued the kind of evidence that he thought would convince sceptics that annuities could and would be paid. Any suggestion of hostility towards emigration had to be challenged because it gave weight to the argument that landlords and parishes would not accept responsibility for money spent in removing paupers to the colonies. For this reason Horton was never able to pass over the opinions of an intransigent witness like Strickland, but always pressed for a qualification.

On the question of payment of annuities it was necessary to treat each country in the United Kingdom separately. In England the poor rates offered a possible source of money. A poor rate also existed in Scotland, but its nature varied markedly from locality to locality. Ireland had no poor rate at all.[22] The only alternative source of local money in the absence of a parish rate would be a voluntary contribution by landlords or their principal tenants. Horton reasoned that a pauper population was a burden on landlords whether or not they paid a poor rate, and for that reason it was in the interest of Irish proprietors to support emigration.[23] The Committees sought to determine to what extent Irish proprietors and English parishes recognized their interests as Horton saw them and how much they were willing to spend to advance these interests.

Evidence was taken from the Home Counties of Middlesex, Surrey, Kent, Hertfordshire, Buckinghamshire, and Sussex, from

[21] *Parl. Pap.* 1826, iv (404), and 1826–7, v (88); C.O. 324/96, Horton to Butler, 29 Mar. 1826, and Horton to Chichester, 16 Apr. 1826; Horton, *A Letter to Sir Francis Burdett*, pp. 15–16.

[22] *Parl. Pap.* 1826, iv (404), 7–8.

[23] See C.O. 324/95, Horton to Townsend, 6 June 1825.

the northern industrial counties of Cheshire and Lancashire, from Cumberland on the Scottish border, Nottinghamshire and Northamptonshire in the Midlands and from Suffolk on the east coast. Two large and important regions were ignored. Not one witness was called from Wales or from the counties of the south-west. Most of the English witnesses came from the Home Counties; geography dictated that, but also it was in the Home Counties that the most favourable evidence was found.

In Lancashire and Cheshire there was great distress among handloom weavers with no prospect of relief. Parishes in these counties appeared willing to contribute towards emigration.[24] Committee members, however, doubted the ability of manufacturing districts to pay annuities. Unlike rural areas these districts would continue to attract population; emigration might well leave the level of poor rates unaffected. Furthermore, Lancashire and Cheshire had not supplied emigrants in the past and there was among their poor no inclination to leave. In Kent, by contrast, some parishes had been sending paupers out to America for several years. The parish of Headcorn had assisted emigrants annually since 1823 by borrowing money against the poor rates.[25] At a cost of £8 a head the parish had transported about twenty individuals a year from Kent to Liverpool and from Liverpool to New York. As a consequence, the cost of poor relief had declined steadily and it was optimistically estimated that the parish could find employment for all of its agricultural labourers if another ten families were removed.

Thomas Law Hodges, chairman of the West Kent Quarter Sessions, told the Committee of 1826 that his parish of Benenden had given twenty-seven men, women, and children their passages to New York at a cost of £13. 10s. 0d. per adult: ten guineas for passage and provisions, 4s. 6d. landing fee at New York, a few shillings for carriage from Kent to the Port of London, and two sovereigns pocket money on arrival.[26] In comparison, Horton estimated that an emigrant could be settled in Upper Canada for £20. The passage to Quebec was actually cheaper than to New York, but Benenden did not assist its emigrants after they had landed. Hodges's testimony provided solid evidence that parishes might accept responsibility for as much as half of the cost of settling emigrants in the manner

24 *Parl. Pap.* 1826–7, v (237), 29–46, 175–85, and (550), 13–14.
25 Ibid. (237), 144–6.
26 Ibid. 1826, iv (404), 133–40.

Robinson followed in 1823 and 1825. Indeed, while the national debate on emigration dragged on, Hodges himself lent £1,150 to his parish to enable 145 men, women, and children to emigrate to America in 1827 and 1828.[27] This example was followed by other parishes in Kent: Marden, Tenterden, Headcorn, Westerham, Deal, Holden, Northbourne, Mongeham, St. Lawrence, Sevenoaks, the Isle of Thanet, and Chatham. By the early 1830s parishes in East Anglia and on the Wiltshire-Somerset border as well as in Sussex and Kent were organizing large parties of emigrants without any encouragement from the national government. There was a role for the government to play in assisting these parishes and in co-ordinating their efforts.

The propertied class in Scotland gave no sign of imitating the positive action that had been taken in Kent. The problem of un-employment in Glasgow was much greater than in the agricultural parishes of England. The cotton industry which dominated the Scottish economy was concentrated in Glasgow. Here the revolution caused by the introduction of the power loom was most acutely felt.[28] One girl operating a pair of looms could produce as much as six hand-loom weavers; 11,000 weavers and their families were reduced to hopeless poverty. Wages were further depressed by Ulster weavers who were brought into Scotland by master manufacturers for 4d. a head. In 1927 at least 40,000 Irishmen lived in the Glasgow area; witnesses predicted that every Scotsman sent to the colonies would be replaced by an Irishman arriving on the steamboat from Belfast; no matter how bad things were in Glasgow, they were worse in Ireland. To replace natives with Irishmen seemed a poor exchange. If there was ever any possibility that Scottish aristocrats might dip into their purses, this consideration held them back. An emigration from Glasgow might be of more benefit to Northern Ireland than to

---

[27] William Day, *An Inquiry into the Poor Laws and Surplus Labour and their Mutual Reaction* (London, 1833), p. 43; W. C. Fonnereau, *Remarks and Suggestions relative to the Management of the Poor in Ipswich* (Ipswich, 1833), p. 76; Thomas Bunn, *A Letter Relative to the Affairs of the Poor of the Parish of Frome Selwood in Somersetshire* (London, 1834), pp. 4–6, 41–3; Charles Barclay, *Letters from the Dorking Emigrants to Upper Canada in the Spring of 1832* (London, 1833), pp. 6–7; T. Sockett, *Emigration. A Letter to a Member of Parliament Containing a Statement of the Methods Pursued by the Petworth Committee* (Petworth, 1834), pp. 3–20; *Parl. Pap.* 1837 (131), 4; W.H.P., Horton to Malthus, May–June 1830. See also Mary D. Wainwright, 'Agencies for the Promotion or Facilitation of Emigration from England to the U.S.A., 1815–1861' (M.A. Thesis, London, 1952), pp. 79–90, 112.

[28] *Parl Pap.* 1827–8, v (237), 9–18, 26–7, 154, and (404), 201.

western Scotland. If it was to be carried out, Scottish landlords thought that the national government should bear the whole cost.

The appointment of a parliamentary committee on emigration had generated powerful feelings among the weavers of Glasgow and Paisley. Many of these weavers could remember better times twenty-five years earlier when work which now brought in 4*s.* or 5*s.* would have earned them four times as much.[29] They could also remember that in 1820 and 1821 the government had conceded assistance to 2,700 paupers from Lanark and Renfrew who had settled in Upper Canada. During the general economic recovery which began in 1822 the weavers' wages had improved and their situation had become tolerable. In 1825 the trend had reversed itself. In 1826 money wages for all labour in Britain declined sharply, but the weavers, who were in the most exposed position, suffered the most acutely. With the steady encroachment of machines on their work, every sign that the weavers could read indicated that their trade was near extinction. At the same time they continued to receive optimistic reports from their friends and relatives in Upper Canada.

By March 1827 at least thirty-three societies had been organized in Lanark and Renfrew by over 2,200 weavers and other tradesmen whose families included almost 12,000 individuals.[30] These people were to a man destitute and incapable of contributing anything towards their passages. They expressed a very strong preference for the British colonies over the United States. If the government would assist them to settle in Upper Canada, they were confident they could repay the entire debt themselves. The knowledge that the government had given similar help in the past and that the entire subject was now under serious study by Horton's Committee raised in them high expectations of success in their petitions.

When witnesses were asked how much money could be raised in the Glasgow area, the answers were discouraging to say the least.[31] All of the money spent on the relief of the able-bodied poor in Renfrew was obtained through charitable donations. Many of these donations came from outside the country. The only people in Scotland with a legal right to maintenance by the parish were the aged and infirm. Excepting some parishes in the border counties, the practice in Scotland had been to confine parish relief to those in-

    [29] *Parl. Pap.* 1827–8, v, (237), 11–12.   [30] Ibid., pp. 19, 51–2.
    [31] Ibid., pp. 21, 23, 25–6, 151, 156–8, 202; W.H.P., Maxwell to Horton, 13 July 1826.

capable of working. There was no poor rate which could be used to finance an emigration of weavers, and because local landlords were unlikely to support such a measure voluntarily, it was apparent that Horton's scheme would not work in Glasgow.

Yet the Committee of 1827 was painfully aware that its very existence had fed the emigration fever that existed in Lanark and Renfrew.[32] Many of the weavers were so confident that they would be leaving for Canada that they had let their leases lapse and had sold their looms. In late February 1827 Horton, on the instructions of the Committee, tabled a short report of two paragraphs stating that voluntary contributions, private or local, ought to form the basis of any emigration. The purpose of this report was to check the expectation that the whole expense would be undertaken by the government and to give the weavers a warning that they would likely receive no assistance at all.

There was one possible source of money. The London Committee for the Relief of the Manufacturing Districts, a charitable organization, had appropriated £25,000 for emigration on the condition that twice that sum be found somewhere else. In response the Emigration Committee issued a second report in early April recommending a parliamentary grant of £50,000 for emigration from the manufacturing districts of England and Scotland.[33] It became apparent, however, that the London Committee did not intend its money to be used for Scottish emigration except in a very limited way. The Committee thought that the Scots had not done enough for their own paupers. Large sums had been sent to Scotland for other relief projects, but the leading people of Scotland had not given the Committee the co-operation it expected. The London Committee had experienced great difficulty not only in securing contributions ('Our receipts from Scotland have been almost none') but also in getting information about the distribution of grants.

Elsewhere in Scotland landlords were as reluctant to support emigration as in Lanark and Renfrew. In the Highlands and Western Islands estates were minutely divided; if over-population had not arrived, it could be seen to be coming very soon. The consequences of further crowding were certain to be serious because the herring fisheries on which so many people depended had been extended to

[32] C.O. 324/97, Horton to Smith, 25 May 1827; Add. MSS. 40392, Horton to Peel, 24 Feb. 1827; *Parl. Pap.* 1826–7, v (88).

[33] *Parl. Pap.* 1826–7, v (237), 4, 201–2.

their limits. Emigration had been under way for many years; in communities where it was popular tenants would make supreme efforts to raise the money to pay for their passages. Yet the witnesses who appeared before the Emigration Committees did not speak of this movement with much enthusiasm.[34] The old paternalism which in the past had governed the relationship of Highland landlords with their tenants was not completely gone. There were still some land-lords who put loyalty ahead of efficient management and refused to turn out tenants although sheep-runs would bring in more income. Those who were less disinterested in income were unlikely to con-tribute towards emigration for other good reasons. If they had many tenants and few sheep, they were in a poor position to raise money. If the reverse condition prevailed, they had no incentive to do so. The Emigration Committee concluded that, with the exception of some of the Western Islands, life in Scotland could not be improved by emigration.[35]

Early in its proceedings, the Committee of 1826 had decided that Ireland should be the focus of any extensive system of emigration. It was argued that Glasgow would not benefit from an emigration of weavers because their places would be immediately filled up by Irish.[36] In London Irish immigrants were seen to depress wages and vagrant Irish boys formed gangs of pickpockets and constituted a major problem for magistrates. Manchester attracted large numbers of Irish and in 1826 the township of Manchester had spent over £1,100 to return 3,660 Irish paupers home. In rural areas Irish immigrants were more welcome. For years Irish harvesters had been coming by Holyhead and Liverpool or by the Bristol Channel and walking inland to earn a few pounds before returning home. They arrived in a season of full employment and left as soon as it was over; they did not threaten the welfare of the local population. Neverthe-less, the Committee of 1827 asserted that a continued increase of the Irish population would inevitably lead to a decline in the living standards of the lower classes throughout England. The depression of wages in the manufacturing districts of western Scotland and England, particularly in Glasgow and Manchester, were held up in proof of this contention.

[34] *Parl. Pap.* 1826 iv (404), 65, 73–81; 1826–7, v (550), 287–90.
[35] Ibid. 1826–7, v (550), 14.
[36] Ibid. 1826–7, v (237), 60–1 and 32–3, 40, 146, 178, and 1826, iv (404), 115, 125, 214–16.

The Committee's analysis was broad but not very thorough. Horton and his colleagues possessed a grand conception of the population problems of the British Isles in which the overcrowding and pauperization of the Irish dwarfed all other questions. England and Scotland would experience no permanent benefit from emigration if Irish labour remained redundant. As a generalization, this assessment was reasonable and useful, but it did not spring from an appreciation of particulars. The Committee did not discern the several elements of the Irish immigration to Great Britain: the harvesters who returned to Ireland before winter; the unskilled labourers who settled in London, Liverpool, and other large cities, the navvies, who moved from job to job, and the families who set up looms in the regions of Manchester and Glasgow.[37] It attached no importance to evidence that it was the textile industry more than any other which was subject to Irish invasion. Nor did it draw attention to the fact that the weavers who settled in Lancashire and western Scotland came from Dublin and from Ulster, the most industrialized parts of Ireland. The Committee was satisfied with the knowledge that Irishmen were entering England and did not attempt to be more specific. A majority of the Irish witnesses came from Munster, the province of the south-west. Horton had more connections with this region than with any other as a result of the two emigrations from Cork; it was this circumstance rather than any design which produced an unbalanced selection of witnesses. Yet it was a poorly constructed argument which emphasized the dangers of an influx of Irish into England without recognizing the role of immigrants from Irish manufacturing districts.

Twenty-five witnesses were examined on Ireland; five were members of the Committees: Stanley, Spring Rice, Parnell, Lord Ennismore, and J. L. Foster. These men were enlightened but business-like landlords who were fully conscious of the fact that overcrowded estates returned low rents. In emigration they saw a way to clear estates in a civilized manner. They insisted that the dispossessed tenant should be a more eligible emigrant than the unemployed craftsman and that a government system of emigration should be coupled with a drive to consolidate farms.[38] Money was

---

[37] C. R. Fay, *Great Britain from Adam Smith to the Present Day* (London, 1950), p. 347; Arthur Redford, *Labour Migration in England, 1800–1850.* (New York, 1968), pp. 132–64.

[38] *Parl. Pap.* 1826, iv (404), 197–200, 212; 1826–7, v (550), 307–11, 446–61.

being spent to employ the poor on public works or to provide a bounty for the linen industry and the fisheries; it should be used instead to supplement the contributions of landlords who sent out emigrants on the condition that those landlords prevent a recurrance of over-population on their estates. The process of clearing estates might be slow. Landlords could not evict until leases had expired and in much of Ireland, leases still had a long time to run. Furthermore, where land was inferior, and this included a great area of the island, the practice of letting small farms would have to prevail until farmers found the capital to make improvements.

Spring Rice and his Irish colleagues saw no reason to grant assistance to emigrants from manufacturing districts.[39] They wanted the government to concentrate on the less heavily populated rural areas; the advantage of such a policy to progressive landlords need not be stressed. It was justified by the observation that only in rural areas could emigration bring a permanent depopulation. If cottages were destroyed and small plots amalgamated into large farms, early marriages and large families could be prevented. Landlords would take these steps if they realized it was in their interest to do so. No such measures could be taken in manufacturing districts. Besides, the disturbances that periodically rocked the country were primarily an agrarian phenomenon; arson and thuggery were usually the work of men who had lost their land. In the manufacturing districts, even of Cork, the population had been quite peaceful. The evidence given to the Committee did not justify any effort to promote Ulster emigration.

Malthus was called to give his opinions on Ireland. He appeared before the Committee on 5 May, 1827 and was questioned at length; his examination fills sixteen large, printed pages. These sixteen pages have been the most frequently thumbed of the hundreds of pages of evidence amassed by the Committees. Students of the classical economists and of the theory of population find this material instructive because it contains Malthus's last published contribution to the subject of emigration. Great emphasis was placed on Malthus's testimony in the final report; much of it was included verbatim. Maria Edgeworth, the novelist, read a draft of the report and felt that the economist was quoted needlessly. 'You do Mr. Malthus great, and no doubt well-deserved, honor by the weight you attach to his opinions,' she wrote to Horton. 'But . . . why not embody the

[39] *Parl. Pap.* 1826, iv (404), 188–91.

opinions as part of your own; since you adopt them, they are in fact yours; and refer to his name in the notes to the text with whatever tribute of respect and admiration you think proper.'[40]

The questions addressed to Malthus were long, complex, and so worded that they demanded a response of either 'yes' or 'no'.[41] His answers were short although sometimes qualified. The whole proceeding had the appearance of a disciple being led through a catechism. Malthus agreed that an increase of population in Ireland would be 'most fatal to the happiness of the labouring classes in England'. He agreed that any population vacuum created by emigration from England or Scotland would be immediately filled up with Irish. At the same time he admitted that wages could be depressed by a small excess of the supply of labour over the demand. From this point it followed that the removal of a comparatively small part of the population might cause a considerable improvement in the condition of those who remained. Although there was always a tendency towards the filling up of a vacuum, Malthus expressed confidence that it could be prevented by the landlords of Ireland if they reformed their estates. He was asked if there was a better way than emigration to make Ireland rich and prosperous. 'I think,' he replied, 'that a judicious system of emigration is one of the most powerful means to accomplish that object.'[42]

Contemporaries found the case for Irish emigration convincing; Malthus gave it more authority. The likelihood that Irish landlords would contribute money was less apparent. None of the witnesses spoke on this matter with much confidence. As Maria Edgeworth put it, the landlords could not help if they would, and would not if they could.[43] Spring Rice himself admitted that a large proportion were not in a position to pay. To a reviewer who read the evidence thoroughly the possibility of raising money in any part of Ireland seemed 'highly problematical'.[44] Yet the Committee of 1827, which recognized the unwillingness or inability of Scottish landlords to support emigration, did not admit that the same situation reigned in Ireland. The evidence from Ireland was interpreted as positively as possible without actual fabrication. Irish proprietors generally

[40] W.H.P., Edgeworth to Horton, 29 July 1827.
[41] Parl. Pap. 1826–7, v (550), 311–27.
[42] Cited in the Committee's Report (550), 10.
[43] W.H.P., Edgeworth to Horton, 9 Nov. 1826. For the evidence of Irish witnesses: Parl. Pap. 1826, iv (404), 143, 191, 196, 198, 208–11.
[44] Eclectic Review, Sept. 1827, p. 242. See also Westminster Review, Oct. 1826, p. 355.

believed that they would be better off if they cleared their estates, the Committee stated: 'this feeling is strong enough, to induce them, in many cases, to make a pecuniary contribution towards the expenses of Emigration.'[45] The accuracy of the Committee's judgement depended entirely on the interpretation intended for the phrase 'in many cases'.

Those who read the evidence should not have been deceived by the conclusions. The strongest part of the argument related to England. There was redundant population in all parts of the British Isles, in the Outer Hebrides as well as in County Cork or Lancashire, but only in rural England was there a strong indication that the Horton system would work. The emphasis the Committee gave to Ireland was not without justification. As long as there was free movement between Ireland and Great Britain, England could not divorce itself from the Irish pauper problem. Yet the Irish members were the ones who expressed the greatest concern that England might be pulled down to Ireland's level. Their purpose was transparent: to persuade Englishmen that they should pay for Irish emigration. As an active minority, their influence in the Committee was of disproportionate importance. They were essential allies for Horton as he was for them. If he thought that a local assessment was imperative, they did not want to insist that it could not be raised. As a consequence, the Committee reached optimistic judgements which did not stand up well to the scrutiny of the sceptical.

[45] *Parl. Pap.* 1826–7 (550), 8.

VII

THE EMIGRATION COMMITTEES: EMIGRATION VERSUS COLONIZATION

HORTON believed that the distinction between emigration and colonization was an important one. In his usage, emigration described a movement of labour without capital. This was a movement which could not proceed safely except on a small scale because it meant that the number of people seeking employment in the colonies would grow faster than the colonial wage funds. A large emigration would create more misery than it would alleviate. Serious dislocation of colonial economies could be avoided only if emigrants were accompanied by capital. The obvious way to use this capital would be to develop wild land. This was colonization. Horton saw colonization as the more effective answer to Britain's excess of population. His arguments were not fully appreciated by other members of the Emigration Committees, a difference of opinion which was disguised without being resolved in the final report.[1]

It would be wrong to suggest that Horton wanted to subsidize pauper settlement on a scale great enough to remove Britain's entire redundant population. He held it unnecessary to remove all who were unemployed in order to provide relief. Moreover, he predicted that if the government made an initial effort the results would be multiplied. Settlements created at government expense would become the nuclei of larger settlements of unassisted emigrants. Paupers who became settlers would soon be in a position to bring over friends and relatives and to provision them until they were established. For each person who received government help, Horton estimated that another three would follow.[2] This could not happen, however, if the Imperial government pursued a restrictive land policy. Terms of settlement

---

[1] See *Parl. Pap.* 1826–7, v (550), 35–8. For Horton's views see his evidence before the Irish Committee, *Parl. Pap.* 1825, viii (129), 15, and W.H.P., Horton to Grenville, Feb. 1826.

[2] R. W. Horton, *Correspondence between the Rt. Hon. Sir Robert Wilmot Horton Bart., and J. B. Robinson Esq., Chief Justice of Upper Canada* (London, 1839), p. 11; W.H.P., Horton to Peel, 1826?

would have to favour the small settler with little capital. Soon after he entered the Colonial Office Horton began to work towards a land reform of this nature. In this respect, his thinking was diametrically opposed to the Wakefieldian theorists who came later. Wakefield argued that great harm was done by giving land to poor settlers and that a high value should be placed on land to force the poor to seek employment and thus keep the price of labour in the colonies low. Horton wanted to put paupers on the land while Wakefield wished to keep them off it.

Between 1783 and 1825 no effort had been made to standardize procedures for granting land in the various British possessions overseas. Regulations developed uniquely in each colony.[3] Colonial statesmen could be excused for tolerating separate policies in agricultural and pastoral colonies, in free and convict colonies, and in American, French, and Dutch populated colonies. To frame a single set of regulations for colonies with different systems and fundamentally different problems was a formidable task. Yet it did not intimidate Horton. In the early 1820s the need to reform land regulations both in Upper Canada and in New South Wales was widely recognized. Changes could have been made in each colony without any attempt to establish a consistent imperial policy. The simplest course for the Colonial Office would have been to leave wide powers of discretion to the governors as in the past. Instead the Colonial Office asserted itself by dictating precise regulations, uniform in principle, for the North American and Australian colonies. If Horton had not been dogmatic by nature, he could not have pushed his views as far as he did. The subject was infinitely complicated. He inevitably met resistance and his system was never given a complete trial.

The Horton system provided a dual set of rules to accommodate both rich and poor settlers.[4] The former could purchase outright large blocks of land. The latter could take small grants and pay an annual quit rent of 5 per cent of the purchase price, redeemable at twenty years' purchase. The terms *grant* and *quit rent* are, perhaps, misleading. In effect, settlers paid 5 per cent interest on the cash price. They were as much purchasers of land as those who paid for it immediately.[5] For the first seven years the quit rent would not be

[3] R. G. Riddell, 'Land Policy of the Colonial Office, 1763–1855', *Canadian Historical Review*, Dec. 1937, p. 387.

[4] *H.R.A.*, Series I, xi. 442.

[5] W.H.P., Horton to Black, 16 Feb. 1831; C.O. 43/66, Horton to J. Robinson, 29 June 1825; C.O. 324/96, Horton to Galt, 8 Mar. 1826.

demanded. As Horton explained it, the system was designed to allow people with little capital to become established; they would not be called upon for payments until they could obtain the money they needed from the soil itself. Land would be available to poor emigrants while the government would preserve the promise of eventual income. Settlement would be advanced without a permanent sacrifice of revenue.

The system was introduced to New South Wales in 1825 and to Upper Canada in 1826. In the spring of 1827 the Governors of Lower Canada, Nova Scotia, and New Brunswick received instructions to adopt the same regulations.[6] Horton even proposed to extend the system to the Cape of Good Hope although he did not get around to it before he resigned; his initial request for information was not answered by the Commissioners of Inquiry whose investigation of affairs at the Cape had bogged down in trivia.[7] As far as New South Wales was concerned, Horton did not see his system as a vehicle for pauper emigration, but he did think that it would help people with a limited amount of money. This in itself involved a basic reassessment of the future of the Australian colony. In the past poor emigrants had not been encouraged to go there. A change would have been welcomed by spokesmen for the emancipated convicts, the largest element in the population of New South Wales. A class of small landholders could have offset the political weight of John Macarthur and the other great proprietors and could have helped the emancipists in their struggle for a more liberal regime. It was not surprising that the colonial elite was prejudiced against poor settlers.[8] Horton was the only individual involved in the administration of New South Wales at that time who believed in a less restrictive land system. His plan for opening wild land to emigrants of modest means was rendered ineffective by colonial officials. For the remainder of the decade the colony continued to be out of bounds to all but convicts and capitalists.

In British North America the new regulations suggested a way in

---

[6] Riddell, 'Land Policy', pp. 390–1.

[7] *R.C.C.*, xxi. 172, Horton to Commissioners of Inquiry, 30 Apr. 1825, and xxxii. 321, Hay to Bourke, 12 Aug. 1827.

[8] See *The Australian*, 13 Sept. 1826 for an emancipist opinion of the new regulations. The colonial government made the regulations more restrictive than Horton intended by adding a scale proportioning the size of the grant to the capital of the grantee. A similar scale had been established in the early 1820s but had not been a part of the instructions for which Horton was responsible.

which assisted emigration might be financed. If quit rents could be the means of selling land to emigrants with little capital, they could also be the means of reclaiming money advanced to paupers. Horton proposed that a loan for emigration purposes could be repaid by a sixty-year annuity. For the first seven years annuity payments would be the responsibility of the landlord or parish. After the seventh year they would be taken over by the emigrant.[9] A yearly quit rent of £3. 10s. 9d. would retire a debt of £80 while paying 4 per cent interest. The success of the scheme would depend on the ability of emigrants to produce a surplus crop and to find a market for that crop.

On this point the Emigration Committees interviewed witnesses from North America at length. They discovered that very little money circulated in Canada in 1826; barter was the usual method of exchange in the backwoods.[10] While colonial witnesses expressed no doubt that settlers could make payments in kind, they spoke less certainly about payments in money. Upper Canadians could sell some flour in York and at Niagara and there was a possibility of sending flour to Montreal for export. The issue hinged mainly on what predictions could be made of the likely growth of this trade; it was necessary to discuss the future prospects of the North American colonies.

The Erie Canal had been completed in 1825, outflanking the St. Lawrence and drawing the trade of the West away from Montreal to New York, but Canadians were convinced of the inherent superiority of the St. Lawrence route which they fully expected to be reasserted as soon as the Welland Canal was opened. The Committees took a great interest in this subject.[11] Did Canadians themselves trade mainly through the Erie Canal? Would the Welland Canal turn the tide of business to Montreal? Would the western states deal through Montreal once the Welland was finished? What disadvantage did Montreal suffer because it was frozen up for part of the year? The witnesses who were examined on these points shared the optimism of most Canadian merchants and politicians and gave the Committee no reason to doubt that prosperity was within easy reach of the Canadas.

In 1826 the Canadas exported very little. Lower Canada was barely able to feed its own population. The Canadian wheat surplus was

[9] A schedule of payments under this plan is depicted in the form of a table in John Strachan, *Remarks on Emigration from the United Kingdom Addressed to Robert Wilmot Horton* (London, 1827), p. 83.

[10] *Parl. Pap.* 1826, iv (404), 17.

[11] Ibid., pp. 19–21, 29–30, 82–3, 171–2.

too small and uncertain for Montreal merchants to undertake to supply the West Indies, the obvious potential market. Canadian flour crudely manufactured in small local mills was inferior to flour from the middle states and was unsuitable for export. Any judgement about the ease with which settlers could raise money in seven years' time was purely speculative. It was already evident that the Lanarkshire weavers were going to resist payment of the money that had been advanced to them. When colonial witnesses spoke confidently of collecting a quit rent of £3. 10s. 0d. or £4 0s. 0d., they did not mean that it was possible under existing conditions. Instead, they counted upon a dramatic development of the colonial economy.[12] One of the principal stimulants of that development would be the great system of colonization that was now being studied. The arrival of large numbers of emigrants would create such a demand for agricultural produce, one witness predicted, that twenty or thirty years would pass before the Canadas would have surplus grain for export. The markets brought into existence by colonization were the very thing that would make colonization pay for itself.

Events soon afterwards proved that emigration, even when it was not supported by public capital, could give the colonial economy a powerful boost. The great influx of the early 1830s had this effect. There was a slump in the latter part of the decade, but in the 1840s, when emigrants again streamed into the province, Upper Canada quickly reached a level of activity in which a system of credit based on newly cleared land could work.[13] The expectations of the witnesses before the Committee of 1826 were not far-fetched. Unfortunately, these witnesses offered little concrete evidence other than their own attitude of assurance. This attitude was not shared by all colonial authorities. Quit rents had a bad name in British North America. In the Maritime provinces the crown possessed the right to a small quit rent of 2s. per 100 acres, which had never been collected consistently and had been allowed to lapse for a half-century.[14] Colonials were opposed to its resurrection; it was predicted that they would object

[12] Ibid., pp. 30, 53–63, 81–2.

[13] After 1842 the Canada Company enjoyed considerable success in disposing of land to settlers with little or no capital. See W. H. Smith, *Canada: Past, Present and Future*, ii (Toronto, 1851), 164.

[14] C.O. 217/146, Kempt to Horton, 30 July 1826; C.O. 217/149, Sir R. George, memorandum on Quit Rents, 27 July 1829; C.O. 188/33, Douglas to Horton, 16 Nov. 1826, and Extract of Report of Committee of Saint John Agricultural and Emigrant Society, 17 Oct. 1826; C.O. 42/222, Kempt to Hay, 24 Feb. 1829; MacNutt, *Atlantic Provinces*, pp. 148–9, 189–90.

strenuously to a new form of quit rent and that their resistance would not be overcome without endless litigation and coercion. Of course, a quit rent of £3 or £4 would be proportionately cheaper to collect than one of 2s.; if it were paid by new settlers who had received help from the government, it would be less odious than a rent imposed on everyone after long lying dormant. Nevertheless, a question mark hung over the whole idea of quit rents. The Committees were convinced that the system was practical, but, with the exception of Horton, members of the government were doubtful.[15]

The witnesses from the North American colonies included the Lieutenant-Governor of Prince Edward Island, Colonel John Ready; the Chief Justice of Lower Canada, Jonathon Sewell; the Attorney-General of Nova Scotia, R. J. Uniacke; four members of the Upper Canadian executive council, Archdeacon Strachan, Solicitor-General Henry John Boulton, George Markland, and Peter Robinson; a member of the Lower Canadian legislative council, W. B. Felton, a member of the Upper Canadian legislative assembly, Dr. John Rolph; the former deputy-quartermaster-general at Quebec, Lieutenant-Colonel Francis Cockburn; and the brother of the British consul at New York and a Lower Canadian merchant, A. C. Buchanan. This was as well-informed a group of colonials as could have been assembled. Yet some of their statements were no more than educated or half-educated guesses. They had only a vague notion of how much land could be opened to settlement and their interest in promoting immigration did not lead them to guard against exaggeration. Uniacke, who thought that Nova Scotia could absorb 12,000 to 15,000 emigrants in a single year, was simply fanciful.[16]

Most of the acreage of Nova Scotia that was fit for cultivation had been alienated during the eighteenth century. What was left was far from main roads and scarcely worth the cost of surveys.[17] In New Brunswick about 10,000,000 acres remained in the possession of the crown. Contemporaries thought there was room for extensive settlements; but much of the soil was rocky; the province contained less than 2,500,000 acres of good farm land and a large part of that had already been granted.[18] Although the Canadas held vast tracts

---

[15] For example see C.O. 324/89, Hay to Ellis, 24 Nov. 1829.

[16] *Parl. Pap.* 1826, iv (404), 39–47. See W.H.P. Kempt to Horton 20 Nov. 1826.

[17] Kempt to Horton, 30 July 1826 (enclosure); J. S. Martell, *Immigration to and Emigration from Nova Scotia, 1815–1838* (Halifax, 1942), p. 20.

[18] By Sept. 1826, a total of 3,593,267 acres had been granted in New Brunswick; 1,603,832 had been escheated, leaving 1,989,435 which were still alienated. See Douglas

of undeveloped fertile land, little of it was easily accessible. Nearly all of the frontage on Lower Canada's river highways had been alienated during the French regime. Seigneurial grants totalled 8,500,000 acres; since the conquest another 3,500,000 had been alienated and, with few exceptions, left unoccupied.[19] The crown lands of Lower Canada lay behind a belt of wilderness made up partly of the rear concessions of the seigneuries and partly of the lands that had subsequently been granted. Thousands of emigrants had gone on from Montreal to Upper Canada or the United States because the available land in Lower Canada was too far from civilized areas. To open up this land would require the construction of major roads at considerable capital expense.

In Upper Canada there were several million acres of first-rate, unsurveyed land and over a million acres surveyed but not yet claimed.[20] Most of this land, however, was well removed from either Lake Ontario or Lake Erie. In the early history of the province the government had squandered a tremendous amount of the land at its disposal. Officials and their families and certain individuals had been given whole townships. The officers and men of several regiments disbanded after 1763 had been assigned from 5,000 to 200 acres each. United Empire Loyalists and their children when they came of age received 200 acres each free of charge. By 1804 4,500,000 acres had been alienated. Between 1804 and 1824 military claimants and United Empire Loyalists received another 1,125,000 acres; reduced officers, soldiers, and sailors were given 346,000; surveyors were allowed 228,000; special large grants accounted for 107,800 acres; and emigrants and other settlers obtained 1,231,000 acres. Great reaches of the province had been alienated without any comparable evidence of settlement. Although the government probably had the power to resume title to grants that had been left unimproved, this move was not considered politically expedient.[21] The selection of tracts of land for pauper emigrants would not have been a simple

---

to Horton, 16 Nov. 1826. Francis Cockburn and John Richards who wrote reports on the lands available in British North America were confident that vast tracts of New Brunswick were open to settlement. See C.O. 384/17 Cockburn to Horton, 17 Sept. 1827, and C.O. 323/163, Richards to Hay, 17 Sept. 1830.

[19] C.O. 42/206, Felton to Horton, 10 Oct. 1825; C.O. 42/209, Dalhousie to Horton, 4 May 1826.

[20] George C. Patterson, *Land Settlement in Upper Canada, 1783–1840* (Toronto, 1921), p. 153.

[21] C.O. 42/197, J. Robinson to Horton, 10 Apr. 1823.

matter. The British North American colonies did not contain such an unlimited expanse of unappropriated, arable territory as most people supposed.

In its final report the Committee of 1827 recommended a three-year experiment in which the second and third emigrations would be 50 per cent greater than their predecessors: first 20,000 people would be sent; then 30,000 and finally 45,000.[22] Parishes and landlords would be charged with the expense of the Atlantic passage while the emigrants would be expected to pay back with interest the money spent on them after they landed. This was a departure in form but not in principle from the original notion of a single annuity first paid by the parish and then by the emigrant. It was now proposed that the emigrant should begin making small payments in the third year after he settled. If these payments were forthcoming, then the experiment would be proved a success and the government would be justified in sending out greater numbers in the years that followed.

Upper and Lower Canada were expected to absorb the largest part of any emigration that might be sent out. The experience of the 1820 settlers discouraged all notion of colonization by British emigrants at the Cape, while the cost of placing a pauper on land in New South Wales would have far exceeded the £22 spent by Peter Robinson. This was evident in spite of Edward Eager's efforts to prove the contrary.[23] Eager was a pardoned convict and emancipist leader. He upheld transportation as an effective punishment and insisted that free and convict settlement could be combined. Convict labour, he argued, provided New South Wales with a great advantage over the North American colonies. If convicts did the work, land could be prepared and shelters erected for arriving immigrants for under £2 per family. Labour would not be so cheap in North America. But this saving was more than offset by the expense of the long passage to Sydney.

'In New South Wales and Van Diemen's Land,' writes R. B.

---

[22] *Parl. Pap.* 1826-7, v (550), 18-20.

[23] Eager's plan was published in W. C. Wentworth, *A Statistical Account of the British Settlements in Australasia*, ii (London, 1824), and separately as *Letters to the Rt. Hon. Robert Peel* (London, 1824), as well as being included as appendix no. 2 to the Emigration Report of 1826, *Parl. Pap.* 1826, iv (404), 237-82. Eager gave evidence before the Committee on 18, 21, and 28 Apr. 1826. See Noel McLachlan, 'Edward Eager: A Colonial Spokesman', *Historical Studies, Australia and New Zealand*, May 1963, pp. 431-56.

Madgwick, the historian of immigration into Eastern Australia, 'the progress of Horton's schemes occasioned considerable interest and the colonists felt aggrieved that the committees should have envisaged emigration only to Canada.' [24] The demand for free labour was growing steadily as capitalists expanded their pastoral and agricultural holdings. Settlers would have applauded the importation of paupers, says Madgwick, but Horton and the British government did not believe that convicts and free labour could work together; for that reason, New South Wales was disregarded.

This is a mistaken assessment. The Australian colonies were not ignored by Horton and his Committees, nor were they rejected as unsuitable for pauper emigrants. The presence of convict labour did not cause Horton any hesitation in recommending the introduction of free labour. In studying the requirements of the various colonies, Horton grasped an essential point which later eluded Gibbon Wakefield: a uniform prescription would not be appropriate for all colonies. The location of assisted emigrants on 100-acre lots of land would not be as practical an undertaking in New South Wales or Cape Colony as in Upper Canada. Yet in the former two colonies existed a relatively small but certain demand for labour springing from factors totally absent in the Canadian situation.

Because most Canadian farmers operated on a subsistence level and were free from any obligation to pay either rent or interest, they hired little help and did as much as possible by themselves. In New South Wales the growth of great sheep-farming enterprises created a separate set of circumstances. Sheep-farmers depended upon convict labour, but the day was approaching when this would be insufficient. Moreover, convict labour when it was available was not very satisfactory. Witnesses estimated that New South Wales could have employed an additional 500 artisans in 1827 and that Van Diemen's Land could have taken some more.[25] They thought that settlers could afford to pay an artisan £20 a year plus provisions and food for his families and give work to his wife and children as well. If this were true, it would be possible for emigrants to repay their passage money out of their wages in four or five years.

At the Cape a shortage of labour was felt most acutely by the 1820 settlers in the Zuurveld or Albany district. Representatives of the 1820 settlers were agitating for government assistance to bring out

[24] *Immigration into Eastern Australia, 1788–1851* (London, 1937), pp. 75, 80.
[25] *Parl. Pap.* 1826, iv (404), 106–11, 1826–7, v (237), 109–10.

almost 800 men, women, and children as indentured servants.[26] The Albany district had not yet produced a wheat surplus; in fact it had been importing wheat from Cape Town. Many of the original settlers had not attempted to develop their estates and had kept a few servants for the sake of personal comfort alone. With more and cheaper labour the district might realize its potential. Because the 1820 settlers considered the government responsible for the hardship they had suffered, they looked for help as a right, not a dispensation. They would not contribute anything towards an emigration of servants themselves but expected the government to advance the money and to seek reimbursement from the emigrants after they began to earn wages. The Emigration Committees were advised that such an arrangement would work for 500–700 emigrants a year.[27] No cause, the Committee of 1827 concluded, was more responsible for retarding the development of the Cape of Good Hope and the Australian colonies than the shortage of labour. If this shortage were redressed by a scheme of assisted emigration, these colonies might become financially self-sufficient and the British Treasury might receive some relief. The Committee felt that government action was warranted even though it would not remove a noticeable portion of Britain's excess population.

In the national system of emigration visualized by the Emigration Committees, large numbers of paupers would be converted into landholders in British North America while much smaller numbers would become indentured servants at the Cape of Good Hope, New South Wales, and Van Diemen's Land. The emigration of labourers, however, would be limited so as to avoid a depression of wages or unemployment in the colonies. Horton was opposed to what he called desultory or casual emigration.[28] Many of his contemporaries believed that emigration should be allowed to take its own course; it should neither be assisted nor restricted. The danger that Horton foresaw in such a policy was that thousands of the starving poor would simply transfer their misery to the United States, their inevitable destination if the government took no interest in their fate. Nor did Horton expect that the Americans would submit to an invasion of British

---

[26] *Parl. Pap.* 1826, iv (404), 87–9; 1826–7, v (550), 304–5.

[27] Ibid., 88; 1826–7, v (237), 110, 115, 123, 127–8, 169.

[28] W.H.P., Horton to Grenville, Feb. 1826; *Lecture VIII*, p. 15; *Parl. Pap.* 1826–7, v (550), 36–8.

paupers if it threatened the welfare of their own people. Yet the lobby in favour of the removal of all restriction on emigration had powerful supporters who were all the more assured because they rested their arguments on the principles of free trade. Horton himself admitted the soundness of these principles. It was inevitable, therefore, that the Emigration Committee should have turned their attention to the Passenger Act and the impediments which it supposedly threw in the way of the free movement of labour.

In the early 1820s under lenient legislation and with more and more vessels competing for the emigrant trade the steerage rate from Ireland to British North America had dropped to less than £3.[29] Under regulations authorized by the Acts of 1816 and 1817 British vessels sailing to the colonies had been permitted to carry more passengers than those sailing to the United States. While the latter had been restricted to one passenger for every 5 tons, the former had been allowed one for every 1½ tons. As a consequence of the cheaper fares to British North America, Quebec had become a major port of entry for emigrants intent on going to the United States. In 1823 the passenger legislation had been revised. A new Act drafted by the Commissioners of the Customs without the advice of either the Board of Trade or the Colonial Office had imposed the same ratio of one passenger to 2 tons on all vessels irrespective of destination.[30] The authors of this Act were apparently motivated by two considerations: a humanitarian desire to eliminate the abuses and hardships of the Atlantic crossing which had earned notoriety in the previous two seasons and an intention inspired by free-trade doctrine to remove the preferential features of the existing legislation.[31] Shipowners immediately complained that the new regulations raised fares to a prohibitive level. As the volume of the emigrant trade fell sharply in 1824 and remained at a lower level in 1825, the clamour for less stringent legislation mounted. In partial response to a stream of protest from Irish shipping merchants the Board of Trade initiated a change in 1825 which permitted vessels sailing from Ireland to British North America to ignore the requirements of the Act respec-

---

[29] *Parl. Pap.* 1825, viii (129), 134.

[30] 4 Geo. IV C. 84. Ships sailing without licences were restricted to one person whether adult or child and including master and crew, for every 5 tons. Ships sailing with licences could carry one adult, including master and crew, or two children under fourteen, or three children under seven for every 2 tons.

[31] Oliver MacDonagh, *A Pattern of Government Growth, The Passenger Acts and their Enforcement* (London, 1961), p. 67.

ting provisions.[32] This change re-created the old distinction between the emigrant trade with the colonies and that with the United States, but did not satisfy the shipping interests.

Wilmot Horton did not object in the beginning to the 1823 Passenger Act. When he appeared as a witness before the Irish Committee in February 1825, his first reaction was to justify the Act.[33] Unregulated emigration meant privation and despair for thousands. In quoting statistics for 1822, 1823, and 1824, Horton appeared to welcome the decline in arrivals at Quebec after the enactment of the new regulations. By the end of 1825 he had acquired another perspective. The cost per person of the transportation of the 2,024 assisted emigrants who left Cork in May 1825, was 15 per cent higher than that of the 571 who had left in July 1823, in spite of the advantages of larger numbers.[34] Horton, although unsympathetic to any efforts to release a flood of helpless emigrants, became interested in an amendment of the Passenger Act which would allow some lowering of fares.

In preparing new legislation Horton exploited the interest and knowledge of A. C. Buchanan, a shipping merchant in the London-derry-British North American trade and joint proprietor with his brother of a saw and grist milling enterprise near Sorel in Lower Canada. Buchanan believed that the Passenger Act could be changed to permit a lowering of fares by 12s. or 14s. without adding to the hazards of the Atlantic passage. In March 1827 he laid before the Committee the draft of a bill designed to accomplish this purpose.[35] His draft bill, like the Acts of 1823 and 1825, would limit the number of passengers to one adult or two children under fourteen or three children under seven for every 2 tons. Buchanan, however, excluded crews in the calculation; this change would raise the legal capacity of a 400-ton vessel from 180 adults to 200. Ships' surgeons were not required in Buchanan's draft; he believed that it was impossible to find enough regular surgeons and that nine-tenths of those who engaged carried fraudulent diplomas. If ships were compelled to have nothing more than a good supply of medicine with instructions, no ill would result. By freeing shipping companies from any obligation

[32] 6 Geo. IV C. 116; C.O. 384/12, Watson and Graves (New Ross) to Bathurst, 6 Mar. 1824; *Parl. Pap.* 1825, viii (129), 133–4.

[33] *Parl. Pap.* 1825, viii (129), 11, 15.

[34] Cost per person in 1823 was £6. 12s. 5d., and in 1825 it was £7. 14s. 7d. See C.O. 384/12, abstract of expenses and *Parl. Pap.* 1826–7, v (550), 347.

[35] *Parl. Pap.* 1826–7, v (237), 73–4; W.H.P., Buchanan to Horton, 22 May 1826.

to carry doctors, Buchanan expected to reduce the costs of a single crossing by £50. He also included a clause allowing emigrants to lay in their own provisions. The Act of 1823 obliged captains to take provisions unsuitable for the potato and herring fed Irish: 'If you give an Irish peasant beef and biscuit and salt pork and coffee, they will be all over scurvy before they get to North America.'[36] There should be some legislation to protect the emigrants against their own ignorance. Irish emigrants would take too little. They would hear of packets going from New York to Liverpool in twenty or twenty-five days and would calculate on a twenty-day passage for themselves. Provisions for seventy-five days would be the minimum that Buchanan would recommend.

Buchanan's views were accepted by Horton, who was determined that they should be adopted by the Emigration Committee and by Parliament. 'I want immediately to bring in a bill to amend the Passenger Act,' Horton told a senior clerk in the Colonial Office; 'the Bill is ready and Mr. Buchanan will explain what additions are to be made to it.'[37] Buchanan was also sent to James Stephen, counsel to the Colonial Office, for his assistance in framing the bill. This meeting was profitless. In Stephen's opinion the changes that were proposed were too sweeping. If the bill originated in the Emigration Committee, it should be confined to purposes 'strictly emigratory'.[38] If the Passenger Act of 1825 were to be repealed, the step should be taken by Huskisson and the Board of Trade because they had drawn it up. The Committee should not interfere with the regulation of the carriage of passengers in general but should confine itself to 'the high objects of facilitating emigration'. This was a fine splitting of hairs. Stephen proposed a less comprehensive measure which would have left the existing Act intact, but exempted pauper emigrants to British North America from its operation.

Stephen's ideas were as unacceptable to Buchanan as Buchanan's had been to Stephen. To one man the Passenger Act was an integral part of the code of Trade and Navigation law and could not be tampered with without raising larger questions. To the other man the Act was essentially an instrument for regulating the emigrant trade; nothing could be more straightforward than to amend the Act where it was ineffective or too restrictive. Buchanan believed very

---

[36] *Parl. Pap.* 1826, iv (404), 173.
[37] W.H.P., Horton to Baillie, 12 March(?) 1827.
[38] W.H.P., Stephen to Horton, 26 and 27 Feb. 1827.

strongly that, for the protection of emigrants, rules governing their condition on board ship should be laid down by the direct authority of Parliament. He completely rejected Stephen's suggestion that ships carrying paupers should be freed from obligations imposed by statute. Such a measure might be legally correct, but it would jeopardize the welfare of emigrants in a most irresponsible way. Stephen very quickly confessed his inability to help Buchanan to draft his bill. Yet the two men must have been equally dismayed by the final resolution of the House of Commons on the recommendation of the Committee.

Although the amendments advocated by Buchanan were warmly supported by Wilmot Horton and although they appeared to satisfy the demands of some of the Irish shipowners,[39] they were attacked by a vocal group in the Committee and in the House of Commons because they did not go far enough. In disregard of the warnings of well-informed witnesses, the Committee was attracted by the idea of total repeal of the Passenger Act. Buchanan sensed this when he first presented an outline of his bill. He called upon Horton to stamp the idea out.[40] Horton failed. The Committee recommended repeal; the House of Commons dropped Buchanan's bill, which had been introduced by Horton, and passed 7 & 8 George IV Cap. 19 which simply voided all of the existing passenger legislation. Consequently, the Committee assumed an anomalous position. It had endorsed unregulated emigration as well as colonization and had revealed an indifference to colonial consequences in sharp contrast with Horton's point of view.

Joseph Hume, who was a member of the Committee in 1826 but not in 1827, was a major critic of Buchanan's bill; indeed he was a major critic of all of the emigration measures associated with Horton. When Buchanan's bill was debated in the Commons, Hume led the attack on it. A year later he refused to admit that repeal of the Passenger Act had been a mistake. One can sympathize with Buchanan who believed that Hume and his supporters had a very erroneous knowledge of the emigrant trade.[41] In part the opposition to passenger legislation emanated from a conviction that it was discriminatory. Hume thought that the Passenger Act prohibited emigration to the

[39] W.H.P., Dublin Chamber of Commerce to Buchanan, 12 Apr. 1827.

[40] W.H.P., Buchanan to Horton, 6 Mar. 1827.

[41] Ibid. 17 Feb. 1827; *Hansard*, 1827, xvi, col. 510, and 1828, xviii, col. 962; K. A. Walpole, 'Emigration to British North America under the Early Passenger Acts, 1803–42' (M.A. Thesis, London, 1929), p. 77.

ports of the United States and had, as a consequence, created an emigration traffic to the United States via British North American ports. He had observed that of the thousands of arrivals in Quebec every year, a majority went on to the United States. The necessity of entering the republic by an indirect route imposed an extra £10 expense on each emigrant, he claimed. If emigration was to be at all effective in relieving Britain of excess population, then all restrictions on the emigrant trade to the United States should be lifted.

Hume had obviously never examined the Passenger Act for himself. His impression of it was so garbled as to be the exact reverse of the truth. The Act of 1823 had placed vessels going to British North America and vessels going to the United States on exactly the same footing. The only alteration in 1825 was the clause allowing vessels sailing from Ireland to British North America to carry cheaper provisions.[42] What Hume did not realize, and what he never seemed to learn, was that pauper emigration directly from Great Britain to the United States was checked not by British legislation but by American legislation. For a brief period after 1817 this had not been true, but the American Passenger Act of 1819 prescribed higher standards and consequently higher fares than the British Acts. Neither amendment nor repeal of passenger regulations by the British Parliament would substantially reduce the transatlantic fare to New York. Only the British North American trade would be affected. Instead of putting the American and colonial trades on a position of equality, abolition of all British regulation could only increase the discrepancies between conditions on vessels bound for Quebec and conditions on vessels bound for New York.

One suspects that the ignorance and foggy thinking displayed by Hume was shared by most of those who clamoured for repeal of the Passenger Act. If emigration was good for anything, it was thought it should be as cheap as possible. Little time was given to a consideration of possible results. As E. G. G. Stanley later admitted, the Committee's decision to recommend repeal of all passenger regulations had been a hasty one.[43] A majority of the Committee members failed to appreciate Buchanan's testimony that the Passenger Act did not prevent much emigration and that repeal would not lower

[42] 6 Geo. IV C. 116 provided that Commissioners of the Treasury could exempt from the operation of the Act or any part of the Act ships carrying passengers from Ireland to British North America. In practice such ships were exempted only from clauses relating to provisions. See Jones, 'Transatlantic Emigrant Trade', pp. 92–3.

[43] *Hansard*, 1828, xviii, col. 963.

the fare to New York by a farthing. A consensus existed in the Committee and in most of the House of Commons that emigration was a desirable outlet for surplus population. Horton did not have to fight to establish that principle. In the past generation the mercantilist belief that a growing population was a source of wealth and power had been largely discredited. To the advocates of repeal the Passenger Act appeared to be mercantilist in its conception and in its operation because they thought that it prohibited the free movement of emigrants to the United States. Their impressions were not groundless. Earlier passenger legislation had discriminated against the emigrant trade to the United States and an element of discrimination remained in the Act of 1825. But it was with a very imperfect understanding of the nature and effect of this Act that members of the House of Commons cast their votes in favour of an unregulated emigrant trade.

The bill repealing the Passenger Act was passed in April and became law at the onset of the 1827 sailing season. Although Horton was chairman of the Committee that recommended this measure, he was never persuaded of its wisdom. One should not attribute Horton's opposition simply to a humanitarian concern for the welfare of emigrants while they were on board ship. The intention of the House of Commons in repealing the Passenger Act was to break down a supposed dam and to release an uncontrolled flood of voluntary emigrants; this was a contradiction of all that Horton believed essential to a practical system of pauper emigration. The day after the bill reached its third reading in the House of Commons Horton wrote to the Governors of British North America asking them for information about the treatment of emigrants during the coming season.[44] His foresight helped to secure new legislation in 1828.

1827 was a typhus year. The disease broke out on crowded emigrant ships and was spread to the inhabitants of the ports of disembarkation. In Halifax 800 out of a population of 7,000 had died of typhus by November.[45] Colonists were quick to point the finger of blame at Parliament. If the emigrant trade had not been freed of all regulation it might have been possible to keep disease under control. Contagion, it was argued, was unavoidable among undernourished passengers on crowded and filthy ships without any medical assist-

---

[44] Walpole, 'Emigration to British North America', p. 79.
[45] *Hansard*, 1828, xviii, col. 962; Cowan, p. 148; MacDonagh, pp. 67–8; Walpole, p. 92.

ance. It is probably accurate to say that the typhus epidemic would have been severe whether or not the Passenger Act had been repealed. The turn of events, nevertheless, made it impossible to construct a powerful case in favour of legislative regulation. Not only did the Governors of British North America report the arrival of disease-ridden ships, they also described instances of starvation and even mutiny. These reports arrived shortly after Huskisson was appointed Colonial Secretary. He was convinced that some moderate legislation was necessary; under his auspices, with the co-operation of Horton and Buchanan, a bill was drafted in the Colonial Office, introduced in the House of Commons, and subsequently enacted.

Joseph Hume and other leading parliamentary Radicals denounced Huskisson's bill as a retrogressive step. The Emigration Committee had advocated the removal of all restrictions after full deliberation, Hume said; there was no reason to reverse their decision. The ensuing debate is characterized by Miss Walpole as a conflict between humanitarians and free traders. The principal speakers, she says, were Huskisson and Hume, 'the one representative of enlightened Toryism . . . the other . . . guided by the light of economic theory.'[46] This is a deceptive simplification. Contemporaries, Oliver MacDonagh tells us, saw the opponents as doctrinaires and practical men.[47] Hume and his supporters were uncompromising in their abhorrence of regulation while Huskisson, though a firm believer in free-trade theory, could not ignore considerations of human safety and welfare. Was Huskisson, as a practical man, compelled to betray his economic principles? It could have been argued that the modest measure introduced by Huskisson in 1828 which imposed the same requirements on all vessels irrespective of destination did not act as a significant restraint on trade. In that light it would have been most accurate to say that the debate divided the informed and the misinformed; Hume rose to the defence of free trade when it was not under attack, to criticize legislation he did not understand.

Throughout the controversy Horton's objectives remained consistent, although his motives were complex. With Buchanan constantly at his elbow, he was never allowed to forget the welfare of the pauper families who boarded emigrant ships. Nor did his concern end once these families were discharged on the shores of North America. Horton's five years in the Colonial Office had taught him

[46] Walpole, p. 93.
[47] MacDonagh, p. 70.

to look for an immediate protest from the colonies if their ports were overrun with paupers. At the same time he considered it neither practical nor desirable to expect the United States to absorb Britain's redundant population. Horton was a serious student of the new science of political economy, but he also believed in the value of colonial possessions. The principles of *laissez-faire* were theoretically correct, but they had to be modified in a world in which nations were frequently at war.[48] Besides, the immigration of large numbers of British paupers would certainly be resisted by the Americans themselves.

The Passenger Act of 1828 answered Horton's requirements. It made no distinction between the emigrant trade to the United States and that to British North America and so accorded with the economic doctrines to which Horton adhered. It introduced a measure of government control over the trade and gave some protection to emigrant passengers. Finally, the standards imposed by the Act were not so high as to push fares back up to the pre-1827 level. Transportation of assisted emigrants to the British Colonies would cost less than it had when Peter Robinson took his settlers out in 1825.

In the context of the proceedings of the Emigration Committees, the most remarkable aspect of the Passenger Act controversy was Horton's failure to sway opinion to his point of view. The members of the Committee of 1827 were not as malleable as some historians suggest. Men like E. G. Stanley were far too capable and independent of thought to follow Horton placidly. Repeal of the Passenger Act appeared to be an attractive means of stimulating emigration; it involved no expenditure by government, landlord, or parish. Irish proprietors and liberal economists could agree on its desirability. Although two well-informed witnesses expressed emphatic opposition to repeal, Horton's influence was insufficient to deflect the Committee from its intention to recommend abolition of all regulation.

Yet one must acknowledge the extent to which Horton did dominate the Committees. The initiative was his. The Committees had been appointed at his insistence; he had recruited their members.[49] No one had devoted more time and energy to the theoretical aspects of the subject than he had. Horton was the only Committee member

[48] *A Letter to Sir Francis Burdett,* p. 51.
[49] W.H.P., Wellesley to Horton, 10 Mar. 1826, Goulburn to Horton, 10 Mar. 1826, Wortley to Horton, no date.

with a complete emigration plan to propose. He knew from the
beginning what kind of a report he wanted to produce. As chairman
Horton was able to guide proceedings into the directions that he
preferred. As an Under-Secretary in the Colonial Office he enjoyed
a superior knowledge of colonial conditions, and needed no assistance from other Committee members in finding colonial witnesses.
His purposefulness, his industry, his access to people and to information and his position in the Committees made it inevitable that his
ideas should be thoroughly aired. Although members of the Committees challenged Horton's opinions, they all allowed him to use
the Committees as a platform for arguing his views. The work of the
Committees became not so much an investigation of the subject of
emigration as an investigation of the Horton system of emigration.
The issues that Horton raised were accepted as the principal issues
that needed to be raised. For the most part, the Committee members
limited themselves to a choice of either admitting or refuting the
soundness of Horton's presuppositions. Intelligent and resourceful
as many of the Committee members were, they conceded to Horton
the definition of the area they were to study, without being aware
that they had done so.

Although Horton believed that the emigration of indentured
labourers to New South Wales, Van Diemen's Land, and the Cape
of Good Hope would mutually benefit the colonies and the mother
country, he was convinced that the capacity of the British North
American provinces to absorb population was much greater. He saw
the experiments conducted by Peter Robinson as models of what
should be done to assist emigrants to these provinces. To remove
significant numbers of paupers in this way would cost millions of
pounds. The problem for Horton was to find a means of raising this
money. From the beginning he had been predisposed towards a
system which would lay the onus of subsidizing emigration on those
who would benefit from a depopulation of estates and parishes. To
call upon the nation as a whole to underwrite all of the costs of
emigration would be to disregard the fundamental precepts of contemporary economic thought. Even if Horton had been less attached
to the teachings of Ricardo he was pessimistic about the possibility
of securing grants from Parliament on the scale that a massive scheme
of emigration would require. In 1822 Horton had first suggested
the parish poor rates as a source of funds for emigration. Between
1822 and 1826 he developed his more complex proposal that loans

for emigration purposes be repaid in part by parishes out of the poor rate and in part by the settlers themselves through the machinery of the quit rent system that he was introducing in the British North American colonies. This proposal was Horton's principal theoretical contribution to the science of emigration. It was this proposal that Horton wanted the Committee to assess fairly and it was to a study of the feasibility of this proposal that the Committee devoted most of its time. The trap into which the Committee fell was to assume that assisted emigration was synonymous with Horton's scheme. Consequently, the opportunity to consider less ambitious but more obtainable alternatives was lost.

VIII

THE RESPONSE OF
POLITICAL ECONOMISTS

THE celebrity of any idea might be measured by the criticism it provokes. In the late 1820s the reports of the Emigration Committees were answered by the publication of a number of tracts and arguments which were as emphatic as they were hostile. The issues that were revealed were larger than the single question whether or not assisted emigration might be practical. What was the responsibility of the state for the poor? What were the rights of the poor? Should the unemployed be given help or would that interfere with necessary, although harsh, natural processes? If a national system of emigration was desirable, should the government attempt to finance or administer it, or should the government remain in the background? Certainly, the feasibility of state-aided emigration was a central point of discussion, but in some quarters it was attacked not just as a hopeless but as a harmful remedy. This opposition fell into two classes: one denied the Malthusian thesis and the necessity of emigration; the other admitted the Principle of Population but drew from it very pessimistic conclusions.

No one assaulted the Malthusian position with more invective than William Cobbett, the Radical journalist and champion of the agricultural labourer.[1] Cobbett's *Political Register*, which was directed at a wide working-class readership, was a major force in the political reform movement. Cobbett, however, took his inspiration from the past and although his re-creation of history was sometimes mistaken and sometimes absurd, his was a peculiarly Tory radicalism. At one time he had applauded Malthus's *Essay on Population*, but at an early date he had identified it as a weapon fashioned against the interests of the lower classes. The Malthusian doctrine became a frequent target of abusive comment. Population had been much

---

[1] See Charles H. Kegel, 'William Cobbett and Malthusianism', *Journal of the History of Ideas*, 1958, pp. 348–62; and John W. Osborne, *William Cobbett: His Thought and His Times* (New Brunswick, N.J., 1966), pp. 114–19.

greater in the Middle Ages, Cobbett insisted. The churches that dotted the countryside had obviously been built for the needs of much larger communities than those in existence in the nineteenth century. Parish churches could hold four, five, and even ten times the number of their present parishioners. 'What should men have built such large churches for?' 'What a lie!' he described one estimate of the Elizabethan population; it was obvious that England then had contained more than nineteen adult men for each parish church, 'including cripples and insane persons, and leaving nobody for cathedrals.'[2] If Cobbett's argument amounted to nonsense, he did at least understand the social prejudices to which Malthusian doctrine gave armour. The privileged were all too willing to attribute the poverty of the labourer to his own worthlessness. Malthus sanctioned the denial of charity in the name of the common good. To Cobbett this was anathema; the poor had a right to relief; charity was a Christian obligation which had been willingly shouldered in the past.

The poor also had a right to live in England. Why should a farm labourer who produced more than he consumed be forced to leave the country? No one, Cobbett observed, proposed to send away a single soul of those who lived upon taxes and tithes. The labouring classes should stay in England where conditions could only improve; 'they have *seen the worst*; at least they have proved that they will not *lie down and die quietly from starvation*;' they would be fools if they did not stay to see what happened and enjoy the consequences.[3] On the other hand, for the middle classes, especially for farmers, emigration offered escape from oppressive taxation. These people should leave before the last shilling was taken from them. It was for their benefit that Cobbett wrote his *Emigrant's Guide*. He warned them not to go to the British Colonies, 'those worthless tracts of rocks, sands and swamps'.[4] Anyone who went to British North America would eventually end up in the United States; he could save himself money by going there in the first place.

Cobbett did not develop his ideas in a coherent work; his attacks drew less notice than those of Michael Thomas Sadler, another Tory radical, and an opponent of Catholic emancipation who was to become parliamentary leader of the movement for a ten-hour working day. Like Cobbett, Sadler maintained that the advocates of emigra-

[2] *Cobbett's Weekly Political Register*, 13 Mar. 1830, p. 350.
[3] Ibid., 20 Mar. 1830, p. 368.
[4] Ibid., 9 Apr. 1831, p. 80.

tion possessed a degraded estimate of the worth of human beings. 'Thank God,' he wrote of the Emigration Report, 'these notions are as absurd and impolitic as they are selfish and cruel.'[5] Sadler's attention was centred on Ireland. He argued that the condition of the Irish peasantry had always been wretched and that the cause was not excess of population but absenteeism. Irish pauperism resulted not from insufficient production but from inequitable distribution. Sadler's remedies included the discouragement of absentee landlords, a poor law for Ireland on the English model, and the protection of Irish agriculture.[6]

With the publication of *The Law of Population* Sadler put forward an entire thesis in contradiction of the Malthusian argument.[7] Dismissing Malthus's preventive checks, Sadler argued that the prolificness of humans varied inversely as their numbers. In crowded conditions fertility declined; where space was abundant it increased. The experience of the United States, in which population was doubling every twenty-five years, gave superficial support to this theory. Sadler insisted that the fears aroused by Malthus were not justified. Population would not expand in geometric proportions until halted by famine, pestilence, or war. Instead, it would be controlled as space became restricted. On this basis Sadler rejected emigration as a measure as inexpedient as it was inhuman. It could not reduce pauperism in Ireland because over-population was not at the root of the problem. Yet it would have the effect of increasing fertility. Sadler's ideas were ridiculed by disciples of the orthodox economists. Malthus did not think they should be dignified by a rebuttal.[8] Yet Sadler was sensitive in a way in which many of his contemporaries were not. The Emigration Committees had recommended the destruction of cottages to prevent repopulation after emigration. This met with the approval of the leading economists. To Sadler the clearing of estates was a measure more merciless than emigration. In combination the two were barbaric.[9]

As self-appointed spokesmen for the labouring classes, Cobbett and Sadler reacted instinctively against a doctrine that justified the

[5] M. T. Sadler, *Ireland: Its Evils and their Remedies being a Refutation of the Errors of the Emigration Committee and Others* (London, 1829), pp. 87–9.

[6] Ibid., pp. 186, 294, 320.

[7] London, 1830.

[8] W.H.P., Malthus to Senior, 24 May 1829.

[9] *Ireland: Its Evils and Remedies*, p. 105. See also *Hansard*, 1830–1, ii, col. 885–92. For a reply see Horton, *Causes and Remedies of Pauperism Considered*, Pt. 1, pp. 1–4.

denial of minimum-wage legislation and the withdrawal of poor relief. Their involvement in the population controversy was not merely academic; they attempted to contradict Malthus's Essay because they fully understood its social implications. Yet it would be true to say that their attitudes were as much Tory as Radical. Certainly, they were poles apart from Radicals of Joseph Hume's outlook. Hume accepted Malthus; he believed that Britain suffered from excess population and he saw emigration as a necessary safety-valve.[10] His opposition to Horton's plans was based on his abhorrence of government expenditure; he was an advocate of voluntary and privately financed emigration and he wished every obstacle in the way of such a movement removed; but he objected to the use of public money. This was a stand consistent in a man who preached retrenchment and attacked restriction. It was also the stand of a Radical Whig, a man who represented the world of commerce and industry and who held great respect for the science of political economy. Distrust of the work of the classical economists was a Tory rather than a Whig trait. The anti-Malthusianism of Sadler and Cobbett was a bias shared by more conventional Tories.

Yet the final Emigration Report was applauded in the *Quarterly*, the principal Tory periodical. The reviewer, Robert Southey the Poet Laureate who frequently contributed articles on economic subjects, revealed a sense of responsibility and obligation towards the poor and a fear of the consequences if nothing were done. He was oblivious of the idea that it would be an injustice to ask the poor to emigrate. There were higher considerations than those recognized by the economists, he wrote. To insist that the poor should avoid marriages and families was to forget Christian values:[11]

The poor are the prolific portion of the community. Increase and multiply they will and must; it is in the order of nature and Providence that they should; and woe be to the nation, whose institutions should strive against that order! Our duty is to provide for this necessary increase; and the time is fast approaching when this must be regarded as one of the most important parts of the business of the state.

Pauperism was increasing, Southey observed, and its rise threatened the foundation and whole fabric of society. Emigration was the

---

[10] *Hansard*, 1827, xvi, col. 510, and xviii, col. 1557. In 1819 Hume had welcomed the expenditure on emigration to the Cape and had gone so far as to suggest that parish paupers who were unwilling to go should be sent without consent. However, one does not expect Hume to speak always with consistent sense. See *Hansard*, 1819, xl, col. 1550.

[11] *Quarterly Review*, Mar. 1828, p. 572.

answer. Southey accepted the evidence and recommendations of the Emigration Committees without reservation. In this he may have been exceptionally uncritical, but his sentiments were of a kind that old-school Tories could respect.

In the late 1820s and early 1830s several articles supporting sponsored emigration appeared in the _Quarterly_. Only once in this period did the review publish a hostile opinion.[12] _Blackwood's_, the other great Tory review, was much more inconsistent, alternately calling for an early adoption of a plan of emigration and then denying that such a plan was needed.[13] Contributors could not agree on emigration, but they all believed in home colonization. The choice between the two, if it was necessary, did not have to involve deep principles. It could be argued simply on the basis of cost. Yet there were reasons for preferring home colonization which had a special Tory appeal. Emigration would subtract from the nation's potential and, still worse, if it became government policy, it would cause Englishmen to lose pride and confidence in their native country.

Tory reviewers were unimpressed by the economic arguments they found in the Emigration Reports. 'This disease of Political Economy prevailed to a most alarming degree in the Committee,' _Blackwood's_ observed.[14] Horton and his collaborators obviously wanted the approval of the economists. They urged members of the propertied classes to act because it was to their advantage rather than because it was their responsibility. It would be a mistake for anyone to think that landlords and manufacturers gained by the existence of a large pool of unemployed labour or that they were in any way compensated for the inevitable expenses which the presence of large numbers of paupers produced. In the final Report the Committee denied that the general prosperity of the country could be in any way compatible with the impoverishment of the labouring class.[15] High profits were not dependent on low wages. On the other hand, low wages meant a smaller home market. If the labouring class was well paid, then the country as a whole would be more prosperous. An emigration of a portion of the working class would force wages up.

---

[12] July 1829, pp. 240–84. See also May 1830, pp. 242–77; Jan. 1831, pp. 1–52; Jan. 1832, pp. 349–89; Dec. 1832, pp. 320–45; Aug. 1834, pp. 233–61.

[13] Apr. 1827, pp. 377–91; Feb. 1828 pp. 191–4; May 1828, pp. 615–20; June 1828, pp. 923–36. Horton lost no time in bringing the favourable June 1828 issue to the attention of the House. See _Hansard_, 1828, xix, col. 1504.

[14] May 1828, p. 615.

[15] _Parl. Pap._ 1826–7, v (550), 17–18.

Assisted emigration would not be a measure of charity but one of sound policy.

The authors of the Emigration Report relied heavily on the testimony of Malthus to make their points. Yet his ideas also inspired criticism of the emigration solution. The only remedies that the most rigid interpreters of Malthus would accept were those designed to prevent marriages. If emigration could be carried out on a large scale, its beneficial effects would be but temporary; very rapidly the population gap which had been created at vast expense would be filled. Disappointment and ruin would be the only result. Among those who made this prediction was Captain Francis Bond Head, the Assistant Poor Law Commissioner for Kent, a man who later gained notoriety as the incompetent colonial governor who provoked rebellion in Upper Canada. Bond Head would have relied entirely upon the preventive checks outlined by Malthus:[16]

We find our population redundant—we know that distress will curb it; yet, the moment its salutary influence comes to our assistance, we writhe under the operation and try to avoid it. If we are willing to bear our distress, (which from political and mercantile causes must fluctuate, like the value of property on the Stock-Exchange) our population will never overwhelm us; but, if, by borrowing money, or by any other unfair means, we shrink from our distress—population, encouraged by our weakness, must increase.

'In our humble opinion,' said Bond Head, 'the remedy is the very evil we wish to avert.' Emigration would be injurious because it would stimulate population by encouraging 'reckless' marriages. No man held this view more firmly than Dr. Thomas Chalmers, Scottish theologian and evangelist notable for his work among the poor of Glasgow.[17] Only by instilling habits of prudence in the lower classes through education and religious sanction could population growth be held in check. Misplaced charity inhibited the acquisition of these habits. This, of course, was exactly the attitude against which Cobbett reacted. It was the existence of this attitude that caused Nassau Senior to say that he found the Principle of Population made 'the stalking horse of negligence and injustice'.[18]

Where did Malthus himself stand on the emigration issue? As a

[16] F. B. Head, *A Few Arguments against the Theory of Emigration* (London, 1828), pp. 59–60.

[17] W.H.P., Chalmers to Horton, 9 June 1827. See 'Dr. Chalmers on *Political Economy*', *Quarterly Review*, Oct. 1832, pp. 39–69.

[18] N. W. Senior, *Two Lectures on Population* (London, 1829), p. 89.

witness before the Emigration Committee he had given his assent to the leading questions he had been asked. He had agreed that emigration in combination with the clearance of estates could bring relief to Ireland. Yet he was as attached to the vacuum theory as any of his disciples; he always maintained that emigration was applicable only as a momentary answer to sudden population increase. This point is stressed by R. N. Ghosh and by Donald Winch.[19] Malthus explained to Horton the way in which they differed: 'I incline to the opinion that we are called upon to make a great temporary effort, in order to relieve a great present difficulty . . . while you incline to a permanent national system of emigration.'[20] Emigration was a solution that would be beneficial only in the short run; in the long run it did not touch the difficulty. Chastity, birth control, or prostitution were the only means by which population could be brought permanently under control. The latter two were unpleasant to contemplate, the former unlikely to be observed. Malthus's conception of the long run was decidedly pessimistic. The future, however, was as much an abstraction to him as to anyone else. He could speak dispassionately about ultimate consequences while feeling a warm awareness of immediate needs. He could believe that an emigration measure was imperative even though its effect would be temporary; this was illustrated in his correspondence with Horton:[21]

But though it would be a contradiction to all theory, and all past experience to deny the strong tendency of population to recover lost numbers, and the extreme difficulty of keeping the labouring classes from increasing beyond the effectual demand for labour; yet I think that both policy and humanity require that we should make every practicable effort to improve their condition, and I feel no doubt that your plan of emigration would essentially contribute to this most desirable end, by affording undoubted present relief and the best chance which offers itself of the means of permanent improvement. I think therefore we are called upon to attempt it, even though it may not be distinctly proved that the first loan will certainly be paid off before there can be necessity for another.

Malthus maintained 'that population is always ready and inclined to increase faster than food, *if the checks which repress it are removed*'. Many of his readers believed that all attempts to mitigate the effects

[19] R. N. Ghosh, 'Malthus on Emigration and Colonization: Letters to Wilmot-Horton', *Economica*, Feb. 1963, p. 61; Donald Winch, *Classical Political Economy and Colonies* (London. 1965) pp. 56–60.
[20] W.H.P., Malthus to Horton, 1829.
[21] Ibid., June 1830.

of expanding population were futile and self-defeating. This was the viewpoint which led men to call remedy an evil. In his correspon-dence Malthus denied that his doctrine supported such an idea.[22] His discovery of the Principle of Population had not led him to fear the consequences of improvements in the condition of the poor. Although increased productivity would be nullified by increased population, it did not follow that larger yields of wheat were un-desirable. A greater population would be a positive advantage if it did not mean greater misery. The pressure of population might be lightened for only a short period, but this would be a period of com-parative ease and its value should not be lightly dismissed. Further-more, Malthus remarked, the experience of such a period might give the labouring classes a taste for better living and encourage them to cohabit with more prudence.

When he spoke of the insuppressible drive of population to replace lost numbers, Malthus did not intend to disarm the advocates of emigration. He wanted only to defeat the notion that emigration could be a complete and final cure. 'I am convinced that it is *Emigra-tion* alone, which in the present state of things, can present any fair prospect of an *essential improvement* in the condition of the labouring classes, consistent with humanity and good policy.'[23] There was some reason for Malthus to describe his differences with Horton as 'trifling'. They agreed on the main point: the immediate value and desirability of emigration. Malthus would have willingly paid his share of any tax necessary to carry out a national system of emigra-tion; he supported the legislation that Horton wished to introduce in 1830. On the filling up of a vacuum created by emigration, Malthus conceded that the danger lay not simply in an absolute increase of population, but rather in such an increase as would bring back pauperism. This was a distinction which he did not make sufficiently clear in his published work. In discussing the theoretical aspects of the question, he foresaw immense hazards in a programme of emigration so extensive that it broke down all economically based caution towards marriage while so costly that it could not be repeated indefinitely. As soon as assisted emigration was discontinued, the labouring classes would experience a very painful readjustment.

---

[22] Senior, *Lectures*, pp. 85–6.
[23] W.H.P., Malthus to Horton [1830?]. His differences with Horton were minimized by Malthus in a letter to him, 5 May 1831. See also Malthus to Horton, 15 Feb. and 23 Aug. 1830.

However, this was a purely hypothetical analysis. Malthus did not expect that emigration would be supported on a dangerous scale. He was not afraid of the effects of Horton's plan or any other plan that was likely to be carried out.

While Malthus supported emigration as a measure of short-term relief, his arguments were cited by those who opposed emigration in any circumstances. He may have welcomed efforts to improve the condition of the poor, but his published opinions encouraged a much less constructive attitude. The difficulty, Nassau Senior thought, was not what Malthus said, but the way in which he said it. Senior was the first Professor of Political Economy at Oxford, a position he held from 1825 to 1830. In the 1830s, after the Whigs came to power, the government turned to him on a number of occasions for advice on economic questions.[24] The most consequential task he carried out was as a member of the Poor Law Commission set up in 1832. He played a large role in drafting the Poor Law Amendment Act of 1834, a reform which did not go so far as to withdraw parish assistance to the unemployed but did seek to make the life of those dependent on relief less 'eligible' than that of the least fortunate independent labourer. Although Senior did not think that public charity was a solution for poverty, he was convinced that government could be the agent of improvement. He was an optimist. He looked on emigration as a valuable weapon against pauperism. In 1831 he helped to draw up an emigration bill that was presented to the Commons by Lord Howick and he was responsible for the insertion into the Poor Law Amendment Act of a clause enabling parishes to raise money for emigration. He became involved in the emigration question at an active as well as a theoretical level.

Senior was not as thorough a disciple of Ricardo as were J. R. McCulloch and James Mill, but he belonged to the same school of economic thought. This was a school that differed with Malthus in some fundamental areas but accepted his population views without reservation. Senior was the first to cast doubts. He was willing to acknowledge the correctness of the Principle of Population in an abstract sense; he was not willing to adopt the pessimistic outlook that the statement of the Principle seemed to suggest. Certainly, Senior said, population has the power to increase faster than the means of subsistence. Under unwise institutions that power might

[24] Marian Bowley, *Nassau Senior and Classical Economics* (New York, 1967), pp. 22, 286–7, 328–9.

be exercised. All that is required to check that power, however, is good government.[25] In fact, Senior observed, the tendency is for the supply of food to increase faster than population. For proof one had only to look at the earliest records of nations now civilized; in every case poverty had declined. Senior did not suggest that prosperity was the result of high population. He believed that the inhabitants of Europe would be richer if their numbers were fewer and he commended Malthus for showing that additional numbers could bring poverty. Unfortunately, Malthus's views were open to the interpretation that what might happen necessarily would happen. They were, as a consequence, an obstacle to constructive efforts to improve the lot of the poor.

Horton believed that the principal and most successful argument used against emigration was the Malthus-inspired notion that any population vacuum would immediately be filled.[26] The argument, Horton contended, was fallacious and he gave good reasons for saying so. Senior agreed. If the birth-rate did not rise, the positive effects of a large emigration would never be obliterated. The vacuum created by such an emigration could not be considered filled at the moment when population was restored to its previous level. Only by means of an increased birth-rate could population reach the level that it could have reached if there had been no emigration. Moreover, it was conceivable that with a reduced population a higher birth-rate could still produce an absolute drop in the number of births. Like Horton, Senior did not think that the birth-rate could go up enough to obliterate the effects of a large emigration; the vacuum might be partially filled but not completely.[27] In any case, pauperism would be reduced. Offsetting any addition to the number of labourers would be an improvement occasioned by higher wages. The condition of the poor would be permanently improved, although not to the extent that would be initially felt.

Senior supported emigration but did not see it as a panacea. The thousands of miles that separated Britain from her colonies made it inconceivable that emigration alone could provide for every member of a population which took no precautions to check its growth.[28]

---

[25] Senior, *Lectures*, pp. 35–6, 52. See H. L. Beal, 'The Historical Context of the *Essay* on Population', D. V. Glass, ed., *Introduction to Malthus* (London, 1953), p. 7.

[26] *Causes and Remedies of Pauperism. Second Series*, p. 34.

[27] W.H.P., Senior to Horton, 12 May 1829, and 4 Feb. 1830.

[28] N. W. Senior, *A Letter to Lord Howick* (London 1831), p. 10; Horton, *Causes and Remedies of Pauperism. Fourth Series. Containing letters to Lord John Russell*, p. 55.

Emigration was neither a self-sufficient remedy, nor the most effective step that could be taken. The labouring classes would benefit far more by the total abolition of the Corn Laws and by the elimination of all restriction upon commerce than by the measure that Horton proposed. These considerations did not make emigration any the less desirable. As prompt and practical relief it would be invaluable. Malthus could not have contradicted Senior's assessment:[29]

The only effectual and permanent means of preventing the undue increase of the number to be maintained, is to raise the moral and intellectual character of the labouring population; to improve, or, I fear we must say, to create the habits of prudence, of self-respect, and of self-restraint, to equalize, as by nature they are equal, the wages of the single and the married, and no longer to make the family the passport to allowance. But these are necessarily gradual measures—they are preventive, not remedies. The only immediate remedy for an actual excess in a class of the population, is the ancient and approved one, *coloniam deducere*.

It is, of great importance to keep in mind, that not only is emigration the sole immediate remedy, but that it is a remedy preparatory to the adoption and necessary to the safety of every other.

In the late 1820s Senior's criticism of Malthusian doctrine had not yet been taken into account by his fellow economists. The problem of the vacuum filling up, a problem which was understood in rather simple terms by men as prominent as J. R. McCulloch, was raised again and again. It was thought quite probable that the long-run effect of emigration could be an increase of pauperism in Britain. Those who held this view did not necessarily object to the scheme proposed by the Emigration Committees, but they did insist that emigration should be accompanied by other measures designed to check the birth-rate. A vigorous levy of cottage and window duties would drive up the cost of housing and make life more difficult for newly married couples, forcing adolescents to wait longer before having children. Landlords could be required to pull down cottages and taxed heavily if they erected new ones. Steps of this kind, Thomas Tooke and J. R. McCulloch thought, could make emigration a workable remedy.[30] But it was agreed that the Emigration Committees had not given enough thought to the subsidiary measures which should accompany their main recommendation.

29 W.H.P., Senior to Horton, Dec. 1830.
30 W.H.P., McCulloch to Horton, 20 June 1828, and 25 May 1829, and T. Tooke to Horton, 3 Sept. 1830.

As a group the economists saw emigration as a palliative of short-term value by itself, or of long-term value if accompanied by other reforms. Approval of emigration, however, did not lead automatically to approval of the Emigration Reports. There were serious reservations about the system of emigration that was proposed. In orthodox Ricardian economics, it was assumed that wages could rise only through an accumulation of capital, and that there could never be a glut of capital. Capital never lay idle; when it was redundant in one field it was reinvested in another. A loss of capital meant a contraction of the wages fund. If large sums were spent in settling emigrants in the colonies, there would be a reduction of capital at home. Such a reduction would add to existing distress if more money were spent to settle one emigrant family than would be sufficient to create work for one pauper in Britain. James Mill had raised this objection in his article on colonization in the 1818 supplement to the *Encyclopaedia Britannica* and it constituted his criticism of the rough draft of the final Emigration Report of 1827.[31] Ricardo, who died in 1823, had held the same reservation.

Three long paragraphs were added to the Emigration Report in answer to Mill.[32] A distinction was made between productive and unproductive capital. Parish paupers were supported by unproductive capital. In the colonies the same people could be employed profitably in cultivating waste land. In effect, a scheme of assisted emigration would turn capital from an unproductive to a productive use. Furthermore, the capital advanced for emigration would produce a direct return in the repayments made by settlers and an indirect return in the creation of a new market overseas. Finally, the interest on an emigration loan would be considerably lower than the annual charge for maintaining paupers at home. The net result would be an improvement in Britain in the ratio of population to capital. Horton thought that this reasoning was conclusive. Mill remained dubious. The only argument that he acknowledged was that paupers might be placed on land in Canada for less than they could be kept at home; on this point he regarded Horton's figures with scepticism. An exchange of letters in 1830 won from Mill a conditional surrender:
'. . . on the footing you now place it, I can cordially go along with

---

[31] W.H.P., E. Tooke to Horton, 1827 (enclosure), and Ricardo to Horton, 19 June 1823.

[32] *Parl. Pap.* 1826–7, v (550), 39–40. See Horton's marginal comment on enclosed letter from Mill forwarded by E. Tooke. Senior thought that Horton had answered the objection. W.H.P., Senior to Horton, 15 Apr. 1829.

you.'[33] Subsequent statements showed that he continued to think that the cost of colonization would be too high.

Robert Torrens provided a more sophisticated reply to Mill. Torrens had been an early advocate of emigration; he was to become the leading adherent to Wakefield among the economists. During the spring of 1826 he volunteered his services to Horton and helped in the preliminary drafting of the Emigration Report.[34] In his ideas on colonization, he moved somewhat ahead of orthodox economic thinking. The belief that an expenditure on emigration would reduce employment-creating capital in Britain, he insisted, was based on a misconception. The wealth of England was retarded not by difficulty in accumulating capital, but by difficulty in putting it to profitable use.[35] As population had increased, new capital had been turned to the development of increasingly inferior soils until profits and wages had dropped to a minimum level. New savings were being invested in foreign loans and adventures. Under these circumstances the accumulation of capital did not influence the rate of wages. Capital could be devoted to emigration without depressing the market for labour. At the same time, a large-scale emigration would make it less necessary to cultivate inferior land. The rate of profit would rise; it would become easier to save; and the capital spent on emigration would soon be replaced. Torrens drew attention to the combined roles of land, labour, and capital in producing wealth. In Ireland labour was redundant in relation to capital; in England labour and capital were redundant in relation to land; in North America, South Africa, and Australia, land was redundant in relation to capital and labour. A system of colonization would simply bring together the redundant labour and capital of the United Kingdom with the redundant land overseas.

This was a line of reasoning that Wakefield was to follow and that John Stuart Mill was to accept. It was a cogent answer to Ricardo's objections to the export of capital. Yet it was not an essential answer. Ricardo's disciples were not uniformly concerned that the expendi-

---

[33] W.H.P., James Mill to Horton, 15 Feb. 1830. See also Mill to Horton, 21 Apr. 1829, 11 June 1830.

[34] W.H.P., Torrens to Horton, 25 Mar., 9 May 1826.

[35] R. Torrens, *Substance of a Speech in the House of Commons, 15 February, 1827 on the Motion for the Re-appointment of a Select Committee on Emigration* (London, 1828), p. 10; W.H.P., Memorandum by Torrens in reply to objections to Emigration Plan by Grenville, 1826?, and Torrens to Horton, 22 Mar. 1826. See also Lionel Robbins, *Robert Torrens and the Evolution of Classical Economics* (London, 1958), p. 250.

ture of capital on emigration would counteract the benefits of emigration. No one did more to popularize Ricardo's ideas or stuck to them more slavishly than J. R. McCulloch, Professor of Political Economy at the University of London from 1828 to 1832 and the *Edinburgh Review*'s principal contributor on economic subjects.[36] But McCulloch did not share the apprehension about colonization that James Mill and Ricardo himself had expressed. There was little doubt in McCulloch's mind that money spent on emigration could not be spent at home with equal benefit. On the question of expenses he thought that the public ought to do more than the Emigration Committee had suggested. He could not agree with the requirement that the emigrants themselves should repay part of the money spent on their behalf. If they were settled in Canada, they would be tempted to move to the United States to escape their debts, or they would be discouraged, or they would resist payment. McCulloch thought that half of the expense should be thrown on the landlords and parishes and that the other half should be borne by the government. The government should not be niggardly but should be prepared to spend between £10,000,000 and £15,000,000.[37]

McCulloch did endorse another criticism of the plan of colonization in the Emigration Reports. He was firmly convinced that colonies were worthless to Britain. In an article in the *Edinburgh Review* in 1825, he defied anyone 'to point out a single benefit of any sort whatever, derived by us from the possession of Canada, and our other colonies in North America'.[38] These colonies produced nothing but expense; they had already cost £60,000,000 or £70,000,000 and their only possible future would be merger with the United States. It followed then that McCulloch saw no advantage in directing emigration to British colonies. The national purpose would be served as well if emigration went to any other part of the commercial world. Indeed, South America deserved first consideration. New South Wales was too far away ever to develop an important trade with Europe; the Cape of Good Hope had been proved unfit for British settlers; the harsh climate of Canada permitted only a half-year of labour and its exports were too similar to those of Europe; the American economy did not need stimulation. The greatest oppor-

[36] See S. G. Checkland, 'The Propagation of Ricardian Economics in England', *Economica*, Feb. 1949, pp. 48–9.

[37] W.H.P., McCulloch to Horton, 21 Sept. 1826.

[38] Aug. 1825, p. 291. See also McCulloch's article in the *Edinburgh Review*, Jan. 1828, pp. 206–7.

tunity to advance British interests lay in South America where the climate was equable, the people susceptible to the influence of British settlers, and the products of the highest exchangeable value in any trade with Europe.

Ideally, McCulloch thought, assisted emigrants should be taken to the colony or country they preferred. If they wished to go to the United States or to South America, the British government should make it possible.[39] British consuls at New York, New Orleans, and other American ports should be empowered to give emigrants money to help them find their way into the interior. Canada might still be the destination of a large portion of the assisted emigrants, but it need not be the destination of them all. There was one consideration which could have induced McCulloch to give preference to British North America. He found unanswerable the unanimous opinion of colonial witnesses that settlers could repay loans of £60 each by annual instalments. If the evidence was sound, it would be more economical to send emigrants to colonies under British jurisdiction where collection could be enforced rather than to foreign countries where the British government would have to write off its expenditure. Yet McCulloch had doubts about the evidence: 'In our view of the case, under the uncertainty of eventual repayment, it remains . . . a very secondary point, what precise direction the stream shall take.'[40]

While McCulloch questioned the practicality of colonization as outlined by the Emigration Committees, he did not dispute the appropriateness of emigration. He was less worried about expenses than Horton. A scheme involving repayment by settlers was not essential except to excuse the location of those settlers in British colonies. Emigration was a subject so momentous that it outweighed in potential consequences the cause or result of any war Britain ever fought 'except perhaps the last'.[41] Over-populated and under-nourished Ireland threatened to bring the rest of the British Isles down to its level. 'The Irish . . . have practically decided, that emigrate they must,—the only question for us to determine, is, whether it shall be to England or America.'[42] The urgency of the problem warranted heavy expenditure. Although Horton's desire to find the least expensive system was laudable, McCulloch believed

[39] *Edinburgh Review*, Dec. 1826, p. 65.
[40] Ibid., Jan. 1828, p. 216. See also W.H.P., McCulloch to Horton, 25 May 1829.
[41] Ibid., p. 212.
[42] Ibid., p. 236.

that the simplest and soundest policy would place the full burden on the government. If an article in the *Edinburgh Review* would help the cause, he was willing to write it.[43] In fact he wrote two long reviews in which he made very positive assertions of his respect for the work of the Emigration Committees.

It was important to Horton to have the backing of men like McCulloch. Horton had pretensions as a political economist and the Emigration Reports were purportedly based on scientific principles. If the leading economists approved these principles, then Horton could demand greater attention from Parliament for his ideas. He corresponded with Malthus, Senior, James Mill, J. R. McCulloch, Colonel Torrens, Archbishop Whately, Thomas Tooke, and James Pennington. His enthusiasm for his subject led him inevitably to exaggerate whatever unanimity existed. He was capable of taking adhesion as positive when it was conditional and when he had not accepted the conditions. 'I have with me all, or almost all, the Political Economists, theoretical and practical,' he boasted.[44] If he meant that these men were confident that his plan of colonization would work, he was guilty of invention. If he meant that they agreed that emigration could bring desirable temporary relief, he did not misrepresent the truth. His contention that settlers would be able to pay back their debts was viewed with scepticism. His single-minded advocacy of emigration was distrusted. He met with the repeated objection that emigration would not work as an isolated measure and that he had not given enough consideration to the reforms that should accompany it. Yet to say that the economists lacked enthusiasm for Horton's work would not reflect the positive manner in which several of them took up the cause. McCulloch's articles in the *Edinburgh Review*, Senior's draft bill of 1831 and his work as Poor Law Commissioner, Torrens's contribution to the Emigration Committee, and Whately's recommendations as chairman of the Irish Poor Laws Commission in 1833 demonstrated the warmth of their belief that assisted emigration could be workable and beneficial.

[43] W.H.P., McCulloch to Horton, 21 Sept. 1826; *Edinburgh Review*, Dec. 1826, pp. 49–74, and Jan. 1828, pp. 204–42.
[44] W.H.P., Horton to Peel [1826?]. See also Horton to Tennant, 22 Apr. 1831.

IX

THE RESPONSE OF
CABINET MINISTERS

In a notebook in which the pages were divided into two columns headed 'Vituperation' and 'Compensation' Wilmot Horton kept a careful record of the abuse and praise that he attracted as an emigration enthusiast. The most painful cuts were those inflicted by his friends. 'As long as it was only a *hobby*,' Horton was told, 'it was bad enough, because it subjected you to ridicule; but it is become now the one engrossing topic.'[1] Another man might have dismissed such a remark; Horton preserved it. When he lost his initial conviction that his views would readily win acceptance he began to take a perverse pleasure in calling attention to the hostility and indifference with which he was confronted. 'I have heard that men of high reputation have expressed their regret "that I would continue to bore the House of Commons with my absurd opinions",' he wrote to Poulett Thomson.[2] No ministry ever took his schemes seriously, he complained; his ideas were ridiculed because they were new and apparently speculative.

You will tell me that nobody reads my Publications, or cares about them—Undoubtedly—The manner in which Parliament, the Government, the Public Press have hitherto treated me has prejudiced me in no small degree, but . . . the day *may arrive* when as much unmerited Praise may be poured over me as has been poured of apathy and contempt.[3]

In constantly returning to this theme, in repeatedly stating that he knew that no one had the patience to hear him out, Horton created the impression that emigration questions were not held to be important by ministers of the crown. One cannot read Horton's pamphlets and speeches on emigration after 1827 without beginning to believe what he said: that all of his enthusiasm was answered by

---

[1] W.H.P., Notebook, volume no. 63.
[2] *Causes and Remedies of Pauperism. First Series*, p. 12.
[3] W.H.P., Horton to Sir James Macdonald, 4 Sept. 1830.

one great yawn. E. G. Wakefield's followers reinforced this picture. Horton's empty speeches and tedious pamphlets, they said, drove men to loathe the mere mention of the word emigration. 'Let him but drop the question—let him emigrate to Canada, only for a year—and the public aversion to the subject, caused and still nourished by his fantastic tricks, will be conquered.'[4]

After reading this it comes as a surprise to discover that Horton held the respect of the most powerful men in the Tory party. Lord Melbourne might have thought Horton 'a particularly silly fellow', but that was not an opinion shared by Bathurst, Goderich, Wellington, or Peel.[5] In Bathurst's judgement, Horton had proved his talent in the Colonial Office and deserved promotion. Horton's emigration activities did not reduce him in the esteem of his superiors. Although he was never offered the position that he most wanted, the Irish Secretaryship, the denial of this office was dictated by his pamphleteering on the Catholic question and not by his enthusiasm for the subject of emigration. Horton, it was decided, had placed Ireland out of bounds to himself, but other offices were open to him. He was offered the vice-presidency of the Board of Trade by Goderich in 1827; and in 1828 Wellington approached him with the intention of bringing him into the Cabinet. The Tories remained friendly towards Horton to the end of their regime. Nor did the advent of the Whigs close doors to him. 'Had I been in Parliament,' he wrote to his father after the formation of the Grey ministry, 'the chances would have been a thousand to one in favor of my having been offered office by the present Government.'[6] As it was, the Whig administration provided him with a knighthood and the governorship of Ceylon in 1831.

Horton claimed that financial difficulties loomed large among the reasons that compelled him first to leave office and second to abandon his seat. Horton had lived beyond his means; he had made an impulsive and imprudent purchase of an estate in the village of Petersham next to Richmond Park. This estate, which he maintained

[4] *Spectator*, 15 Jan. 1831.

[5] Lord Melbourne's remark: Lloyd C. Sanders, ed., *Lord Melbourne's Papers* (London, 1889), p. 376. Bathurst's assessment: B.M. Loan 57/59, Bathurst to Hay, 14 Apr. 1827. The Irish secretaryship: W.H.P., Horton to Littleton, 8 Nov. 1827; Hatherton Correspondence, Horton to Littleton, 22, 27, 30 Nov. 1827, 24 Sept. 1834, and Littleton to Horton, Nov. 1827. The Board of Trade: W.H.P., Horton to Huskisson, 5 Dec. 1827; Jones, 'Wilmot Horton', p. 87. Wellington's overture: W.H.P., Statement by Horton, 6 July 1828; *Journal of Mrs. Arbuthnot*, ii. 190.

[6] W.H.P., Horton to father, 26 Nov. 1830.

as a London home in addition to a town house in Montague Street, was a millstone round his neck until he disposed of it.[7] His own impecuniousness and his want of a generous father or benefactor made the likelihood of his gaining re-election after 1826 dim. Newcastle-under-Lyme, Horton's constituency, was an expensive borough in which to campaign. It had cost Horton 6,000 guineas to win election there in 1818.[8] The borough had been controlled by a coalition between the Corporation and the principal landlord, Earl Gower, the Second Marquis of Stafford. Without the ballots cast by the tenants of Earl Gower and the towhead voters created by the Corporation, Horton could not have been elected. In the 1820s, however, Gower began to extricate himself, selling property on which he had formerly tolerated large arrears in rent. At the same time the borough's electorate was becoming too large to manage. By adding names to the rolls the Corporation had secured victories for Horton in the past, but the accumulative effect of this practice was to raise the cost of purchasing a majority to a prohibitive level.

Horton was not a popular candidate in Newcastle. He made no effort to cultivate the favour of his constituents between elections. His association with the Gower-Corporation machine and his firm stand in favour of Catholic emancipation aroused the antagonism of the independent voter. In 1826 Horton avoided a contest and held on to his seat, but he knew that his chances for re-election were slight. For that reason he hesitated to accept the vice-presidency of the Board of Trade in 1827; he dared not vacate his seat to seek the approval of his constituents as the practice required.[9] Yet there were other considerations that led him to turn down the vice-presidency of the Board of Trade. Re-election at Newcastle was not the only way for him to extend his parliamentary life. Lord Goderich offered him the riding of Hastings which could have been purchased for £1,000. Possibly this modest sum exceeded Horton's means; more likely, he did not want the appointment badly enough to spend anything. Horton professed to see some advantage in going out of office. He wanted to follow an independent line on three public issues, the slave trade, Catholic emancipation, and emigration. Had he remained

---

[7] Jones, 'Wilmot Horton', pp. 34–5; W.H.P., Chad to Horton, 22 July 1826.

[8] W.H.P., Horton to Goderich, 18 Oct. 1827; Hardy, 'The Downfall of the Gower Interest', pp. 293–4.

[9] Add. MSS. 38751, Horton to Huskisson, 27 Oct. 1827; W.H.P., Statement by Horton, 6 July 1828, and Horton to Goderich, 18 Oct. 1827.

in the government his freedom to express his opinions on these subjects would have been inhibited; 'I therefore relinquished office voluntarily.'[10] In the expectation that Horton would accept a promotion, Huskisson had offered the Colonial Office under-secretaryship to E. G. G. Stanley. Horton brooded over his alternatives for three months with both Huskisson and Goderich showing unusual consideration for his predilection. In late October 1827 he decided to retire from the Colonial Office on 5 January 1828. In early December he advised Goderich that he would not take the vice-presidency of the Board of Trade. By coincidence, he left office three days before the Goderich government collapsed.

If Horton had conducted himself in a different manner he would have come closer to achieving high office. Lord Bathurst thought that he had done himself much harm and 'given persons of abilities very inferior to his, opportunities of undervaluing him, by not having stuck to the duties of his Official table'.[11] He would have been better advised to have worked methodically at Colonial Office business without attempting to attract distinction by doing anything uncommon. Horton, nevertheless, enjoyed Bathurst's respect and received friendly counsel from him from time to time. In his criticism of Horton's activities, Bathurst was referring to publications on Catholic emancipation, and not to the promotion of emigration.

Other ministers also appreciated Horton's abilities. Peel valued him as a House of Commons speaker and urged Wellington to bring him into the Cabinet for that reason. After Horton gave up his seat in 1830, Peel wrote him a friendly letter for which there was no obvious motive other than respect: 'I think it a great reflection on the Constituent Body of this Country, and a great misfortune to the public, that you are *allowed* to be out of Parliament.'[12] Lord Goderich held Horton in high regard. If he failed to find a position satisfactory to him in the government that he formed after Canning's death, it was not for want of a desire to do so.[13] In 1830 Goderich made some

[10] Statement by Horton, 6 July 1828; Add MSS. 38751, Horton to Huskisson, 27 Oct. 1827; W.H.P., Huskisson to Horton, 6 Dec. 1827.

[11] B.M. Loan 57/59, Bathurst to Hay, 24 Dec. 1828.

[12] W.H.P., Peel to Horton, 5 Sept. 1830. For Peel's desire to have Horton in Wellington's Cabinet: *Journal of Mrs. Arbuthnot*, ii. 190.

[13] B.M. Loan 57/59, Bathurst to Hay, 14 Apr. 1827; Louis J. Jennings, ed., *The Croker Papers*, i (London, 1884), 388; W.H.P., Goderich to Horton, 24 July 1830, and Horton to Goderich, 18 Jan. 1831.

effort to keep him in the House of Commons and in 1831 he was directly responsible for Horton's appointment as Governor of Ceylon.

One should not underestimate Wilmot Horton. His intense conviction that he had discovered the panacea for the nation's ills makes him an easy target. He tackled his subject with more academic zeal than pragmatic sense, yet he was treated with greater seriousness at the time than he has been in retrospect. No one could have predicted that his political life was over when he left the Colonial Office in 1828. He left of his own accord, for his own highly complex reasons. The most powerful political figures in the country still considered him cabinet material. His emigration speeches gave them no cause to suspect his judgement. Indeed, he had been encouraged to take up the cause of emigration. He had not been the only member of the government concerned with the subject; nor had the Emigration Committees been created simply to indulge his eccentricities.

Yet Horton was destined for disappointment. He did not think that emigration would be effective as a partial or piecemeal measure. It would have to involve hundreds of thousands of individuals and millions of pounds. His reasoning was sound. If assisted emigration was to be the means of a serious attack on pauperism, then a programme on the scale that Horton projected would be necessary. But it was possible for men to speak of emigration as a radical cure for pauperism while envisaging a very modest role for the government to play. Many hoped that emigration could be promoted without great cost. Even if it was not likely to make a large dint in Britain's pauper problem, it could provide a critical release of tension. Fear of lower-class unrest was an underlying fact of life in the early nineteenth century. For this reason the Liverpool Cabinet was prepared to endorse emigration measures of modest expense and consequence. For this reason, Horton was given encouragement, even though the Cabinet was not prepared to go beyond a small-scale test of his ideas.

None of the Cabinet ministers was over-impressed by the support that Horton claimed to have from the political economists. 'I cannot help the big wigs you bring forward,' wrote Frederick Robinson, later Lord Goderich; 'They look at it solely in the abstract and I could not give a farthing for McCulloch's opinion on Ireland.'[14] Of course, Robinson was quite capable of citing the economists when it suited his purpose. He did not maintain the same lofty disregard for

[14] W.H.P., F. Robinson to Horton, 25 Mar. 1826.

science affected by some of his colleagues. But very few principles of political economy were firmly established and it was possible to quote the economists both for and against Horton.

Robinson did not believe that the population of England was redundant. There might be local pockets of unemployment, but in the nation as a whole there was no excess of labour. The colonies held out no attractions to the English who were comfortable at home. Only the idle would emigrate: 'whatever we might gain by getting rid of them, the Colony would lose by acquiring them.'[15] Ireland, Robinson admitted, presented a different problem. Here the pressure of population was perfectly evident. But no conceivable private or public effort could transport enough people from Ireland to make more than a temporary hole in the total number. Robinson had read his Malthus, and he subscribed to the vacuum theory which others had derived from the same source. As a consequence, he did not consider emigration as a particularly promising cure for Great Britain's domestic ills.

Yet with all of his reservations about emigration as a measure of relief for England and Ireland, Robinson looked for benefits from it. A carefully executed programme on a limited scale might help the people of selected localities and certainly would benefit the colonies to which settlers were sent. 'It is not therefore with me so much a question of principle as one of degree.'[16] Government-sponsored emigration could be justified simply as a measure to strengthen an infant colony with resources of great potential. When Chancellor of the Exchequer, Frederick Robinson had said that the government might be advised to pay a large part or even all of the cost according to the circumstances. He had expressed the strongest disapproval of the financial arrangements that Horton advocated. A direct government grant, in his eyes, was infinitely preferable to any scheme of government-guaranteed annuities which were to be repaid by Irish landlords. In March 1826 Robinson summarized his ideas in a letter to Horton:[17]

If Emigration be carried on upon such a scale as to make any . . . impression upon the mass of the people of Ireland, it would be too unwieldly to manage . . . if on a scale to be manageable in the Colonies, it would be too small to relieve Ireland. I say, therefore, let it be confined to a gradual extension of the population in the Colonies and let the Govern't assist in

[15] W.H.P., F. Robinson to Horton, 25 Mar. 1826.
[16] Ibid.   [17] Ibid.

the work: but let the assistance be direct and simple, not complicated & complex. Give up all notion of making *great holes* in your population . . . the holes would necessarily be filled up with alarming rapidity.

These views were expressed by other members of the government. Lord Palmerston, Henry Goulburn, and Robert Peel expressed themselves in terms almost identical to those used by Robinson. 'Emigration,' said Peel, 'is an excellent thing for colonies like the North American Colonies—is worthy of encouragement for their sake—but it will never answer to this Country—with the mere view of diminishing an excessive population.'[18] 'I confess', Palmerston wrote, 'that I cannot bring my mind to see the emigration measure in any other light than that of a Colonial Question, and as such its adoption . . . would certainly be highly advantageous.'[19] Emigration, Goulburn thought, might be beneficial to the Colonies, but it would do nothing for Ireland. Agreement went beyond this basic assessment. Like Robinson, Peel distrusted the involved financial arrangements that Horton proposed. If the government were to administer a scheme of emigration and settlement, it should bear the whole charge. To expect repayment from settlers would not be realistic. To attempt to work in conjunction with parish authorities would be impractical. 'I am quite sure,' Peel told Horton, 'that a simple Plan—though more expensive is the preferable one—a plan I mean in which there was one single superintending authority bound down by no contracts with local authorities and looking rather to colonial advantages than to the relief of the Mother Country.'[20]

In the spring of 1826 Robinson and Peel, the Chancellor of the Exchequer and the Home Secretary, were of one mind on the subject of emigration. They were unimpressed by Horton's reasoning and arithmetic, but they were not indifferent to his work. In a friendly yet straightforward manner they told him to develop a less ambitious and more feasible plan. As long as the number of emigrants was limited, the government could safely undertake the bulk of the expense: this would be preferable to the system of annuities, guarantees, poor rates and quit rents that Horton described. The experiments of 1823 and 1825 were seen as sound examples to follow. If the primary objectives were to bolster the defence and to

[18] W.H.P., Peel to Horton, 12 July 1826.
[19] W.H.P., Palmerston to Horton, 13 Sept. 1826. For a reference to Goulburn's viewpoint see W.H.P., Horton to Peel, 1827?.
[20] Peel to Horton, 12 July 1826.

stimulate the economy of a North American colony, then an expenditure of £20 per person would not be too high. The Prime Minister, Lord Liverpool, supported liberal advances for emigration.[21] Although Horton's comprehensive scheme was not warmly entertained, the Cabinet was sympathetic to the idea of government-sponsored emigration.

The evidence amassed by the Select Committee of 1826 deeply impressed Robinson. 'I am sure,' he told Horton, 'some gov't plan might be adopted with great relief to expenditure at home, & great benefit, commercial and political, to our colonies abroad.'[22] The findings of the Committee convinced Goderich that emigration could improve conditions in depressed English parishes as well as in Ireland and in Scotland. His reservations respecting Horton's project, however, remained strong: to guarantee loans that Irish landlords and emigrant settlers were to repay would invite disaster; an open-ended, self-perpetuating scheme such as Horton proposed would involve risks that no government should take. The question was where to find a fund to support a government-directed system. Robinson provided an answer in his own plan which he circulated among Cabinet ministers in August 1826. 'When you read it . . .,' he admonished Peel, 'pray forget that Emigration is one of the children of Wilmot's ardent imagination.'[23]

Frederick Robinson's plan called for modifications in the Corn Laws to produce new revenues which could be used for emigration purposes. Robinson, who accepted liberal economic doctrine, thought the promotion of emigration could be combined with a move to open up the grain trade. If the prohibition on imports of barley, oats, rye, peas, and beans were lifted and if wheat were admitted at duties on a sliding scale, an estimated additional revenue of £600,000 would be produced.[24] This could be used for emigration purposes: 50 per cent for Ireland, 33 per cent for England, and 17 per cent for Scotland. The government would pay three-quarters of the costs and parishes or individuals one-quarter. Irish parishes would need to be empowered by law to raise their share by assessment. The total sum available for emigration would be £800,000

[21] B.M. Loan 57/15, Liverpool to Bathurst, 15 May 182[3].
[22] W.H.P., Frederick Robinson to Horton, 28 Aug. 1826.
[23] Add. MSS. 40389, Robinson to Peel, 17 Sept. 1826.
[24] B.M. Loan 57/23, Robinson memorandum 'Suggestions on Emigration and the Corn Laws'. See W. D. Jones, *'Prosperity Robinson', The Life Viscount Goderich 1782–1859* (New York, 1967), p. 127.

which would remove 8,000 families or 40,000 individuals at the Emigration Committee's figure of £100 per family. British North America would take an annual influx of 4,000 families, the Cape of Good Hope 500, and New South Wales 3,500. This emigration system, Robinson concluded, would be one of the most powerful means of defence which England could provide its colonies; at the same time the establishment of flourishing settlements would lead to an increased demand for British shipping and manufactures.

Wilmot Horton could never have conceived anything so grand and yet so simple. Indeed, one could say of Horton the least complicated solution was always the last to occur to him. His great fault was that in attempting to anticipate every objection, his solutions became too elaborate. The great fault in Robinson's plan was that it failed to anticipate the most obvious objection, the objection immediately raised by the conservative Tories in the Cabinet. 'I cannot admire your project,' Lord Bathurst informed Robinson. 'It proposes to mix the two Questions of Corn Laws and Emigration together. I doubt the Policy of this.'[25] What disturbed Bathurst was the suggestion that the Corn Laws might be used to raise revenue. A duty that brought in revenue would not protect British agriculture. If emigration meant the wholesale importation of foreign grain, then Bathurst would be opposed to both measures. His attitude represented that of the Duke of Wellington and other old-school Tories. The spectre of free trade in Robinson's plan turned them against it. As a result, the plan was rejected by the Cabinet and abandoned by its author.

Bathurst and the Duke were willing to discuss emigration as a separate measure. In over a decade as colonial secretary Bathurst had taken responsibility for the settlement of several thousand emigrants in the colonies. His attention had always been concentrated on the colonial rather than the domestic benefits of emigration. He felt little confidence that either the landed interest or the country as a whole gained much by the transportation of paupers to the colonies. He would concede that only a few agricultural districts in England might find an emigration project advantageous.[26] The issue did not elicit from him a very profound response, either in a positive or in a

---

[25] B.M. Loan 57/19, Bathurst's memorandum to F. Robinson; W.H.P., Bathurst's minute on emigration, Oct. 1826, and Palmerston to Horton, 13 Sept. 1826.
[26] Bathurst's memorandum to Robinson.

negative sense. He tolerated the emigration activities of his Under-Secretary, never protesting against them but never displaying much earnest interest in them.

The Duke of Wellington set out his ideas on emigration with characteristic certainty. Redundancy of population was not the cause of the nation's ills and emigration was not the answer. Nor was emigration necessary for the defence of the North American colonies or even desirable for permanent British interests there. Canadians, Nova Scotians, and New Brunswickers were already numerous enough to withstand, with the assistance of the mother country, an attack by the democratic armies of the United States. If there were more colonists, they would begin to produce their own manufactured articles in competition with the United Kingdom, and then they would become impatient with rule from overseas. Yet, Wellington said, 'I do believe that it is expedient to encourage emigration from each of the United Kingdoms by public authority, and with the aid of public money.'[27]

Wellington's vision of empire was an eighteenth-century one. On the other hand, his opinion of the Poor Laws was remarkably similar to that of the Whig economist, Nassau Senior. The real cause of England's troubles, Wellington stated, was that over-population had been encouraged by abuses in the administration of the Poor Laws; reform of the Poor Laws was the only solution. He recognized an excess of population in Ireland, and he attributed this to the potato culture and to minute subdivision of land. The habits of the Irish country labourer had to be changed by laws which would force him to give up his garden to seek remunerative employment. In England Wellington would abolish the system of hiring out labourers by parishes and he would pay paupers working under the parish over-seer in kind and not in money. In Ireland he would compel the pay-ment of rent for land in cash. He believed that legislation of this nature would accomplish far more than the most extensive system of emigration. Yet a programme of government-assisted emigration would make the necessary measures more palatable. In conjunction with more fundamental remedies, the promotion of emigration made sense and government expenditure for this purpose could be justified.[28]

---

[27] *Despatches, Correspondence and Memoranda of the Duke of Wellington* (Last Series), iii, Wellington to F. Robinson, 20 Oct. 1826, p. 432.
[28] Ibid., p. 437.

Wilmot Horton did not make any special effort to gain Wellington's support for his plans. Robinson and Peel were the men who he hoped would throw their weight behind him. They were the Cabinet ministers who were most closely associated with his projects. On Peel's initiative and with Robinson's consent preparations were made for a large emigration in 1827.[29] Parliament voted £10,000 to send an agent to North America to select suitable places for settlements and to make other arrangements. Peel had raised the question of the need for advance surveys early in December 1826. His suggestion had come during the interval between the report of the Emigration Committee in 1826 and the resurrection of the Committee in 1827 and at the end of a year of exceptional distress which had seen a revival of Luddite rioting. Through his reading of the Committee's minutes of evidence for 1826 and some supplementary material that Horton had given him, Peel perceived that nobody knew how much land was immediately available for colonization in British North America.

This was information which it was imperative to obtain without delay. If no land was fit for settlement then some should be prepared. Roads should be built and huts thrown up in anticipation of the arrival of emigrants. When Peel recommended these steps to Wilmot Horton, his expectation that the government would undertake some scheme of emigration was obviously very real. This does not mean that he had surrendered to the logic of Horton's arguments. The weavers of Glasgow were waiting for an answer to their petitions for assistance to go to Canada; Peel was willing to give them a favourable reply. While he could accede to government sponsorship of a special group for special reasons, he still distrusted Horton's larger objective of providing extensive facilities for English parishes and Irish landlords.

Lieutenant-Colonel Francis Cockburn, the former superintendent of the Rideau Settlement, was given the task of going to the colonies to make arrangements for the reception of emigrants.[30] If the nomination had been in Horton's hands alone, Cockburn would not have been a first choice. Horton and Cockburn had had strong differences of opinion during the negotiations for the sale of crown

[29] Add. MSS. 40390, Horton to Peel, 24 Dec. 1826; C.O. 324/97, Horton to Sir George Cockburn, 27 Mar. 1827; W.H.P., Peel to Horton, 6 Dec. 1826.

[30] C.O. 384/17 F. Cockburn to Horton, 18 Dec. 1826; Add. MSS. 40385, Horton to Peel, 8 Mar. 1826.

reserves to the Canada Company. Yet Cockburn was well qualified by experience for the present job. He was, moreover, known to Peel who earlier in the year had considered him as a possible Lieutenant-Governor of the Isle of Wight. These circumstances and the haste with which the decision was taken left Horton with little alternative but to acquiesce in Cockburn's appointment. The resolution to send a one-man mission to North America had been a resolution of the Cabinet, not just of the Colonial Office; the selection of Colonel Cockburn underlines this fact.

Cockburn spent the spring and summer of 1827 in British North America, visiting the provincial capitals and examining land records.[31] He worked on the assumption that 10,000 persons or 2,000 families would be transported in the first year. If each family were to receive 100 acres then 300,000 acres would be required to leave a safe margin. The scale of this undertaking was to be about five times greater than the emigration conducted by Peter Robinson in 1825. The total expense, if the project had been carried out, would have been £200,000. In 1825 the Cabinet had asked Parliament for £30,000 to cover all of the expenses of the Irish emigration of that year. In 1827 it asked for £10,000 just for Cockburn's advance mission. Of course Cockburn was warned not to spend anything on the purchase of rations or the building of storehouses until the last moment in case the emigration should not take place. The government never did commit itself publicly to the project and there was never any certainty that it would be carried out. The dispatch of Cockburn to North America must, nevertheless, be taken as a sign of serious intention.

There remained a great distance between the kind of scheme that the Cabinet would support and the action recommended by Horton and the Emigration Committee. Horton wanted to create for emigration self-regulating machinery that would operate over a long period of time. Frederick Robinson, the Chancellor of the Exchequer, insisted that projects of assisted emigration should be undertaken on the merits of each separate case. The idea that emigration was an answer to the population problems of the United Kingdom was too visionary to move the Cabinet. Ministers would have been more impressed if Horton had argued that emigration could alleviate distress in specific instances while bringing benefit to the colonies.

---

[31] C.O. 384/17, F. Cockburn to Horton, 16 Dec. 1826, and 17 Sept. 1827; C.O. 324/97, Horton to F. Cockburn, 7 Feb. 1827.

Emigration could be seen as an indispensable safety-valve without being considered a fundamental answer to over-population. The Liverpool Cabinet was prepared to sanction expenditure for an immediate project of emigration, but it was not going to saddle the public with a permanent and open-ended responsibility for a national system.

These attitudes remained constant from the time the question arose until Lord Liverpool stepped down. Horton was reluctant to accept them as final, but by April 1827 much of his optimism had been crushed. In early March he had stated in a memorandum to the Emigration Committee that the simplest means by which the government could guarantee an emigration loan would be to use the sinking fund. Peel and Robinson reacted with alarm. Robinson had strong objections to a government guarantee of any form.[32] The idea of abusing the sinking fund in the manner which Horton suggested was intolerable. That a person holding an important office in the government should have hinted that the sinking fund was not inviolate was regrettable. 'It is in vain to make a distinction between the Chairman of a Committee, and an Under-Secretary of State,' Peel had declared. 'How can an Under-Secretary of State in a matter immediately relating to his own Department strip himself of his *official* capacity?'[33] Peel asked the Chancellor of the Exchequer to make a plain statement to the Emigration Committee of the limits of the government's willingness to give or to advance money. It was important not to raise false hopes.

The likelihood that the government would refuse a collateral guarantee had never entered into Horton's calculations. 'What was it expected that the Committee could recommend?'[34] If these were the ground rules, then his efforts as chairman of the Emigration Committees were futile. He told Robinson on 10 March 1827 that he intended to put an end to the Committee immediately. Although this threat was not carried out, Horton's disillusionment with the government was permanent. He began to concentrate his search for support outside the government, relaxing his expectation that Peel and Robinson could be converted. It appeared to him that the government had intended from the beginning to refuse either a grant of money or a guarantee. 'I regret', he wrote in a letter which may never

[32] Add. MSS. 40392, Robinson to Peel, 12 Mar. 1827.
[33] Ibid., Peel to Robinson, 12 Mar. 1827.
[34] W.H.P., Horton to Robinson, 10 Mar. 1827.

have been sent, 'that the Committee was granted at all, and personally regret that I had anything whatever to do with it.'[35]

If Horton recovered from his despondency, it was not because he had received any indication that the attitude of the Cabinet would change. He persevered with the Emigration Committee in spite of a realization that the present government was unlikely to adopt his recommendations. After March 1827 he directed his arguments at the public. Outside the Cabinet, outside the House of Commons, existed an audience whose opinion could be decisive.[36] This audience might be persuaded by the final report of the Emigration Committee even if Peel and Robinson were not. It was this consideration that subsequently inspired him. Education of the public, however, was a larger task than education of the public's leaders; his goal retreated into the distance. For Horton theoretical issues began to take precedence over immediate measures.

There were two questions at stake in the spring of 1827. Only one of them had been dismissed: a government guarantee for an emigration loan to operate over a series of years had been ruled out. A direct grant for an emigration of weavers was still under consideration. On 3 May Horton wrote to Cockburn to explain that a decision had not yet been made. 'I will . . . say,' he added, 'that the bias of my mind is that something will be done, but that bias must not be construed to sanction any sort of expense.'[37] At root of Horton's uncertainty was the recent reconstruction of the Cabinet. On 17 February a stroke had abruptly ended Lord Liverpool's political life. Without his leadership the coalition he had held together in spite of deep divisions on the Catholic question, the Corn Laws, and Foreign Policy had come apart. No one had been able to carry on in Liverpool's place. Weeks of manoeuvre had followed before Canning had formed a new Cabinet. Six of the old ministers including Peel, Wellington, and Bathurst had resigned, and Canning had been forced to turn to the Whigs for support. It was for the decision of a vastly altered Cabinet that Horton waited when he wrote to Cockburn in early May.

All unfinished business is jeopardized by the decease of an administration. No decision on an emigration grant had been made before Lord Liverpool's retirement. Now Peel had left the Cabinet. It had been with Peel's support and in part on his initiative that pre-

[35] W.H.P., Horton to ?, no date. See also Horton to Peel, 9 Mar. 1827.

[36] C.O. 324/97, Horton to Drummond, 31 Aug. 1827; *Hansard*, 1828, xix, col. 1503.

[37] Ibid., Horton to F. Cockburn, 3 May 1827.

parations for an emigration of weavers had been carried as far as they were. Had he continued in the government he could not have ignored a project for which he already bore responsibility. Sturges Bourne who replaced Peel at the Home Office did not treat the emigration issue lightly but he was not involved in this particular project and had no reason to champion it.[38] Peel's departure, Canning's promotion, and Robinson's move from the Exchequer to the Colonial Office made the new Cabinet less friendly to emigration than its preccessor. Robinson, who became Lord Goderich when he accepted the secretaryship of the Colonial Office and the leadership of the House of Lords, was no longer in a position to sanction direct expenditure for emigration. Any appeal for money went directly to Canning who acted as his own Chancellor of the Exchequer as well as First Lord of the Treasury. The hands that drew the strings of the public purse after April 1827 belonged to a man who took no interest in the question of emigration. The whole subject was beneath Canning's consideration; he refused to form an opinion on it. He could not be persuaded to read the Select Committee's Report.[39] Emigration had been given serious attention by Lord Liverpool; it was depreciated by Canning. It is not surprising that expectation of government help for weavers dissolved during Canning's administration.

If Lord Liverpool had remained in good health, the anticipated emigration of Glasgow weavers might have been carried out. The disposition of his administration cannot be judged by the inactivity of its successor. A grant towards emigration in 1827 would scarcely have been an innovation. The government had sent 3,500 emigrants to the Cape of Good Hope in 1819–20, 2,700 to Canada in 1820–1, 900 to Canada and the Cape in 1823, and 2,000 to Canada in 1825. A special set of circumstances motivated the government to act in each instance. Nevertheless, there was in these ventures an emerging pattern of regular government expenditure on emigration. If a grant had been made in 1827, the precedents for government involvement in future emigrations would have been well established. It is not inconceivable that Liverpool's Cabinet would have tried to finish what it began when it sent Colonel Cockburn to North America.

For a few weeks after Canning became Prime Minister Horton

[38] W.H.P., Sturges Bourne to Horton, 25 June 1827: 'I agree in all of your general principles and in most of the practical applications of them.'
[39] W.H.P., Granville to Horton, 20 Nov. 1826; Horton to F. Cockburn, 3 May 1827.

expected a positive decision to grant assistance to emigrant weavers. The Emigration Committee was aware of the extreme hardship that weavers had faced since wages had fallen dramatically in 1826. In early April 1827 the Committee produced a short report of seven pages supporting the petitions of weavers who wished to emigrate. If £25,000 from the London Relief Committee were matched by a parliamentary grant of double that size, assistance could be granted to 1,200 families. Canning, however, intervened personally to urge the Emigration Committee to withdraw its recommendations.[40] He had received reports of an improvement in the manufacturing districts. He claimed that there was no longer a shortage of employment and in these circumstances he did not think that a grant for emigration was justified. The Committee acquiesced. The question of a grant was dropped. By the end of May it was decided that nothing would be done.

The distress of the weavers was not the passing phenomenon that Canning portrayed. While wages of artisans generally rose in 1827–8, wages among textile workers continued to fall. During the boom period of 1824–5 the number of power looms had rapidly increased.[41] As a consequence, the skills of hand-loom weavers had been further depreciated and these people did not gain from the upward turn of the economy in 1827. Their condition was determined by a process more relentless than the fluctuations of the market. The decision not to assist weavers to emigrate was not excused by their true situation.

For Canning, an over-all improvement in wages was a pretext to say no to a measure in which he believed the government should not normally be involved. Yet in opposing a grant on these grounds he admitted by implication that there were circumstances in which government-sponsored emigration was warranted. Indeed, the value he placed on such measures was revealed by the praise he paid to the Emigration Committee which, he said, 'had kept the country through a period of peril in a state of tranquillity'.[42] The benefit could be best appreciated by those who remembered what had happened during earlier years of distress. This was as frank an explanation of the whole emigration inquiry as any Cabinet minister had given.

Horton, however, had pitifully little to show for the fifteen months

[40] *Hansard*, 1827, xvii, col. 927–30; C.O. 324/97, Horton to Smith, 25 May 1827. Horton asked the London Committee to consider granting money to re-purchase looms for weavers who had sold theirs in the expectation of emigrating.

[41] Gayer, Rostow, and Swartz, *Growth and Fluctuation*, p. 239.

[42] *Hansard*, 1827, xvii, col. 929.

that he spent on the Committees. The Cabinet neither accepted the larger proposals that had been set forth nor agreed to the limited expenditure that had been recommended on behalf of the weavers. Canning's death in August 1827 brought Lord Goderich into power briefly as first minister, but there was no noticeable change in attitude. Shortly before Wellington formed his Cabinet in January 1828, Horton left office.[43] As a private member from January 1828, until July 1830, he continued to press for action.

His experience outside government was as frustrating as it had been inside. Not once in two and a half years did Horton succeed in having a major motion put to a vote.[44] In June 1828 he asked the Commons to pledge itself to consider emigration and other measures of relief to Ireland early in the next session. Peel objected that such a procedure would be unparliamentary and Horton withdrew his motion. A year later his efforts to secure a committee of the whole on the state of the poor were similarly aborted. In 1830 a bill to permit parishes to mortgage poor rates reached second reading but died for lack of House of Commons time.

Cabinet ministers still treated Horton with deference. Peel took pains to assure the House of Commons that he did not underrate the importance of emigration. Both Peel and Huskisson publicly commended Horton for the ability and perserverence with which he had handled the subject.[45] Horton's plan to bring in a bill on parish emigration was greeted in a reserved but friendly manner. The impressive point was that the Cabinet continued to discuss the emigration question. Wellington's colleagues were not going to act in haste, but they made a pretence at least of moving towards the adoption of some plan of emigration. Sir George Murray, the Colonial Secretary, thought that Horton's schemes involved too much government interference; yet he spoke of emigration as the most effective means of alleviating pauperism and looked for an economical way to promote it.[46]

This was an attitude which members on both sides of the Commons could respect. In March 1828 Sir Francis Burdett, the Radical

[43] Horton's resignation was effective 5 Jan. 1828; Goderich resigned as Prime Minister on 8 Jan.

[44] *Hansard*, 1828, xviii, col. 1554, 1828, xix, cols. 1502–18, 1829, xxi, cols. 1719–41; and 1830 xxv, col. 783; *Causes and Remedies of Pauperism. Fourth Series*, p. 52; W.H.P., Horton to Peel, 4 June 1830, and Peel to Horton, 8 June 1830; Add. MSS., 40401, Horton to Peel, 7 July 1830, and Peel to Horton, 8 July 1830.

[45] *Hansard*, 1828, xviii, cols. 1555, 1557.   [46] Ibid., 1830–1, ii, col. 879.

spokesman, told the House that no issue was of greater importance than emigration; neither the question of free trade nor that of Catholic emancipation was more deserving of attention.[47] Yet Burdett reserved judgement on Horton's plan. Like Burdett, many members were alive to the potential value of sponsored emigration but mistrustful of the recommendations of the Emigration Reports. They would not endorse an expenditure of several million pounds; they were repelled by the suggestion that parishes should borrow money against the poor rates; they did not believe that repayment could be expected from emigrant settlers. Henry Bright, the member for Bristol who had called for a Committee on Emigration in 1825, had hoped that a more effective system would be discovered than that followed by Peter Robinson. He was disappointed by the results of the work of the Committee; a practical question had been dealt with too theoretically.[48]

While the possible advantages of emigration had attracted wide attention, interest was never translated into a public demand for a programme of heavy expenditure. Spending was resisted both by Radicals like Joseph Hume and by the country gentry. There was no precedent for the extensive use of public funds to correct social problems and liberal thought preached retrenchment rather than the reverse. Early on, Horton had been told by his Cabinet colleagues that the government would not assist in financing a measure extensive enough to answer the population problems of Great Britain. Emigration might relieve the distress of certain groups or communities, they said, but it could be justified as a national responsibility only if weight were given to the arguments that it contributed to imperial defence and that it created new markets for British trade overseas. Horton refused to limit his vision. He looked for a major attack upon the domestic problems of over-population, unemployment, and low wages. But he advanced his plans in an age in which governments and parliaments were incapable of responding to the great problem of poverty with anything but paltry and ineffective measures. Even if he were right, one of his contemporaries observed, 'it is enough that the public are not ripe to act'.[49] In this light Horton's ideas and the recommendations of the Emigration Committees were indeed theoretical and impractical.

[47] *Hansard*, 1828, xviii, col. 955.   [48] Ibid., 1827, xvi, col. 495.
[49] W.H.P., Sir James Macdonald to Horton, 5 Sept. 1830.

X

HORTON AND WAKEFIELD

HORTON'S failure by no means ended discussion of the emigration solution. Although few positive steps were taken and a growing transatlantic movement proceeded with little help from the public purse, the idea that emigration could reduce pauperism remained a respectable one. In years of social and economic disturbance it gained in credibility. Individuals and committees continued to press for government action while the promoters of private colonization ventures used the language of emigration enthusiasts to justify their projects.

When Lord Grey's Whig ministry was formed in the autumn of 1830, the rural south of England was agitated by the 'labourers last revolt' while the mood of workmen in northern manufacturing districts was belligerent. Fear of working-class violence, which brought on the Great Reform Bill, also produced more talk of assisted emigration.[1] In February 1831 Lord Howick, the new Under-Secretary in the Colonial Office and the son of the Prime Minister, brought a bill on parish emigration before Parliament.[2] Four months later the government created a commission of five to gather information on the feasibility of emigration to the British colonies. In the same year,

[1] On 24 June 1832, Sydney Smith wrote to Horton in Ceylon: 'The King is frightened at the state of the Country, so is the Queen and I believe the Tories will not come on; I am sure if they are wise (what a supposition!!!) they will not attempt it. The reform is all over and established; remains to be seen what it will effect. In the popular places the Common people seem inclined to choose men of property and character; you have a great triumph, I think, on the subject of Emigration; we all laughed at you, but we are now following your advice; don't be proud of this, for what shall we say of the advocate who cannot get heard when in the right? or being heard cannot convince. Eloquence is almost expected to sanction error, much more to establish truth.' See W.H.P.

[2] On Howick's bill: W.H.P., Horton to Page, 7 Mar. 1831, Horton to Goderich, 11 Apr. 1831, Horton to Richards, 2 Apr. 1831, Richards to Horton, 4 Apr. 1831, Howick to Horton, 22 Apr. 1831; Grey Papers, Horton to Howick, 20 Feb. 1831, enclosure; C.O. 43/43, Goderich to Colborne, 31 Oct. 1831; *Hansard*, 1830–1, ii, cols. 875–906. On the Emigration Commission made up of Howick, the Duke of Richmond, R. W. Hay, F. T. Baring, and H. Ellis: Cowan, pp. 97–8; *Canadian Archives Report*, 1935, p. 265; C.O. 385/6, Emigration Commissioners to Goderich, 15 Mar. 1832. On assisted emigration to Australia: Peter Burroughs, *Britain and Australia, 1831–1855: A Study in Imperial Relations and Crown Lands Administration* (Oxford, 1967), pp. 59–75.

the Treasury approved a plan of assisted emigration to Australia, financed by revenue raised in the colony. With this decision the extensive movement of later years of assisted emigration to Australia had its small beginnings. Howick's bill on parish emigration, on the other hand, did not reach second reading. In some respects, this bill was a revival of Horton's proposed legislation; but it retreated from the idea of pauper settlement and did not have his backing. Even in its less ambitious form the bill was given a cool reception by the country gentry and did not reach second reading before the dissolution of Parliament in April 1831. Howick let the question drop. An unprecedented movement of voluntary and unassisted emigrants in 1830 and 1831 undercut the arguments of those who wanted the government to encourage immigration to British North America; in March 1832 the Emigration Commissioners concluded that an official agency to stimulate emigration to British North America would be superfluous.

Yet the idea of parish-sponsored emigration did not die easily. Nassau Senior, the most energetic member of the Poor Law Commission of 1832-4, believed that an emigration measure would complement Poor Law reform. The Poor Law Amendment Act of 1834, passed virtually as Senior conceived it, included a clause enabling parishes to raise money for emigration.[3] On the eve of the enactment of the legislation Senior wrote to Horton in Ceylon: 'I find everywhere a general regret that you above all people are not here to assist in carrying your own views (for the views of the Commissioners & of the Bill are all, or nearly all, your views).'[4] This claim was exaggerated. The emigration provisions of the Poor Law Amendment Act were far less comprehensive than those advocated by the Emigration Committees. Moreover, the effect of the Act as a whole was to leave parish authorities with less incentive to organize the emigration of paupers. In 1835 about 5,000 assisted emigrants were sent from English parishes, but less than 10,000 went out during the following ten years. Senior, in his turn, began to see less value in the emigration remedy except as applied to Ireland.

It was with respect to Ireland that the vision of relief by emigration was most persistent. The Emigration Committee had emphasized

[3] Bowley, *Nassau Senior*, pp. 286-7. See also Cowan, p. 208; Winch, *Classical Political Economy*, p. 67; and Herman Merivale, *Lectures on Colonization and Colonies* (London, 1928), pp. 151-2.

[4] Hatherton Collection, Horton to Littleton, 24 Sept. 1834. Horton was quoting a letter from Senior dated 11 April.

the importance of Ireland in any attacks upon the population problems of Great Britain. They maintained that there would be no permanent or extensive advantage from any system of emigration which did not give priority to Ireland. This view was seconded by others in the succeeding decade.[5] In 1830 Spring Rice's Committee on the Irish Poor declared that the emigration remedy was most applicable to Ireland. Whately's Commission on the Irish Poor Laws, appointed in 1833, envisaged emigration as the principal means of offering relief to the able-bodied; the Imperial government, the Commission suggested, should bear half of the expense and local taxpayers and landlords the remainder. These recommendations did not lead to effective action. The Irish Poor Law Act of 1838 authorized the use of local funds for the emigration of evicted tenants but did not provide a possible means to do it.

The pattern was predictable. In the years before the Great Famine the emigration topic was revived repeatedly with no concrete results. Responsible ministers refused to believe that over-population could be eased by emigration. The government was unprepared for the consequences of the total collapse of the potato crop in 1846 which created suffering on a scale memorable among a people who had often known famine and which launched a spontaneous and unsponsored emigration of proportions never before experienced. In the years from 1847 to 1854, over 1·6 million Irish emigrated overseas, embarking in wretched circumstances and travelling under deplorable conditions.[6] The effect of this exodus in combination with a decline in marriages and births was to produce an absolute loss of population. A progression was reversed and Ireland became a country of shrinking numbers. The emigration that Horton considered necessary did take place, with the results that he predicted. If he had lived long enough, he would have considered himself vindicated. Yet he would have taken no satisfaction from the vision of such a massive and desperate movement carried out without government foresight or assistance or control or guidance.

[5] See Horton, *Ireland and Canada*, pp. 25–6; W. S. O'Brien, *Speech on Moving Resolutions Relative to Emigration in the House of Commons*, 2 June 1840 (London, 1840), pp. 7, 15; Nassau W. Senior, *Journals, Conversations and Essays Relating to Ireland*, i (London, 1868), 225–8; and Black, *Economic Thought and the Irish Question*, pp. 220–35.

[6] See D. V. Glass, 'Malthus and the Limitation of Population Growth', *Introduction to Malthus* (London, 1953), pp. 31–2; Marcus Hansen, *The Atlantic Migration, 1607–1860* (New York, 1961), pp. 246–61; O. MacDonagh, 'Emigration during the Famine', R. D. Edwards and T. D. Williams, eds., *The Great Famine* (Dublin, 1956), pp. 320–1.

When Horton died in 1841 the influence of Edward Gibbon Wakefield was at its height. In the Australian colonies particularly, imperial immigration and land settlement policy rested in no small way on the theories which Wakefield first published in 1829.[7] Many of those who had supported Horton in the 1820s were seduced by Wakefield's ideas in the 1830s. In this respect Wakefield was Horton's successor. Both men argued the advantage to Britain of developing her colonies through the export of excess population. Yet there was a subtle and important difference in their emphasis. The undeniable foundation of Horton's argument was a belief in the value of pauper emigration. The essential part of Wakefield's system was a theory about the ideal management of colonial lands.[8] He devoted far more attention to an analysis of conditions in the colonies, specifically in New South Wales, than to those in the home country. Economically and socially the colony suffered, he reasoned, because land was too easy to acquire. No one would work for wages if he could obtain land for himself. When land was cheap, there was a shortage of labour; capitalists could not employ their money profitably; settlement was dispersed and the possibility of developing a truly civilized way of life prohibited. All this could be corrected, Wakefield claimed, if land were sold for a sufficient price. A happy by-product of such a policy would be a fund which could be used to bring emigrants from Great Britain. This, he observed, would 'supply the desideratum, so anxiously sought by the Parliamentary Emigration Committee', a method of assisting pauper emigrants without any expense to the mother country.[9] Wakefield could have justified his concept of colonization without reference to the over-population of Great Britain. The relief of British unemployed was an important but not the central feature of his system.

When Wakefield's friends formed the National Colonization Society in 1830, they asked Horton to become a member. In their view, his backing was worth at least an attempt at flattery. Robert Gouger sent him a pamphlet on systematic colonization with the explanation that the author sought anonymity and that he considered

[7] See Burroughs, *Britain and Australia*, pp. 226–8.

[8] For recent discussion of Wakefieldian theory see Burroughs, pp. 12–34; and Winch *Classical Political Economy*, pp. 73–104.

[9] E. G. Wakefield, *A Letter from Sydney* (London, 1829), Appendix, p. iv. In a postscript to the *Letter* Wakefield suggested the application of his principles to the emigration of Chinese to Australia, indicating a greater interest in colonization than in pauper relief. See pp. 201–22.

his plan properly belonged to Horton 'through whose public exertions alone he was led to think on the subject'.[10] Horton chaired the first meeting of a provisional committee of the incipient society in February 1830 and he continued to participate in the affairs of the society until July. His association with the Wakefieldians, however, was not a pleasant one. He was unable to accept Wakefield's doctrines of sufficient price and concentrated settlement. He did not think that a very large fund could be raised through the sale of colonial land and he was convinced that a policy which made land difficult to acquire would discourage immigration. The possibility that members of the society were motivated by selfish and speculative considerations did not escape him.[11] He held firmly to the opinion that the British government should direct and control emigration and he opposed the idea that it should be managed by a private association. He had no sympathy for the Wakefieldian ambition to create a colony largely free of Colonial Office supervision. These were fundamental objections. Added to them was the apparent focus of Wakefieldian attention on Australia. If the National Colonization Society intended to restrict consideration to this continent, Horton argued that it should change its name to one which would suggest its limited objectives.

After an attempt to find common ground, Horton broke with the National Colonization Society. As a consequence, the Wakefieldians became his most unkind critics. Having failed to convert him, they depreciated him. His emigration experiments, they declared, were 'futile' and 'obnoxious'.[12] His theories were founded on not a single sound principle but were 'utterly unmeaning' and 'irrational'. His speeches were empty and his pamphlets tiresome. He was himself

---

[10] W.H.P., Gouger to Horton, 3 Feb. 1830. This letter and sixteen others from Horton's correspondence with members of the National Colonization Society have been published by Douglas Pike in 'Wilmot Horton and the National Colonization Society', *Historical Studies: Australia and New Zealand*, May 1957, pp. 205–10. Most of these letters and some others appear in Jones, 'Wilmot Horton', pp. 280–331.

[11] W.H.P., Horton to Howick, not sent, 18 Jan. 1831. In addition to the letters in Pike and Jones see Charles Tennant, *A letter to the Right Hon. Sir George Murray on Systematic Colonization* (London, 1830), pp. 39–52; Tennant, *Letters forming part of a Correspondence with Nassau William Senior* (London, 1831), pp. 42–3; Horton, *Causes and Remedies of Pauperism, Fourth Series. Explanation of Mr. Wilmot Horton's Bill*, pp. 95–6; Robbins, *Robert Torrens*, pp. 168–9; R.N. Ghosh, 'The Colonization Controversy: R. J. Wilmot-Horton and the Classical Economists', *Economica*, Nov. 1964, pp. 385–400.

[12] 'Mr. Wilmot Horton and the Mechanics' Institution', *Spectator*, 15 Jan. 1831, p. 58; 'P——— to Viscount Howick', *Spectator*, 5 Mar. 1831; p. 236; E. G. Wakefield, *England and America*, ii (London, 1833), 160.

'an insufferable political bore' who pursued great ends but was 'contemptible by his impotence, heedlessness, and inordinate vanity'. It had been a capital error, the Wakefieldians claimed, to have invited Horton to be a member of their society: 'His name alone was sufficient to throw disrepute on their cause.'[13] These judgements have generally been accepted at face value. Yet they were in no way objective and were far from fair.

There was a purpose in the Wakefieldian attacks on Horton and that was to puff up their own plan of colonization. They agreed with him on one point only, the importance of emigration. On the means of carrying it out, they differed entirely. His system, they charged, was ruinously expensive, totally ineffective, and distasteful to the lower class. It was merely a system of emigration intended to relieve ratepayers without consideration for the benefit of the emigrants or for the proper development of the colonies. It was, as Charles Buller put it, simply a plan for 'shovelling out paupers'.[14] These objections contained a sufficient measure of truth to give them lasting credibility.

In subsequent literature Horton's ideas have continued to be dismissed as grossly expensive. As a reflection of the opinion of Horton's contemporaries this is justified. Yet it should be observed that a question of values was involved. How great a burden was it assumed that taxpayers should bear? How deeply did the poverty of the unemployed trouble the consciences of those who were better off? It was estimated that Ireland contained a redundant population of about one million.[15] According to the Emigration Committee, this population could have been transplanted to the colonies for less than £20,000,000. With this expenditure the Committee believed it possible to eliminate Irish pauperism and to relieve England from the consequences of an influx of Irish labour. For the right cause the money would have been available. The compensation granted to West Indian planters after the abolition of slavery in 1833 was a free gift of £20,000,000.[16] The country had the capacity to pay for emigration on the scale that Horton projected. It was not for this reason that

[13] *Spectator*, 15 Jan. 1831, p. 58.
[14] *Hansard*, 1843, lxviii, col. 522.
[15] W.H.P., Horton to Place, Sept. 1830; *Parl. Pap.* 1826–7, v (550), 39.
[16] R. Coupland, *The British Anit-Slavery Movement* (London, 1933), p. 141. Horton did not fail to point this out in arguing for expenditure on emigration. R. W. Horton, *Correspondence between the Rt. Hon. Sir Robert Wilmot Horton Bart., and J. B. Robinson Esq., Chief Justice of Upper Canada* (London, 1839), pp. 11, 17.

his plan was considered too expensive, but because it would have cost more than people thought it was worth.

In an uncompromising view of the question, the Wakefieldians were right when they ridiculed Horton's emigration experiments as totally inadequate. Helen Cowan observes that as a means of alleviating misery in the home country, assisted emigration was ineffective.[17] The removal of 800 weavers and dependents in 1820 brought no noticeable improvement in wages in Glasgow. Horton's experiments made no dint in the problem of pauperism in Cork. Yet Horton did not expect any demonstrable results of this nature. He realized that his experiments did not involve enough people. Large emigrations were for the future when he had proved that settlers could be established in the colonies for the amount he had predicted and when he had persuaded Parliament and the Cabinet of the validity of his case. He did not pretend that Peter Robinson's efforts were of any great significance except as experiments. It was pointless to object that these efforts produced no noticeable benefit.

There was some justification for describing Horton's scheme as 'shovelling out paupers'. Of course, he was opposed to any hint of compulsion; it was essential that emigrants should go because they wanted to. Nor did he approve any plan which gave emigrants the means to cross the Atlantic without ensuring them with a livelihood after they landed. For that reason he proposed lavish assistance. On these points his position was emphatic. Yet his assumption that emigration was the best answer for paupers and that paupers should leave in large numbers revealed the considerable social bias and insensitivity that was so immediately recognized by Cobbett.

On the other hand, there was no foundation for the charge that paupers and other potential emigrants were deterred by knowledge of the hardships faced by Peter Robinson's settlers. Even though government-assisted emigration had been managed in a haphazard manner in every instance, the settlers themselves had written optimistic letters to their friends and relatives at home. This was true not only of the Irish who had gone out in 1823 and 1825 but also of the weavers who had emigrated in 1820 and 1821 and the Scottish settlers who had left in 1815. The exceptions were the 1820 emigrants to the Cape whose unhappy accounts were widely reported in the British press. The net effect of the Canadian experiments was to stimulate interest in emigration. However inefficient the Colonial

[17] Cowan, p. 236.

Office was in executing its projects, those who were sent out were grateful for the help they had received. The expectations of most of the assisted emigrants were not high. It was so manifestly preferable to go under the auspices of government instead of going on their own that they were not disposed to complain. In many cases the conditions that they left at home prepared them to tolerate a precarious existence in the colonies. Under these circumstances it was possible for Horton to carry out his experiments with inadequate foresight and knowledge without damaging his cause in the eyes of prospective emigrants.

The claim that Horton's experiments had done harm was not a central part of the case that the Wakefieldians made against him. One great weakness in his system, as they saw it, was the lack of an acceptable guarantee that money spent on emigration would be repaid. The other was that it was not based on any 'principles of colonization'.[18] Horton's vision, they insisted, was too limited. He did not realize that emigration was simply an aspect of colonization. He did not see that there was anything more involved than transporting emigrants to the colonies and helping them to become established. Consequently, he did not give enough attention to the disposal of waste lands and the requirements of the colonial labour market. The Wakefieldians insisted that the question of emigration was subordinate to that of colonization. Only through the application of the techniques they had discovered could the growth of a balanced colonial society be achieved or could emigration reach its full potential.

Horton himself made a distinction between the terms emigration and colonization, but not in the special sense used by Wakefield. To Horton emigration meant labourers going out to a colony with the intention of finding employment for wages. Colonization described the settlement of immigrants on land. Emigration could proceed with a minimum of assistance from the government while colonization would require an initial heavy expenditure. But the number of labourers that a colony could absorb was limited. Once the colonial labour market reached the point of saturation it would be necessary to resort to colonization, to place emigrants on the land or else expose colonials and emigrants alike to great misery and distress. Colonization, as Horton understood it, was self-perpetuating

---

[18] Tennant, *Correspondence with Nassau William Senior*, p. 15; *Spectator*, 15 Jan. 1831, p. 59; Mills, *Colonization of Australia*, p. 51.

while emigration was not. Those who became settlers would be able to offer help to friends and relatives who would follow them from Britain and also take up land. Moreover, colonization could open the way for further emigration; in time settlers would become employers of labour and the opportunities for emigrants looking for work would be expanded.

Far from viewing colonization in the Wakefieldian sense as the correct means of land management to attract private capital, Horton insisted that colonial investments would never return a high rate of interest except in unique circumstances.[19] It was unrealistic to expect capitalists to develop large estates or to provide funds to subsidize immigration. Wakefield's desire to create a pool of labour for capitalists was misplaced, especially in the North American colonies. At the same time, while colonial lands would not provide quick or easy profit, they were attractive to people of modest means to whom they offered all of the necessities of life and the prospect of steady improvement. It was in the accommodation of small landholders that the future of the colonies lay. This was a well-founded judgement and a corner-stone of Horton's theory. When this judgement is acknowledged, his ideas on colonization appear somewhat more sophisticated than those of his detractors.

Wakefieldian assertions to the contrary, Horton's schemes were projected with close reference to their potential impact on the colonies. Although he found his enthusiasm for state-aided emigration in the conviction that it could relieve pauperism, he always conceived such a programme as an instrument of colonial advancement. The domestic and colonial advantages of sponsored emigration were inseparable in his mind. He never surrendered to the opinion that it would serve Britain as well to send excess population to the United States as to Canada. He echoed the familiar refrain that immigration to that country built up its strength at the expense of the colonies. His knowledge of political economy did not inspire any doubt of the value of colonial possessions. The colonies produced wealth which could not be directly shown in balance sheets and documents but which existed nevertheless. If colonial markets were lost, there was no certainty that they could be replaced. As it was, colonial wealth could be considered as national wealth and the growth of the colonies as equivalent to the growth of the nation. There could be no hesitation in identifying the ideal destination of emigrants, especially when

[19] Ibid., *Letter to Sir George Murray*, pp. 51–2.

it could be shown that an increase of population would do more than anything else to keep British North America from falling into foreign possession.

On the other hand, Horton believed that it would be a gross mistake to allow an indiscriminate movement of emigrants to the colonies. 'Nothing would be more easy,' he wrote, 'than to drug the Canadas with labour.'[20] This was a danger of which Wakefield's disciples did not seem to be sufficiently aware. This was the reason why Horton wished to establish large numbers of emigrants on the land. But pauper settlement did not represent his complete system. It was desirable to supply the colonies with as much labour as they could absorb both because it would be economical and because it would promote colonial development. New South Wales and Cape Colony in particular were experiencing labour shortages. While Horton did not believe that pauper settlement would be possible in these colonies he did think that they could absorb a limited number of pauper labourers each year. British North America could also provide places for some emigrants who came in search of wages. Horton, however, was aware as Wakefield was not that the nature of the demand for labour varied from colony to colony. For this reason he could not treat the questions of emigration and colonization in Wakefield's coherent terms.

Horton did not need to be reminded that emigration involved the colonies as well as the home country. His appreciation of colonial problems was at least as acute as Wakefield's. At the same time, he approached the subject of pauper emigration with a far greater sense of urgency. The Wakefieldians did not pretend that Systematic Colonization would provide immediate machinery for a large-scale movement of population. Britain, they observed, had been engaged in colonization for 200 years without achieving any relief from over-population; 'we are not inclined to attach much importance to a question of a few years more or less; provided that, as we firmly believe the new theory of colonization offers the means of effectively curing and preventing, sooner or later, the evils of redundant population.'[21] Horton did not possess the same perspective. He was concerned with the possibilities of the present and he addressed himself squarely to the problem of assisting a maximum number of emigrants within a minimum number of years. If emigration was to do

[20] W.H.P., Horton to Richards, 2 Apr. 1831.
[21] Tennant, *Letter to Sir George Murray*, p. 44.

any good within the near future, the government would have to assume responsibility for an ambitious and expensive programme. Horton saw no alternative to government action. Yet he did not expect direct support from national taxation. Instead, he thought that a national system of emigration could be paid for by those who would obtain the greatest benefit, the landlords and parishes on one hand and the emigrants on the other. By means of an emigration loan guaranteed by the government and charged against poor rates and other assessments in Great Britain and quit rents in the colonies, Horton thought that a great effort could be made without delay. His system was not an ideal one, but one which he thought could work under existing circumstances. Consequently it was both complex and, in a peculiar way, realistic.

'Your plan,' a friend remarked to Horton, 'is no less difficult to refute than to execute.'[22] The comment was appropriate. There was little fault in Horton's reasoning as far as it went. If a parish was permanently encumbered with a number of unemployed, it could conceivably find advantage in supporting emigration on the basis that Horton suggested. If conditions in the colonies were as he described them, then it would be practical to expect repayment of part of the expense by the emigrants themselves. Assuming that his information was correct, the idea that emigration could be financed by long-term annuities was not at all absurd. Nor was the plan of pauper settlement based on shallow observations. Horton's system did not lack sophistication. He could defend it with subtle argument and there were few people who could match his over-all knowledge of his subject. Yet Horton's proposals did not inspire confidence. They were far too novel, far too ambitious, and their consequences were far too unpredictable. Cabinet ministers were repelled by the prospect of extensive involvement in a measure of public relief built on such conjectural foundations. Their fear of complications and difficulties outweighed any consideration of possible benefits. Pauper assistance of any form aroused in them great apprehension. As a consequence, it was inevitable that the government should fail to advance from theoretical speculation to practical application.

The fruitlessness of Horton's efforts was scarcely surprising. Yet he was not entirely out of step with his colleagues. Although Peel and Goderich did not share his optimism, they gave him more than a

22 W.H.P., Wm. Tooke to Horton, 13 Mar. 1830.

little encouragement. If the Liverpool Cabinet had not supported him, he could not have attempted his emigration experiments or chaired his Emigration Committees. Horton's ideas were viewed sceptically, but his interest in emigration was welcomed. He presented a desirable spectacle of active concern. Cabinet ministers may have been unprepared to act positively, but they were equally unprepared to speak negatively. They were happy to see the subject studied and discussed while they remained uncommitted. Assisted emigration deserved serious attention not because any special group in Parliament was demanding government initiative, but because it might become the hope of the lower classes. In the uneasy atmosphere of post-Waterloo Britain the Cabinet saw no wisdom in resolutely closing a door. In moments of greatest tension it made small gestures of intention to open it. The decisions to conduct experiments in 1819, 1820, and 1823 followed this pattern. The appointment of the Emigration Committee of 1826 came after a serious economic reverse which, by the end of the year, had produced an outbreak of machine smashing. The effectiveness of emigration as a safety-valve was not underrated; in this respect Horton's work was valued.

Beyond this, there was a conviction that emigration could bring larger benefits. Cobbett and his ilk aside, its potential usefulness was generally admitted, if not as a permanent or long-term remedy, at least as an effective short-term or local one. The Cabinet and Parliament admitted the need to smooth the path to remove all obstacles as far as was prudent in the name of humanity. Nor did agreement with Horton end there. The advantage to the colonies of a policy of assisted emigration was widely recognized. The utility of colonial possessions was not questioned at the Cabinet level. Lord Liverpool and his colleagues were not philosophically opposed to expenditure for the purpose of colonial development. On these foundations rested Cabinet sympathy for the campaign which Horton undertook. What was lacking was belief in the capacity of the government to act and a certainty that Horton had not lost all sense of proportion.

BIBLIOGRAPHY

A. MANUSCRIPT COLLECTIONS

1. *British Museum Additional Manuscripts*
Goderich Papers 40862
Huskisson Papers 38745–62
Liverpool Papers 38290–3302
Peel Papers 40242–401

2. *British Museum Loans*
Bathurst Papers 57

3. *Derby Central Library*
Wilmot Horton Papers

4. *University of Durham*
3rd Earl Grey Papers

5. *Surrey Record Office*
Goulburn Papers

6. *Staffordshire Record Office*
Hatherton Collection

7. *Public Record Office*
 i. Audit Office

    A.O. 1/2131 Settlers in America
    A.O. 2/34 pp. 48–55 Peter Robinson's accounts
 ii. Home Office
    H.O. 102/30–3 Scotland—original correspondence, 1819, 1820
    H.O. 41/4 Disturbances—entry book 1818–19
    H.O. 100/208 Ireland—original correspondence, 1823
    H.O. 79/8 Ireland—private and secret correspondence, 1822–9
    H.O. 122/13 Ireland—general entry book, 1820–7
 iii. Foreign Office
    F.O. 5/116, 125, 135, 144, 152, 161 British Consuls in America—
    original correspondence 1816–21
 iv. Colonial Office
    C.O. 42/– Upper and Lower Canada—original correspondence particu-
    larly 1814–34

C.O. 43/- Upper and Lower Canada—entry books—particularly 1814-34

C.O. 48/36-61 Cape of Good Hope—original correspondence 1815-23

C.O. 48/75-9, 88, 100 Commissioners of Enquiry at the Cape 1822-5

C.O. 48/87 Mr. Parker's complaints against the colonial government 1820-6

C.O. 49/10-23 Cape of Good Hope—entry books 1806-31

C.O. 188/31-44 New Brunswick—original correspondence 1825-32

C.O. 189/12-13 New Brunswick 1819-34

C.O. 201/114-15, 117 Commissioners of Enquiry into state of New South Wales 1822

C.O. 217/144-56 Nova Scotia and Cape Breton—original correspondence 1825-34

C.O. 218/30-1 Nova Scotia and Cape Breton entry books 1823-37

C.O. 226/42-8 Prince Edward Island original correspondence 1825-31

C.O. 227/7 Prince Edward Island—entry book 1801-32

C.O. 323/142-75 Colonies general—original correspondence 1824-35

C.O. 324/73-102 Colonies general—entry books 1821-36

C.O. 325/36 Regulations respecting grants of land in the Australian colonies and North America

C.O. 384/1-26 Emigration—original correspondence 1817-31

C.O. 385/2 List of Scottish assisted emigrants of 1815

C.O. 385/5 Emigration to North America—entry book

B. PRINTED MATERIAL

1. *List of Parliamentary Papers*

1817, vi (462), Select Committee on the Poor Laws

1819, ii (529), Select Committee on the Poor Laws

1822, v (165, 346), Select Committee on the State of Agriculture

1823, vi (561), Select Committee on the Employment of the Poor in Ireland

1825, viii (129), Select Committee on the State of Ireland

1826, iv (404), Select Committee on Emigration

1826-7, v (88, 237, 550), Select Committee on Emigration

1828, xxi (109, 148), Report by Lieutenant-Colonel Cockburn on Emigration

2. *Select List of Parliamentary Debates in Hansard*

15 April 1825, xii, Emigration from Ireland

14 March 1826, xiv, Emigration

7 December 1826, xvi, Emigration

15 February 1827, xvi, Emigration

4 March 1828, xviii, Emigration

17 April 1828, xviii, Emigration

24 June 1828, xix, Emigration
4 June 1829, xxi, Distress of Labouring Classes—Redundant Population
22 February 1831, ii, Emigration

3. *Collections of Documents and Works of Reference*
BAMFORD, FRANCIS, and WELLINGTON, THE DUKE OF, ed. *The Journals of Mrs. Arbuthnot 1820–1832*, ii. London, 1950.
BICKLEY, FRANCIS, ed. *Report of the Manuscripts of Earl Bathurst*. London, 1923.
Canadian Archive Report
CLARK, C. M. H., ed. *Select Documents in Australian History, 1788–1850*. Sydney, 1950.
Dictionary of National Biography
DOUGLAS, DAVID D., ed., *English Historical Documents, 1783–1832*. London, 1959.
FIRTH, EDITH, G., ed. *The Town of York, 1815–1834*. Toronto, 1966.
Historical Records of Australia
HOUGHTON, WALTER E., ed. *The Wellesley Index to Victorian Periodicals, 1824–1900*, i. Toronto, 1966.
INNIS, H. A., and LOWER, A. R. M., ed., *Select Documents in Canadian Economic History, 1783–1885*. Toronto, 1933.
JENNINGS, LOUIS J., ed., *The Croker Papers*, i. London, 1884.
MELLVILLE, LEWIS, ed., *The Huskisson Papers*. London, 1931.
PIKE, DOUGLAS, *Australian Dictionary of Biography*, i. Melbourne, 1966.
Records of Cape Colony
REEVE, HENRY, ed., *The Greville Memoirs*, ii, iii. London, 1888.
SANDERS, LLOYD C., ed., *Lord Melbourne's Papers*. London, 1889.

4. *Contemporary Periodicals*
Blackwood's Edinburgh Magazine, 1817–30.
Caledonian Mercury, 1815, 1819.
Cobbett's Weekly Political Register, 1830–1.
Colonial Advocate (Upper Canada), 1825.
The *Courier*, 1819.
Eclectic Review, 1827.
Edinburgh Review, 1805–30.
Evening Mail, 1819.
Glasgow Chronicle, 1827.
Glasgow Herald, 1820, 1827.
Gentleman's Magazine, 1819–30.
Monthly Review, 1820–30.
Morning Post, 1819.
Morning Herald, 1819.

The Pamphleteer, 1817.
Quarterly Review, 1814–34.
The South African Commercial Advertiser, 1824.
The Times, 1819.
Westminster Review, 1826–30.

5. *Contemporary Books and Pamphlets*

ANONYMOUS, *Hints and Observations on the Disadvantages of Emigration to British America*. London, 1833.

ANONYMOUS, *Poor Laws: The Injustice, Impolicy and Inhumanity of the Present System*. London, 1822.

ABEONA SURVIVORS, *Narrative of the Loss of the Abeona*. Glasgow, 1821.

BANFILL, SAMUEL, *A Second Letter to Sir T. D. Acland, Bart., M.P., on the Means of improving the Condition of the Labouring Classes and Reducing Parochial Assessments*. Exeter, 1818.

BANNISTER, JOHN WILLIAM, *On Emigration to Upper Canada*. London, 1831.

— *Sketch of a Plan for Settling in Upper Canada a Portion of the Unemployed Labourers of England. By a Settler*. London, 1821.

BARKLAY, CHARLES, *Letters from the Dorking Emigrants to Upper Canada in the Spring of 1832*. London, 1833.

BARTON, JOHN, *On the Depreciation of Labour*. London, 1820.

BIRD, W. WILBERFORCE, *State of the Cape of Good Hope in 1822*. H. T. Colebrooke, ed. London, 1823.

BLISS, HENRY, *The Colonial System. Statistics of the Trade, Industry and Resources of Canada and the other Plantations in British America*. London, 1833.

BRERETON, C. D., *The Subordinate Magistracy and Parish System Considered*. London, 1827.

BRUCE, THOMAS, LORD ELGIN, *View of the Present State of Pauperism in Scotland*. London, 1830.

BRYDGES, EGERTON, *Arguments in favour of the Practicability of Relieving the Able-Bodied Poor, By finding Employment for Them*. London, 1817.

BRYDONE, JAMES MARR, *Narrative of a Voyage with a Party of Emigrants, sent out from Sussex in 1834*. Petworth, 1834.

BUCHANAN, A. C., *Emigration Practically Considered, with detailed directions to emigrants proceeding to British North America in a letter to the Right Hon. R. Wilmot Horton M.P.* London, 1828.

BUCHANAN, JAMES, *Project for the Formation of a Depot in Upper Canada with a view to receive the whole pauper population of England*. New York, 1834.

BUNN, THOMAS, *A Letter Relative to the Affairs of the Poor of the Parish of Frome Selwood in Somersetshire*. London, 1834.

COLQUHOUN, PATRICK, *Considerations on the Means of Affording Profitable*

Employment to the Redundant Population of Great Britain and Ireland through the medium of an Improved and Correct System of Colonization in the British Territories in Southern Africa. London, 1818.

COLQUHOUN, PATRICK, *A Treatise on the Wealth, Power, and Resources of the British Empire.* London, 1814.

COURTENAY, THOMAS PEREGRINE, *A Treatise upon the Poor Laws.* London, 1818.

DAVIDSON, JOHN, *Considerations on the Poor Laws.* Oxford, 1817.

DAVIS, WILLIAM, *Hints to Philanthropists; or, a Collective View of Practical Means of Improving the Condition of the Poor and Labouring Classes of Society.* Bath, 1821.

DAY, WILLIAM, *An Inquiry into the Poor Laws and Surplus Labour and their Mutual Reaction.* London, 1833.

DONKIN, RUFANE, *A Letter on the Government of the Cape of Good Hope.* London, 1827.

DOYLE, MARTIN, *Hints on Emigration to Upper Canada especially addressed to the Middle and Lower Classes in Great Britain and Ireland.* Dublin, 1834.

DUGMORE, HENRY HARE, *The Reminiscences of an Albany Settler.* Grahamstown, 1958.

EDE, JOHN, *Reflections on the Employment, Wages, and Condition of the Poor.* London, 1829.

ELMORE, J. E., *Letters to the Right Hon. the Earl of Darnley on the State of Ireland.* London, 1828.

ENGLISH, HENRY, *A Complete View of the Joint Stock Companies formed during the years 1824 and 1825.* London, 1827.

ENGLISH, JOHN, *No Emigration. The Testimony of Experience.* London, 1828.

FERGUSON, ADAM, *Practical Notes made during a tour in Canada and a portion of the United States in 1831.* London, 1833.

— *Practical Notes made during a second visit to Canada in 1833.* London, 1834.

FONNEREAU, WM. C., *Remarks and Suggestions relative to the Management of the Poor in Ipswich.* Ipswich, 1833.

GASCOIGNE, HENRY BARNET, *Suggestions for the Employment of the Poor of the Metropolis.* London, 1817.

GODLONTON, ROBERT, *Sketches of the Eastern Districts of the Cape of Good Hope.* Grahamstown, 1842.

GOLDSWAIN, JEREMIAH, *Chronicle, Albany Settler of 1820.* Una Long, ed. Cape Town, 1946.

GOULD, NATHANIEL, *Emigration. Practical Advice to Emigrants.* London, 1834.

GOURLAY, ROBERT FLEMING, *General Introduction to Statistical Accounts of Upper Canada.* London, 1822.

HALE, WILLIAM, *A Letter to Samuel Whitbread, Esq., M.P., Containing Observations on the Distress Peculiar to the Poor of Spitalfields.* London, 1816.

HALL, BASIL, *Travels in North America in the years 1827 and 1828.* 3 vols. Edinburgh, 1829.

HAYTER, W. G., *Proposals for the Redemption of the Poor's Rates by means of Emigration.* London, 1817.

HEAD, FRANCIS BOND, *A Few Arguments against the Theory of Emigration.* London, 1828.

HORTON, R. W., *A Letter to Sir Francis Burdett.* London, 1826.

— *The Causes and Remedies to Pauperism in the United Kingdom Considered.* London, 1829.

— *An Inquiry into the Causes and Remedies of Pauperism. First Series. Containing Correspondence with Poulett Thomson. Second Series. Containing Correspondence with M. Duchatel, with an Explanatory Preface. Third Series. Containing Letters to Sir Francis Burdett. Fourth Series. Containing Letters to Lord John Russell.* London, 1830.

— *An Inquiry into the Causes and Remedies of Pauperism.* (The *First* and *Third Series* are the same as in the previous entry. The *Second Series* does not have a preface.) *Fourth Series. Containing a Letter and Queries addressed to N. W. Senior.* London, 1830.

— *Correspondence between the Rt. Hon. R. Wilmot Horton and a Select Class of the London Mechanics' Institution.* London, 1830.

— *Speech in the House of Commons 9th March, 1830, on Moving for a Committee to Consider the State of the Poor of the United Kingdom,* London, 1830.

— *Ten Lectures Delivered at the London Mechanics' Institution.* London, 1831.

— *Exposition and Defence of Earl Bathurst's Administration of the Affairs of Canada.* London, 1938.

— *A Letter to Dr. Birkbeck.* Richmond, 1839.

— *Correspondence between the Right Honorable Sir Robert Wilmot Horton, Bart., and J. B. Robinson, Esq., Chief Justice of Upper Canada,* London, 1839.

— *Ireland and Canada; Supported by Local evidence.* London, 1839.

— *Letters Containing Observations on Colonial Policy.* London, 1839.

JERRAM, CHARLES, *Considerations on the Impolicy and Pernicious Tendency of the Poor Laws.* London, 1818.

KENNEDY, L., *On Cultivation of the Waste Lands in the United Kingdom.* London, 1829.

KEPPEL-JONES, ARTHUR, ed., *Philipps, 1820 Settler,* Pietermaritzburg, 1960.

LAMOND, ROBERT, 'A Narrative of the Rise and Progress of Emigration from the Counties of Lanark and Renfrew to the New Settlement in

Upper Canada, Glasgow, 1821'. Sutro Branch, California State Library, *Occasional Papers* Jan., 1940.

LEWIS, G. C., *On Local Disturbances in Ireland*. London, 1834.

MCDONALD, JOHN, *Narrative of a Voyage to Quebec*. London, 1926.

MACGREGOR, J., *Observations on Emigration to British America*. London, 1829.

MALCOLM, J. D., *An Enquiry into the Expediency of Emigration as it respects the British North American Colonies*. London, 1828.

MALTHUS, T. R., *An Essay on the Principle of Population*. London, 1817.

MARTIN, R., MONTGOMERY, *History of the British Colonies*, iii, London, 1834.

— *Statistics of the Colonies of the British Empire*. London, 1839.

MERIVALE, HERMAN, *Lectures on Colonization and Colonies*. London, 1928.

MOORSOM, W., *Letters from Nova Scotia comprising Sketches of a young Country*. London, 1830.

NICHOL, S. W., *A Summary View of the Report and Evidence Relative to the Poor Laws Published by the House of Commons*. York, 1818.

O'BRIEN, W. S., *Emigration*. London, 1840.

PARKER, WILLIAM, *Proofs of the Delusions of His Majesty's Representative at the Cape of Good Hope*. Cork, 1826.

PRINGLE, THOMAS, *Some Account of the Present State of the English Settlers in Albany South Africa*. London, 1824.

— *Narrative of a Residence in South Africa*. London, 1835.

ROLPH, THOMAS, *Emigration and Colonization*. London, 1844.

SADLER, MICHAEL THOMAS, *Ireland: Its Evils and their Remedies*, London, 1829.

— *The Law of Population*, London, 1830.

SEDGWICK, J., *A Letter to the rate-payers of Great Britain on the Repeal of the Poor Laws*. London, 1833.

SENIOR, NASSAU, *Journals, Conversations and Essays Relating to Ireland*, i. London, 1868.

— *Remarks on Emigration with a draft of a Bill*. London, 1831.

— *Outline of the Poor Law Amendment Act*. London, 1834.

— *Two Lectures on Population*. London, 1829.

— *A Letter to Lord Howick on a Legal Provision for the Irish Poor*. London, 1831.

SHERLEY, FREDERICK, *Practical Observations on the Poor Laws*. London, 1829.

SOCKETT, THOMAS, *Emigration. A Letter to a Member of Parliament containing a statement of the method produced by the Petworth Committee in sending out emigrants to Upper Canada in the years 1832 and 1833*. Petworth, 1834.

STANLEY, E. G. G., *Journal of a Tour in America, 1824–1825*. Privately Printed, 1930.

STEPHEN, JAMES, *Address on the British Colonies and Colonization*. Liverpool, 1859.

STRACHAN, JOHN, *Remarks on Emigration from the United Kingdom Addressed to Robert Wilmot Horton Esq., M.P.* London, 1827.

STRICKLAND, GEORGE, *A Discourse on the Poor Laws of England and Scotland and on the state of the poor of Ireland and on Emigration*. London, 1827.

TALBOT, EDWARD ALLEN, *Five Years' Residence in the Canadas: including a Tour through Part of the United States of America in the year 1823*, 2 vols., London, 1824.

TAYLOR, HENRY, *Autobiography*, i. London, 1885.

TENNANT, CHARLES, *Letters Forming Part of a Correspondence with Nassau William Senior Esq. Concerning Systematic Colonization and the Bill now before Parliament for Promoting Emigration*. London, 1831.

WAKEFIELD, E. G., *England and America: A Comparison*. London, 1833.

— *A Letter to the Right Hon. Sir George Murray on Systematic Colonization*. Attributed to Charles Tennant. London, 1830.

— *A Statement of the Principles and Objects of a proposed National Society for the Cure and Prevention of Pauperism by Means of Systematic Colonization*. London, 1830.

— *A Letter from Sydney the Principal Town of Australasia*. London, 1829.

WENTWORTH, W. C., *A Statistical Account of the British Settlements in Australasia*, 2 vols., London, 1824.

6. *Secondary Works*

ADAMS, LEONARD P., *Agricultural Depression and Farm Relief in England 1813–1852*. London, 1932.

ADAMS, W. F., *Ireland and Irish Education to the New World from 1815 to the Famine*. New Haven, 1932.

ARMYTAGE, W. H., 'Thomas Talbot and Lord Wharncliffe: Some New Letters Hitherto Unpublished', *Ontario History*, Autumn, 1953.

BERTHOFF, ROWLAND TAPPAN, *British Immigrants in Industrial America 1790–1950*. Cambridge, 1953.

BLACK, R. D. COLLISON, *Economic Thought and the Irish Question, 1817–1870*. Cambridge, 1960.

BLAUG, MARK, *Ricardian Economics: in a Historical Study*. New Haven. 1958.

BONAR, JAMES, *Malthus and his Work*. London, 1885.

BOWLEY, MARIAN, *Nassau Senior and Classical Economics*. New York, 1967.

BROCK, W. R., *Lord Liverpool and Liberal Toryism, 1820–27*. Cambridge, 1941.

BURROUGHS, PETER, *Britain and Australia 1831–1855 : a study in Imperial Relations and Crown Lands Administration*. Oxford, 1967.

CARROTHERS, W. A., *Emigration from the British Isles*. London, 1929.

CASSELMAN, A. C., 'Pioneer Settlements', *Canada and its Provinces*, xvii. Toronto, 1914.

CHECKLAND, S. G., 'The Propagation of Ricardian Economics in England', *Economica*, February 1949.

CLAPHAM, J. H., *An Economic History of Modern Britain, The Railway Age, 1820–1850*. Cambridge, 1930.

COLE, G. D. H., *The Life of William Cobbett*. London, 1947.

— *A Short History of the British Working-Class Movement, 1789–1947*. London, 1948.

— and POSTGATE, RAYMOND, *The Common People 1746–1946*. New York, 1961.

CORRY, G. E., *The Rise of South Africa*, ii. London, 1913.

COWAN, HELEN I., *British Emigration to British North America*. Toronto, 1961.

CRAIG, G. M., *Upper Canada : the Formative Years, 1784–1841*. Toronto, 1963.

DARVALL, FRANK ONGLEY, *Popular Disturbances in Regency England*. London, 1934.

DE KIEWIET, C. W., *A History of South Africa, Social and Political*. Oxford, 1941.

DONALDSON, GORDON, *The Scots Overseas*. London, 1966.

DUNAWAY, WAYLAND F., *The Scotch-Irish of Colonial Pennsylvania*, London, 1962.

EDWARDS, I. E., *The 1820 Settlers in South Africa*. London, 1934.

EDWARDS, R. D., and WILLIAMS, T. D., ed., *The Great Famine : Studies in Irish History, 1845–52*. Dublin, 1954.

EYRE-TODD, GEORGE, *History of Glasgow*, iii. Glasgow, 1934.

FAY, C. R., *Great Britain from Adam Smith to the Present Day, An Economic and Social Survey*. London, 1950.

— *Huskisson and His Age*. London, 1951.

FETTER, FRANK W., 'Economic Controversy in the British Reviews, 1802–1850', *Economica*, November 1965.

FLICK, CARLOS, 'The Fall of Wellington's Government', *The Journal of Modern History*, March 1965.

FORD, HENRY JAMES, *The Scotch-Irish in America*. Princeton, 1915.

GALBRAITH, JOHN S., *Reluctant Empire, British Policy on the South African Frontier, 1834–1854*. Los Angeles, 1963.

GARNETT, R., *Edward Gibbon Wakefield. The Colonization of South Australia and New Zealand*. London, 1898.

GASH, NORMAN, *Mr. Secretary Peel, the Life of Sir Robert Peel to 1830*. London, 1961.

GATES, LILLIAN F., *Land Policies of Upper Canada*. Toronto, 1968.

GAYER, A. D., ROSTOW, W. W., and SWARTZ, A. J., *The Growth and Fluctuation of the British Economy 1790–1850*. Oxford, 1953.

GHOSH, R. N., 'Malthus on Emigration and Colonization: Letters to Wilmot-Horton', *Economica*, February 1963.

— 'The Colonization Controversy: R. J. Wilmot-Horton and the Classical Economists', *Economica*, November 1964.

GLASS, D. V., ed., *Introduction to Malthus*. London, 1953.

GRAHAM, GERALD S., 'Views of General Murray on the Defence of Upper Canada, 1815', *Canadian Historical Review*, June 1953.

GRAHAM, I. C. C., *Colonists from Scotland: Emigration to North America, 1704–1783*. Ithaca, 1956.

GREENWOOD, GORDON, ed., *Australia, A Social and Political History*. Sydney, 1955.

GRENFELL-PRICE, A., *The Foundation and Settlement of South Australia, 1829–1845*. Adelaide, 1924.

GRIFFITH, TALBOT, *Population Problems in the Age of Malthus*. Cambridge, 1926.

GUILLET, E. C., *The Great Migration*. Toronto, 1963.

HAMIL, FRED COYNE, *Lake Erie Baron*. Toronto, 1955.

HAMILTON, HENRY, *An Economic History of Scotland in the Eighteenth Century*. Oxford, 1963.

HANSEN, MARCUS, *The Atlantic Migration, 1607–1860*. New York, 1961.

HARDY, S. M., 'William Huskisson, 1770–1830, Imperial Statesman and Economist'. Ph.D. Thesis, London, 1943.

HARDY, S. M., and BAILEY, R. C., 'The Downfall of the Gower Interest in the Staffordshire Boroughs, 1800–30', *Collections for a History of Staffordshire*. Staffordshire Record Society, 1954.

HARROP, A. J., *The Amazing Career of Edward Gibbon Wakefield*. London, 1928.

HOBSBAWM, E. J., *The Age of Revolution, 1789–1848*. New York, 1962.

HOCKLY, H. E., *The Story of the British Settlers of 1820 in South Africa*. Cape Town, 1948.

JOHNSON, J. K., 'Colonel James FitzGibbon—Suppression of Irish Riots', *Ontario History*, September 1966.

JOHNSON, S. C., *A History of Emigration from the United Kingdom to North America, 1763–1912*. London, 1913.

JONES, E. G., 'Sir R. J. Wilmot Horton Bart. Politician and Pamphleteer'. M.A. Thesis. Bristol, 1936.

JONES, E. L., and MINGAY, G. E., eds., *Land, Labour and Population in the Industrial Revolution*. London, 1967.

JONES, M. A., 'The Role of the United Kingdom in the Transatlantic emigrant trade, 1815–1875'. D.Phil. Thesis, Oxford, 1956.
— *American Immigration*. Chicago, 1960.
JONES, WILBUR DEVEREAUX, *'Prosperity Robinson', The Life of Viscount Goderich, 1782–1859*. New York, 1967.
KEGEL, CHARLES H., 'William Cobbett and Malthusianism', *Journal of the History of Ideas*, xix, 1958.
KNAPLUND, PAUL, 'Colonial Problems and Colonial Policy, 1815–1837', *The Cambridge History of the British Empire*, ii. Cambridge, 1940.
KNORR, KLAUS E., *British Colonial Theories, 1570–1850*. Toronto, 1944.
KOHLER, MAX J., *An Important European Mission to investigate American Immigration Conditions and John Quincy Adams' Relations thereto, 1817–1818*. Chicago, 1919.
LEYBURN, JAMES G., *The Scotch-Irish. A Social History*. Durham, North Carolina, 1962.
LOWER, A. R. M., 'Immigration and Settlement in Canada 1812–1820', *Canadian Historical Review*, March 1922.
MACDONAGH, OLIVER, *A Pattern of Government Growth, 1800–60. The Passenger Acts and their Enforcement*. London, 1961.
MACDONALD, NORMAN, *Canada 1763–1841; Immigration and Settlement*. London, 1939.
MCLACHLAN, NOEL, 'Edward Eager: A Colonial Spokesman', *Historical Studies: Australia and New Zealand*. May 1963.
MACMILLAN, W. M., *Bantu, Boer, and Briton: the making of the South African Native Problem*. Oxford, 1963.
MACNUTT, W. S., *The Atlantic Provinces. The Emergence of Colonial Society, 1712–1857*. Toronto, 1965.
MADGWICK, R. B., *Immigration into Eastern Australia, 1788–1851*. London, 1937.
MANNING, HELEN TAFT, *British Colonial Government After the American Revolution*. New Haven, 1933.
— *The Revolt of French Canada, 1800–1835*. London, 1962.
MARTELL, J. S., *Immigration to and Emigration from Nova Scotia, 1815–1838*. Halifax, 1942.
MILLAR, ANTHONY KENDAL, *Plantagenet in South Africa, Lord Charles Somerset*. London, 1965.
MILLS, R. C., *The Colonization of Australia (1829–42)*. London, 1915.
NESBITT, GEORGE L., *Benthamite Reviewing, the First Twelve Years of the Westminster Review*. New York, 1934.
O'BRIEN, ERIS, *The Foundation of Australia, 1786–1800*. London, 1950.
OSBORNE, JOHN W., *William Cobbett: His Thought and His Time*. New Brunswick, N.J., 1966.
PAMMETT, HOWARD, T., 'Assisted Emigration from Ireland to Upper

Canada under Peter Robinson in 1825', *Ontario Historical Society Papers and Records*, 1936.

PATTERSON, GEORGE C., *Land Settlement in Upper Canada 1783–1840*. Toronto, 1921.

PIKE, DOUGLAS, 'Wilmot Horton and the National Colonization Society', *Historical Studies: Australia and New Zealand*, May, 1957.

— *Paradise of Dissent, South Australia 1829–57*. Melbourne, 1957.

PLAYTER, GEORGE F., 'An Account of the Founding of Three Military Settlements in Eastern Ontario—Perth, Lanark and Richmond, 1815–20', *Ontario Historical Society Papers and Records*, 1923.

PRYDE, GEORGE S., *Scotland from 1603 to the present day*. London, 1962.

ROBBINS, LIONEL, *Robert Torrens and the Evolution of Classical Economics*. London, 1958.

RIDDELL, R. G., 'A Study in Imperial Land Policy 1783–1848'. B.Litt. Thesis, Oxford, 1934.

— 'Land Policy of the Colonial Office, 1763–1855', *Canadian Historical Review*, December, 1937.

ROBERTS, STEPHEN H., *History of Australian Land Settlement, 1788–1920*. Melbourne, 1924.

ROBINSON, A. M. L., 'Thomas Pringle and Sir Walter Scott', *Quarterly Bulletin of the South African Library*, December 1951.

ROBINSON, C. W., *Life of Sir John Beverley Robinson*. London, 1904.

SHEPPERSON, W. S., *British Emigration to North America*. Minneapolis, 1957.

SMITH, KENNETH, *The Malthusian Controversy*. London, 1951.

THEAL, G. M., *History of South Africa Since September, 1795*, i, ii. London, 1908.

WAGNER, DONALD O., 'British Economists and the Empire', *Political Science Quarterly*. June 1931.

WAINWRIGHT, MARY D., 'Agencies for the Promotion or Facilitation of Emigration from England to the U.S.A. 1815–1861'. M.A. Thesis, London, 1952.

WALPOLE, KATHLEEN A., 'Emigration to British North America under the Early Passenger Acts 1803–1842'. M.A. Thesis, London, 1929.

WEBB, SIDNEY and BEATRICE. *English Local Government: English Poor Law History: Part I: The Old Poor Law*. London, 1927.

— *English Poor Law History: Part II: The Last Hundred Years*, i. London, 1929.

WEIR, A. J., 'British Opinion and Colonial Policy, 1783–1839'. Ph.D. Thesis, Edinburgh, 1924.

WHITE, R. J., *Waterloo to Peterloo*. London, 1963.

WILSON, M., and THOMPSON, L., eds., *The Oxford History of South Africa*. Oxford, 1969.

WINCH, D. N., 'Classical Economics and the Case for Colonization', *Economica.* November 1963.

— *Classical Political Economy and Colonies.* London, 1965.

WITCOMB, J. D., 'Emigration from Great Britain to South Africa, 1820 to 1840'. M.A. Thesis, Birmingham, 1953.

WOODWARD, LLEWELLYN, *The Age of Reform, 1815–1870.* Oxford, 1962.

YONGE, C. D., *The Life and Administration of Robert Banks Second Earl of Liverpool,* ii. London, 1868.

YOUNG, D. M., *The Colonial Office in the Early Nineteenth Century.* London, 1961.

INDEX

British North America, 1817, 29; assisted to Upper Canada, 1, 17–23, 28–31, 32, 52–6, 77–90, 159; assisted to Cape of Good Hope, 1, 27–8, 30, 32–48, 50–1, 56, 72–5, 90, 159; organized by parishes, 66, 100–1; as a remedy for pauperism, 4–5, 8–9, 11–14, 30, 59–60, 62, 64–8, 96–107, 108, 129–44, 150–4, 169; for colonial defence, 10, 15–17, 27, 32–5, 60, 154; and popular disturbances, 35–7, 48–52, 56, 69–71, 83, 92, 155, 160, 174; cost, 29, 54n., 65, 89–90, 100, 120, 121, 126, 142, 108–9; critics, 88, 95, 122, 129–32, 134, 138, 140–1, 142–3, 145, 150–1, 162, 168–9; Emigration Commissioners, 164; see also Select Committees on Emigration, Horton, Malthus, Passenger Acts, population problem

Emily Township, Upper Canada, 88–9
England: and pauperism, 5–6; and emigration after 1815, 7; assisted emigration from, 1815, 19–20; redundant population, 61, 66, 150, 152, 154; rural poor, 64; and Emigration Committees, 99–101, 107; and Irish influx, 105, 143; and Torrens views on colonization, 141; and F. J. Robinson's emigration plan, 152–3
Ennismore, Richard Hare, Viscount, 71–2, 73, 105–6
Erie Canal, 88
Essay on the Principle of Population, 2, 12, 129, 132
Estcourt, T. G. Buchnall, 67n.

Felton, W. B., 26, 114
Fermoy, 72
Fifth Kaffir War, 35
Finlay, Kirkman, 52, 53, 56, 67n.
Fisher, Thomas, 67n.
Fisher, R. B., The Importance of the Cape of Good Hope, 38
Fitzgerald, Rt. Hon. Maurice, 95
Forster, Charles, 67n.
Foster, J. L., 105–6
Foreign Office: authorizes expenditure on emigrants, 24
Fort Wellington, Upper Canada, 21
Fredericksburg, Cape Colony, 45
Free trade, 4, 125–6, 162

Galt, John, 67n.

Gaika, paramount chief of the Xhosa, 46
Galway, 69
Gaspé, 82
Georgia, 6
Ghosh, R. N., 135
Gibraltar, 15
Gisborne, Thomas, 67n.
Glasgow, 20, 58, 169; distress of weavers in, 35–6, 101–2; and assisted emigration to Cape, 39–40; strike, 48–50; decision to assist weavers from, 52; continued desire to emigrate, 56, 102–3; and Irish, 101, 104; wages in after assisted emigrants leave; see weavers
Glasgow Chronicle, 55
Glasgow Herald, 55
Glengarry, Upper Canada, 19
Goderich, Frederick John Robinson, Viscount, 59; and assisted emigration to the Cape, 1820, 34n.; and Horton's plan, 66, 155; and experiment in Irish emigration, 71, 83; suggests emigration committee, 68, 91; on Irish landlords, 95; opinion of Horton, 146–9; government collapses, 148; opinion of political economists, 149–50; on value of emigration, 150–1; emigration plan, 152–3; and recommendations of Emigration Committees, 156–8; becomes Colonial Secretary, 159; becomes Prime Minister, 161; encourages Horton, 173–4
Goodenough, G. Tren., 67n.
Goulburn, Henry: and emigration policy in the Colonial Office, 10; and pauper emigrants, 14; role in Colonial Office, 15; and assisted emigration to Upper Canada, 1815, 17–23; and assisted emigration, 1818–1819, 28–30, 33; on advantages of South Africa, 38; selecting emigrants to the Cape, 39; and decision to assist weavers, 48, 52–3; leaves Colonial Office, 57; and emigration to United States, 60; and crisis in Ireland, 69; and Irish emigrants, 71; and Emigration Committees, 92; on value of emigration, 151
Gourlay, Robert, 12, 16
Graaf Reinet, 47
Grahamstown, 35, 45, 47
Grangemouth, 53
Great Fish River, 27, 33, 34
Greenock, 7, 49, 52, 53, 54
Grey, Charles Grey, 2nd Earl, 163